Student Study Guide

for use with

Traditions and Encounters
A Global Perspective on the Past
Volume I
From the Beginnings to 1500

Second Edition

Jerry H. Bentley
University of Hawai'i

Herbert F. Ziegler
University of Hawai'i

Prepared by
Anne M. Will and Barbara Moburg
Skagit Valley College

Boston   Burr Ridge, IL   Dubuque, IA   Madison, WI   New York   San Francisco   St. Louis
Bangkok   Bogotá   Caracas   Kuala Lumpur   Lisbon   London   Madrid   Mexico City
Milan   Montreal   New Delhi   Santiago   Seoul   Singapore   Sydney   Taipei   Toronto

Student Study Guide for use with
TRADITIONS AND ENCOUNTERS: A GLOBAL PERSPECTIVE ON THE PAST: VOLUME I: FROM
THE BEGINNINGS TO 1500
Jerry H. Bentley, Herbert F. Ziegler

2 3 4 5 6 7 8 9 0 BKM/BKM 0 9 8 7 6 5 4 3 2

ISBN 0-07-256583-7

www.mhhe.com

CONTENTS

INTRODUCTION

This study guide has been designed to help students improve their understanding of the world history textbook, *Traditions and Encounters: A Global Perspective on the Past,* 2nd Edition (Volume I: From the Beginnings to 1600) by Jerry H. Bentley and Herbert F. Ziegler. The intention of this volume is to promote student learning through a variety of formats that address different learning styles and strategies. People learn differently, and students are encouraged to make this study guide work for them.

CHAPTER INTRODUCTION

This section provides an introduction to the major themes and events in each chapter. Connections are emphasized within chapters and also to material from previous chapters. Students might find it useful to read this introduction before reading the chapter in the textbook in order to have a framework for approaching the text.

CHAPTER OUTLINE

The chapter outline follows the structure of the textbook closely, although not in as much detail. The outline can be useful in reviewing the chapter and also for clarifying a section that may have been difficult to understand. It should be understood, however, that the outline is a simplification and cannot be a substitute for the full text. Space has been provided for students to take notes as they read.

IDENTIFICATION: PEOPLE

The significant players in each chapter are listed here, and space has been provided to note the significant accomplishments of each. To do this efficiently, students should wait until completing the chapter before deciding what is most important about each figure. Notes should include the country of origin, dates, and significance to world history. Here is a sample:

> *Tokugawa Ieyasu*: Seventeenth-century Japanese shogun (military governor) who ended a period of civil war, unified Japan, and established a military dynasty that lasted until 1867.

IDENTIFICATION: TERMS/CONCEPTS

Likewise, the major terms and concepts for each chapter are listed with space for definitions. Students should be able to explain in their own words what each term means and why it is important to world history. Terms that involve difficult religious or political concepts or terms that appear in several chapters have been defined in the glossary at the end of the study guide. These terms are indicated with an asterisk (*). Here is a sample definition:

> *indulgences*: the practice by the Catholic Church of reducing time in purgatory (after death) in exchange for a donation to the Church; by the sixteenth century, subject to widespread abuse and the spark of the Protestant Reformation.

STUDY QUESTIONS AND INQUIRY QUESTIONS

These questions are offered to help frame students' reading of the text. There are two kinds of questions here: study questions ask for recall and comprehension of information, while inquiry questions ask for interpretation and application of new learning. Inquiry questions could easily become the subject of further research and discussion.

STUDENT QUIZ

A practice quiz is provided to help students review the details in each chapter. Students would do well to read the chapter first, take notes on the people, terms, and study questions, and then take the student quiz to test for overall comprehension. These are multiple choice quizzes, with the answers provided in the back of the study guide.

MATCHING

This review activity targets the people, groups, places, or terms presented in the chapter. Again, students should first read the chapter carefully and then try the matching activity. Answers are provided.

SEQUENCING

In this exercise, student are given four to seven related events and asked to put them in chronological order. These are not random and isolated incidents, but rather connected events. This exercise helps students recognize that global events are often related. Answers are provided.

QUOTATIONS

A series of quotes relevant to the chapter content are presented in this section. Students should be able to identify either the speaker or the point of view and explain the significance of the passage. Some quotes are taken directly from the text, while others reflect perspectives from the textbook and should be clear from the content. Answers are given at the end of the study guide.

EXERCISES

These exercises ask students to work with visual displays of information. In some cases, students are asked to label geographic information onto outline maps in the study guide as an aid to learning. In other exercises, they are asked to interpret geographic information from maps in the textbook. At times other sorts of exercises, like graphing population trends, are included in this section.

CONNECTIONS

A pair—of people, concepts, or events—is suggested, and students must try to establish a historic connection. In some instances the connection is direct and causal, but in others it may be subtler. Students can use these pairs to test their own comprehension. Or the connections might be the basis of a small group activity or an in-class writing exercise.

GROUP ACTIVITIES

Many students learn best in collaboration with other learners. These activities are offered to help students internalize their learning through role-playing, debate, and other group exercises. These are useful activities for study groups in or outside of class.

FEATURE FILMS

Ours is a highly visual culture, and it often helps to see history enacted in order to understand how it has unfolded in human terms. To this end, a list of feature films has been provided to help students see world history as they read about it. Unfortunately, this section is uneven: there are far more films made about recent events and about western history. Some films suggested here are excellent, and others are more entertainment than history. All the films can be purchased in the United States, but some of the foreign films may be more difficult to rent.

CHAPTER 1
BEFORE HISTORY

INTRODUCTION

The first chapter of *Traditions and Encounters* sets the stage for the drama of world history by presenting the major milestones in the development of humans from their earliest appearance on earth to the dawn of civilization. This chapter addresses the physical evolution of the species and their migrations throughout the globe as well as the revolutionary transformation from all humans surviving by hunting and gathering to the majority living in agricultural societies. The results of this remarkable transformation include

- An unprecedented population explosion due to the increase in the food supply
- Permanent settlement in villages and, later, in cities
- The specialization of labor, which led to the development of craft industries and other professions
- The opportunity to accumulate wealth and the resulting emergence of social class differences
- The development of fertility-based religions and the increasing elaboration of religious institutions

OUTLINE

I. The evolution of *Homo sapiens*

  A. The hominids

    1. *Australopithecus*

      a. Appeared in east Africa about four million to one million years ago

      b. Walked upright on two legs; well-developed hands

      c. Stone tools; fire later

    2. *Homo erectus*

      a. 2.5 million to two hundred thousand years ago, east Africa

      b. Large brain; sophisticated tools; definitely knew how to control fire

      c. Developed language skills in well-coordinated hunts of large animals

      d. Migrated to Asia and Europe; established throughout by two hundred thousand years ago

  B. *Homo sapiens;* evolved as early as two hundred thousand years ago

    1. Brain with large frontal regions for conscious and reflective thought

    2. Spread throughout Eurasia beginning more than one hundred thousand years ago,

    3. Ice age land bridges enabled them to populate other continents

    4. The natural environment

1

a. *Homo sapiens* used knives, spears, bows, and arrows

b. Brought tremendous pressure on other species

II. Paleolithic society

A. Economy and society of hunting and gathering peoples

1. Economic life

   a. Prevented individuals from accumulating private property

   b. Lived an egalitarian existence

   c. Lived in small bands, about thirty to fifty members in each group

2. Big game hunting with special tools and tactics

3. Some permanent Paleolithic settlements, if area rich in resources

   a. Natufians in eastern Mediterranean

   b. Jomon in central Japan

   c. Chinook in Pacific northwest area of North America

B. Paleolithic culture

1. Neandertal peoples

   a. Europe and southwest Asia between one hundred thousand and thirty-five thousand years ago

   b. Careful, deliberate burials were evidence of a capacity for emotion and feelings

2. Cro-Magnon peoples *(Homo sapiens sapiens)*

   a. The first human beings of fully modern type; appeared forty thousand years ago

   b. Venus figurines—fertility

   c. Cave paintings of animals—sympathetic magic

III. The neolithic era and the transition to agriculture

A. The origins of agriculture

1. Neolithic era; new stone age; refined tools and agriculture

   a. From about twelve thousand to six thousand years ago

   b. Neolithic women began systematic cultivation of plants

   c. Neolithic men began to domesticate animals

2. Early agriculture around 9000 B.C.E.

   a. Agriculture emerged independently in several parts of the world

   b. Merchants, migrants, and travelers spread food knowledge

   c. Slash-and-burn cultivation involved frequent movement of farmers

   d. Agriculture more work than hunting/gathering but steady, large supply of food

B. Early agricultural society; population explosion caused by surplus

1. Emergence of villages and towns
    a. Jericho, earliest known neolithic village
    b. Mud huts and defensive walls
2. Specialization of labor
    a. Neolithic site of Çatal Hüyük, eight thousand people
    b. Prehistoric craft industries: pottery, metallurgy, and textile production
3. Social distinctions, due to private land ownership
C. Neolithic culture; calendars and life cycle deities
D. The origins of urban life
    1. Emergence of cities, larger and more complex than villages
    2. Earliest cities in the valley of the Tigris and Euphrates Rivers, 4000 to 3500 B.C.E.

IDENTIFICATION: PEOPLE

What is the contribution of each of the following individuals to world history? (Identification should include answers to the questions *who, what, where, when, how,* and *why is this person important.*) The first one is written for you as an example.

Lucy: Nickname given to reconstructed skeleton of 3.5-million-year-old woman that proved that humans of this era walked upright, freeing their arms and hands for using tools.

Richard E. Leakey

IDENTIFICATION: TERMS/CONCEPTS

State in your own words what each of the following terms means and why it is significant to a study of world history. (Those terms with an asterisk may be defined in the glossary.)

Australopithecus

Homo erectus

Homo sapiens

Paleolithic

Hunting/gathering cultures*

Natufian

Jomon

Chinook

Neandertal

Cro-Magnon

Venus figurines

Sympathetic magic

Neolithic

Agricultural transition*

Jericho

Çatal Hüyük

Metallurgy*

STUDY QUESTIONS

1. What was the significance of the discovery of Lucy's bones?

2. What set the genus *Australopithecus* apart from other animal species of the time?

3. What were the most important changes in the evolution from *Australopithecus* to *Homo erectus*?

4. What advantages did *Homo sapiens* possess over *Homo erectus*?

5. What were the differences between the Neandertal and Cro-Magnon people?

6. What is the significance of the cave art? The Venus figurines?

7. How did the gradual transformation from hunting and gathering to agriculture probably occur? How did it spread?

8. What were the most significant positive and negative effects of the agricultural transition on human society?

9. What were the earliest craft industries to emerge and how did they benefit those living in neolithic villages?

10. How did early cities differ from neolithic villages and towns?

INQUIRY QUESTIONS

1. Would you say that early hunting/gathering cultures were based more on cooperation or competition? Justify your response.

2. What does the appearance of art forms like sculpture and painting tell us about Paleolithic cultures?

3. The development of human societies discussed in this chapter all point to the increasing complexity in people's lives and cultures. What strategies or institutions did people have to develop to cope with this complexity and why?

STUDENT QUIZ

1. By scholarly convention, *prehistory* refers to the period
    a. before the emergence of cities.
    b. before modern humans were born.
    c. before the invention of writing.
    d. before *Homo sapiens* appeared.
    e. none of the above.

2. Human beings and large apes are significantly different in
    a. genetic makeup.
    b. body chemistry.
    c. level of intelligence.
    d. the structure of the brain.
    e. none of the above.

3. The famous Lucy was
    a. a female ape.
    b. an *Australopithecus*.
    c. a *Homo erectus*.
    d. an archeologist.
    e. none of the above.

4. The family of hominids includes all of the following species except
    a. apes and monkeys.
    b. *Australopithecus* and *Homo erectus*.
    c. *Homo sapiens* and *Homo sapiens sapiens*.
    d. Neandertal and Cro-Magnon.
    e. modern humans.

5. A major difference between *Homo erectus* and *Australopithecus* was the ability to
    a. walk upright on two legs.
    b. domesticate animals.
    c. communicate through language.
    d. make stone tools.
    e. all of the above.

6. *Homo sapiens* were better hunters than *Australopithecus* and *Homo erectus* because they
   a. organized larger hunting bands than their ancestors did.
   b. were smaller in body size but swifter in action.
   c. had larger brains and higher intelligence.
   d. had more animals to hunt.
   e. all of the above.

7. The most significant defining characteristic of the paleolithic era was that
   a. human beings used stone and bone tools in their cultivation of crops.
   b. peoples relied on hunting and gathering for subsistence.
   c. men and women engaged in the same economic activities.
   d. people domesticated animals.
   e. none of the above.

8. What is the significance of the Natufian, Jomon, and Chinook cultures?
   a. They show that some paleolithic cultures settled permanently.
   b. They show that some paleolithic peoples lived in much larger groups.
   c. They show that some paleolithic cultures had specialization of labor.
   d. They show that some paleolithic cultures had hierarchies of authority.
   e. all of the above.

9. Neandertal peoples developed a capacity for emotion and feelings, which can be seen from their
   a. elaborate burials.
   b. cave paintings.
   c. ancestor worship.
   d. Venus figurines.
   e. all of the above.

10. Cro-Magnon peoples were
    a. *Australopithecus.*
    b. Neandertals.
    c. *Homo erectus.*
    d. *Homo sapiens sapiens.*
    e. none of the above.

11. The prominent sexual features of Venus figurines at Cro-Magnon sites indicate that the Cro-Magnon peoples
    a. worshipped the goddess of love forty thousand years ago.
    b. had a deep interest in love-making activities.
    c. were strongly concerned with fertility and the generation of new life.
    d. used sympathetic magic to succeed in hunting.
    e. all of the above.

12. What was a likely purpose of Cro-Magnon cave painting?
    a. to warn competing groups of people of their presence.
    b. to practice telepathy.
    c. to draw portraits of each other.
    d. to exercise sympathetic magic.
    e. none of the above.

13. The term *neolithic era* refers to
    a. the early stages of a cultivating society.
    b. the agricultural transition.
    c. the era in which the peoples began to use polished stone tools.
    d. the era in which people began to live permanently in villages.
    e. all of the above.

14. By about 5000 B.C.E., agriculture had displaced hunting and gathering societies in several regions of the world primarily because
    a. cultivation required much less work than hunting and gathering.
    b. cultivation provided a relatively stable and regular supply of food.
    c. human beings had mastered agricultural knowledge and technique.
    d. agriculture led to a more varied diet.
    e. none of the above.

15. All of the following social changes were brought about by agriculture except
    a. population growth.
    b. the emergence of villages and towns.
    c. the invention of writing.
    d. the specialization of labor.
    e. the emergence of social classes.

16. The site of Jericho was one of the earliest known
    a. agricultural sites.
    b. towns.
    c. cities.
    d. villages.
    e. temples.

17. Three neolithic industries that illustrate the greatest potential of specialized labor include
    a. stone tool making, leather, and jewelry.
    b. wood carving, beads, and baskets.
    c. pottery, metallurgy, and textiles.
    d. furs, fish, and grain.
    e. none of the above.

18. Çatal Hüyük is an archaeological site in Anatolia from neolithic times in which one can readily see evidence of
    a. specialization of labor.
    b. iron production.
    c. long-distance trade.
    d. writing.
    e. all of the above.

19. The belief that neolithic religious thought clearly reflected the natural world of early agricultural society is based on observation of
    a. religious texts.
    b. representations of gods and goddesses.
    c. cave paintings.
    d. fossils.
    e. priests' burial sites.

20. Cities first emerged from agricultural villages and towns in
    a. the valleys of the Tigris and Euphrates rivers.
    b. Egypt.
    c. China.
    d. India.
    e. South America.

MATCHING

Match these terms with the statements that follow.

A.	Çatal Hüyük	E.	*Australopithecus*
B.	*Homo erectus*	F.	Neandertal
C.	Lucy	G.	Chinook
D.	Lascaux	H.	Cro-Magnon

1. ___ This foraging culture of the northwest coast of North America lived in permanent settlements.

2. ___ This is the site of some of the most well-known cave paintings; most of them depict animals and are believed to reflect an effort to influence the outcome of the hunt.

3. ___ One of the most significant archeological finds in history, this skeleton dates back about 3.5 million years.

4. ___ Earliest known hominid genus (from four to one million years ago), these creatures walked upright, used tools, and traveled purposefully.

5. ___ These paleolithic people adorned themselves, created works of art, and worshipped fertility figures.

6. ___ This site originated as a neolithic village and evolved into a large town with possibly eight thousand inhabitants, many of whom were in specialized occupations.

7. ___ These paleolithic peoples are associated with the first evidence of reflective thought because of their careful ritualized burial practices.

8. ___ This species flourished from about 1.5 million to two hundred thousand years ago; they knew how to control fire and could communicate complex ideas.

SEQUENCING

Place the following clusters of events in chronological order. Consider carefully how one event leads to another, and try to determine the internal logic of each sequence.

A.

_____ The last ice age cools the earth's temperature and lowers the sea levels.

_____ Neolithic peoples in South America begin cultivating potatoes, maize, and beans.

_____ The last ice age ends; the glaciers melt; the Americas are isolated from the other continents.

_____ *Homo sapiens* use their intelligence to fashion warm clothes and build better shelters, making it possible for them to live in colder climates.

_____ Paleolithic people hunt many large mammal species to extinction in the Americas; the remaining species are largely unsuited for domestication.

_____ Humans migrate across the land bridge between Asia and North America.

B.

_____ Women of hunting/gathering cultures contribute the bulk of the calories to the community's diet by foraging.

_____ Scarcity of game animals forces communities to rely more and more on agriculture.

_____ Slash-and-burn cultivation results in fertile land that could sustain healthy harvests for a few years.

_____ Techniques of cultivation improve until a steady surplus of food is provided.

_____ Specialists perfect the manufacture of pottery.

MAP EXERCISES

1. Using the outline map of the world on the next page, show the spread of *Homo sapiens* by shading in the areas to which they migrated with different colors reflecting different eras. Make a key for your map, matching the colors with spans of years. What does this map tell you about the migrations of humans? Why do you think they did not migrate more quickly?

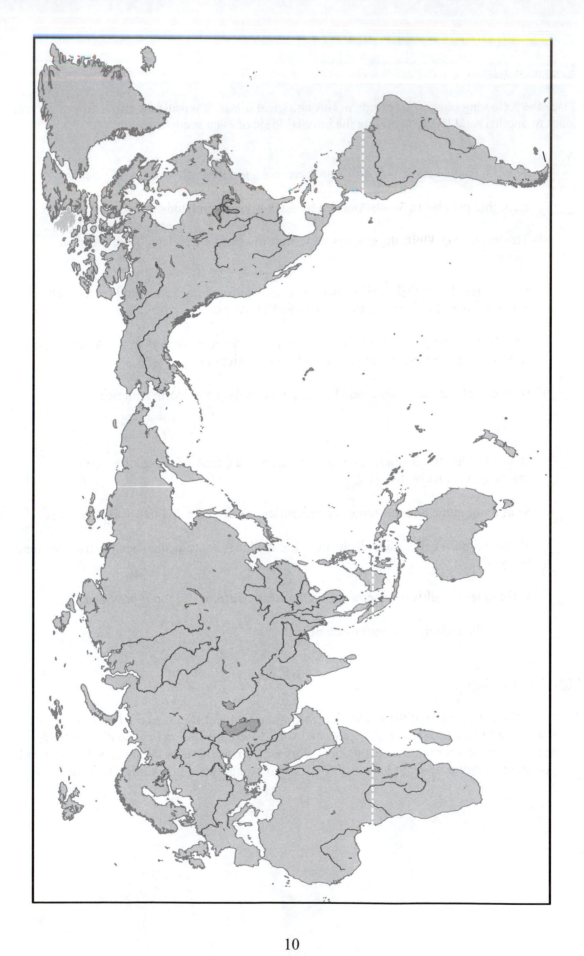

10

2. Graph the population data shown on page 22, placing the years along the X axis and the population in millions along the Y axis. What does this graph indicate to you about the rate of population growth in the first two and a half millennia of world history?

CONNECTIONS

In fifty words or less explain the relationship between each of the following pairs. How does one lead to or foster the other? Be specific in your response. (May be done individually or in small groups.)

- Metallurgy and agriculture
- Neandertal and Cro-Magnon
- Jericho and specialization of labor
- Cave painting and Venus figurines
- Jomon and agricultural transition

GROUP ACTIVITIES

1. Imagine you are a group of archeologists excavating a site of a village in western Asia. So far you have found several decorated pieces of pottery, cast copper knives and jewelry, sewing needles, and what appears to be the foundation of a wall surrounding the settlement. What can you infer about this culture based on this information? What would be the earliest you can date it?

2. Make lists of the advantages and disadvantages of living in the types of hunting/gathering societies described in the text. Then make lists of the advantages and disadvantages of living in early agricultural societies. What was gained and what was lost by the agricultural transition that took place twelve thousand to five thousand years ago?

FEATURE FILMS

Quest for Fire (1982). Paleolithic hunter/gatherers have many adventures and clash with a more sophisticated culture while they search for the secret of creating fire. With Ron Perlman.

CHAPTER 2
EARLY SOCIETIES IN SOUTHWEST ASIA AND THE INDO-EUROPEAN MIGRATIONS

<u>INTRODUCTION</u>

Because of the agricultural transition, societies could sustain larger populations and could become increasingly complex. Thus urban societies emerged in the fourth millennium B.C.E., particularly in the region known as Mesopotamia ("the land between the rivers") along the fertile river valleys of the Tigris and the Euphrates. Some of the world's earliest cities developed and prospered in that region. Mesopotamian prosperity and sophisticated culture attracted many migrants and influenced many neighbors, including the Hebrews, the Phoenicians, and the Indo-Europeans. Some of the characteristics of Mesopotamian societies were

- The establishment of governmental institutions to provide order and stability and to resolve disputes. These institutions evolved into hereditary kingships and, at times, into empires when states sought to expand their dominion to neighboring lands.
- The emergence of social classes as the result of specialization of labor and accumulation of wealth. The agricultural surplus and the accompanying specialization allowed individuals and groups to produce goods of high quality. The desire for these goods, in turn, helped to stimulate trade with other societies, greatly expanding intercultural contact.
- Distinctive cultural traditions that developed including a system of writing that would endure for thousands of years and more elaborate religious institutions than had previously existed.

<u>OUTLINE</u>

I. **The quest for order**

    A. Mesopotamia: "the land between the rivers"

        1. Valleys of the Tigris and Euphrates

        2. Little rain, so area needs irrigation (small scale by 6000 B.C.E.)

        3. Food supplies increase

            a. Human population increases

            b. Migrants to the area increase—especially Semites

            c. Sumer (in south) becomes population center

        4. First cities emerge, 4000 B.C.E.

            a. Between 3200 and 2350 B.C.E., they evolve into city-states (control of surrounding region)

            b. Governments sponsor building projects and irrigation

            c. Attacks by others led to wall building and military development

      d.   Kingships evolve with cooperation of noble families

  B. The course of empire

      1. Sargon of Akkad (2370–2315 B.C.E.)

         a. Coup against king of Kish

         b. Seizes trade routes and natural resources

         c. Gradually empire weakens and collapses about 2000 B.C.E.

      2. Hammurabi (1792–1750 B.C.E.)

         a. Centralizes the bureaucracy and regulates taxation

         b. Capital is Babylon

         c. Law Code: law of retribution and importance of social status

         d. Hittite assault and empire crumbles in 1595 B.C.E.

  C. The later Mesopotamian empires

      1. Assyrians (northern Mesopotamia), about 1300–612 B.C.E.

         a. Cities: Assur and Ninevah

         b. Powerful army: professional officers (merit), chariots, archers, iron weapons

         c. Unpopular rule leads to rebellions; ends 612 B.C.E.

      2. New Babylonian empire, 600–550 B.C.E.

         a. Nebuchadnezzar (605–562 B.C.E.)

         b. Hanging gardens of palace shows wealth and luxury

II. The formation of a complex society and sophisticated cultural traditions

  A. Economic specialization and trade

      1. Bronze (made from copper and tin); used in weapons and later agricultural tools

      2. Iron (about 1000 B.C.E.), cheaper and more widely available; used in weapons and tools

      3. Wheel (about 3500 B.C.E.) helps trade; carts can carry more goods further

      4. Shipbuilding: maritime trade increases in all directions; network develops

  B. The emergence of a stratified patriarchal society

      1. Social classes

         a. Cities: more opportunities to accumulate wealth

         b. Kings (hereditary) and nobles (royal family and supporters) are highest class

         c. Priests and priestesses rule temple communities with large incomes and staff

         d. Free commoners (peasants), dependent clients (no property); pay taxes and labor on building projects

         e. Slaves (POWs, criminals, debt servitude): mostly domestic servants

      2. Patriarchy

          a.   Hammurabi's code: men are head of the household

          b.   Women get fewer rights after 2000 B.C.E.; by 1500 B.C.E. are wearing veils

  C. The development of written cultural traditions

      1. Cuneiform, Mesopotamian writing style, becomes standard

          a.   Reed stylus (wedge-shaped) pressed in clay then baked

          b.   Mostly commercial and tax documents

      2. Education: vocational to be scribe or government official

      3. Literature: astronomy, mathematics, abstract (religious and literary like Gilgamesh)

III. The broader influence of mesopotamian society

  A. Hebrews, Israelites, and Jews

      1. Early Hebrews are pastoral nomads between Mesopotamia and Egypt (second millennium B.C.E.)

          a.   Settle in some cities

          b.   Abraham leads group to Palestine 1850 B.C.E.

          c.   Descendents borrow law of retribution and flood story from Mesopotamia

      2. Some migrate to Egypt in eighteenth century B.C.E. then back to Palestine with Moses

          a.   Twelve tribes become Israelites

          b.   Mesopotamian-style monarchs with Jerusalem as capital

          c.   David (1000–970 B.C.E.) then Solomon (970–930 B.C.E.)

      3. Moses and monotheism

          a.   Ten Commandments: moral and ethical standards for followers

          b.   Compilation of teachings into Torah (1000–400 B.C.E.)

      4. Assyrians conquer

          a.   Conquer Israel in north and Judah in south and destroy Jerusalem

          b.   Deportees return to Judea; become known as Jews (586 B.C.E.)

          c.   Prophets in this period increase devotion of people

          d.   Build distinct Jewish community in Judea with strong group identity

  B. The Phoenicians

      1. First settlers about 3000 B.C.E.; develop into kingdoms of independent city-states

      2. Little agriculture; live on trade and communications networks

          a.   Overland trade to Mesopotamia; influence on culture

          b.   Sea trade most important; get raw materials, trade for manufactured goods

      3. Have early alphabetical script (1500 B.C.E.)

IV. The Indo-European migrations

A. Indo-European origins

1. Linguists discover similarities between many languages; they must be related

2. Originate in steppes of central Asia; pastoral people; 4500–2500 B.C.E.

3. Domesticate horses; learn to ride; use horses with carts, then chariots

B. Indo-European expansion and its effects

1. Indo-European society breaks up about 3000 B.C.E.; peoples gradually migrate

2. Hittites settle in central Anatolia about 2000 B.C.E.

    a. Build powerful kingdoms

    b. Conquer Babylonian empire 1595 B.C.E.

    c. Dissolve by about 1200 B.C.E.

    d. Technology: light horse-drawn chariots (spokes) and iron metallurgy

3. Some migrate into central Asia by 2000 B.C.E.

4. Other migrations: Greece, Italy, central Europe, western Europe, Britain

    a. All pastoral agriculturalists

    b. All speak related languages and worship similar deities

5. Later wave of migrations to Iran and India ("Aryan")

IDENTIFICATION: PEOPLE

What is the contribution of each of the following individuals to world history? (Identification should include answers to the questions *who, what, where, when, how,* and *why is this person important.*)

Gilgamesh

Sargon of Akkad

Hammurabi

Nebuchadnezzar

King David

King Solomon

Moses

IDENTIFICATION: TERMS/CONCEPTS

State in your own words what each of the following terms means and why it is significant to a study of world history. (Those terms with an asterisk may be defined in the glossary.)

Epic of Gilgamesh

Mesopotamia*

Sumer

Tigris

Euphrates

Ziggurat

Akkad

Hammurabi's Code

Lex talionis

Assyrians

New Babylonia

Hanging gardens

Bronze

Iron

Patriarchy*

Cuneiform

Hebrews

Palestine

Israel

Judea

Ten Commandments

Torah

Phoenicians

Astarte

Indo-Europeans

Hittites

STUDY QUESTIONS

1. What does the *Epic of Gilgamesh* tell us about the culture in which it emerged?

2. What was the significance of the need for irrigation to the political development of Mesopotamia?

3. What were the underlying principles of Hammurabi's code of laws and what does the law code tell us about the kind of society that existed in Mesopotamia at the time?

4. Why were the Assyrians such formidable conquerors?

5. What were the technological innovations of the early Mesopotamians and how did they contribute to the development of the culture and to its overall economic prosperity?

6. What were the social strata in ancient Mesopotamia and, in general, what roles did women play?

7. What is the significance of the development of cuneiform writing to the Mesopotamian culture and the surrounding areas?

8. Compare and contrast the history of the early Jewish community and the Phoenician culture. How did the Mesopotamians influence each?

9. What were the origins and early development of the Indo-Europeans?

10. Discuss where and how the Indo-European cultures spread through Eurasia.

INQUIRY QUESTIONS

1. Some historians refer to Mesopotamia as the "cradle of civilization." Why is this? Do you agree that "civilization" originated there? Why or why not?

2. Compare and contrast the *lasting* contributions of the Sumerians, Jews, Phoenicians, and Indo-Europeans. Which culture do you believe made the most significant contributions? Why?

3. Warfare was a significant factor in the development of all the cultures discussed in this chapter. Analyze how political institutions, economic factors, social factors, and technology interplayed to create conflict and war throughout this region.

STUDENT QUIZ

1. Gilgamesh was
    a. a king of the city-state of Uruk.
    b. a hero in a popular Mesopotamian epic.
    c. a warrior in conflict with the city of Kish.
    d. a legendary loyal friend of Enkidu.
    e. all of the above.

2. Which of the following is *not* true of the land called Mesopotamia?
    a. It lies between the Tigris and Euphrates rivers.
    b. It is a land of abundant rainfall and fertile plains.
    c. It is located in modern-day Iraq.
    d. It was the home of the Sumerians.
    e. It attracted many Semitic-speaking migrants.

3. Which of the following did Sumerian cities and their governments do?
    a. organize work on building projects.
    b. rule over the area surrounding the city.
    c. oversee the construction and maintenance of irrigation systems.
    d. organize the defense of the city against attacks.
    e. all of the above.

4. Sargon of Akkad
    a. was a Sumerian ruler.
    b. built the capital city of Babylon.
    c. inherited the kingship from his father.
    d. was a gifted administrator and warrior.
    e. all of the above.

5. In Hammurabi's code you would be *unlikely* to find
    a. laws with punishments that differ according to social class.
    b. laws that prescribe the death penalty.
    c. laws that indicate a suspect is innocent until proven guilty.
    d. laws regulating commercial transactions, wages, and prices.
    e. laws relying the on the principle of retaliation.

6. Which of the following peoples did *not* rule a Mesopotamian empire?
    a. the Assyrians.
    b. the Hittites.
    c. the Jews.
    d. the Chaldeans
    e. the Akkadians.

7. Which of the following was the latest invention?
    a. bronze metallurgy.
    b. the wheel.
    c. ships.
    d. iron metallurgy.
    e. the chariot.

8. Which of the following is true of the social classes of ancient Mesopotamia?
   a. People became kings by winning battles.
   b. The nobility were continually fighting with the kings for power.
   c. Priests and priestesses were powerful rulers over temple communities.
   d. There was no slavery.
   e. all of the above.

9. Cuneiform writing
   a. evolved from Egyptian hieroglyphics.
   b. was usually written on papyrus.
   c. did not last for the duration of the Sumerian culture.
   d. involved wedge-shaped symbols pressed onto clay with a reed.
   e. all of the above.

10. Which of the following was *not* a form of written documentation from Mesopotamia?
    a. commercial and taxation documents.
    b. instructions on mummification of bodies.
    c. documents on astronomy and mathematics.
    d. epic literature.
    e. All of the above *were* Mesopotamian documents.

11. The *Epic of Gilgamesh*
    a. recounts the adventures of Gilgamesh and his friend.
    b. describes the hero's efforts to attain immortality.
    c. explored relations between humans and the gods.
    d. contemplates the meaning of life and death.
    e. all of the above.

12. The Hebrews
    a. were settled agriculturalists.
    b. were led out of Palestine by Abraham.
    c. were always monotheists.
    d. were the first Indo-Europeans to settle in southwest Asia.
    e. none of the above.

13. The religious beliefs of the Israelites after Moses included
    a. the worship of Mesopotamian gods.
    b. monotheism.
    c. the worship of Allah.
    d. the building of ziggurats.
    e. none of the above.

14. After the tenth century B.C.E., the Israelites experienced
    a. the division of the kingdom of Israel.
    b. conquest by the Assyrians.
    c. the destruction of Jerusalem by the New Babylonian empire.
    d. the return of deportees to Judea where they became known as Jews
    e. all of the above.

15. The Phoenicians
    a. were prosperous based on their sea trade and commercial networks.
    b. built a large empire through conquest.
    c. were an Indo-European people.
    d. first settled in the Mediterranean in the tenth century.
    e. all of the above.

16. According to the excerpt "Israelites' Relations with Neighboring Peoples,"
    a. the Israelites conquered the Phoenician city of Tyre.
    b. Solomon gave cedar trees to Hiram for his temple.
    c. Solomon sent laborers to Hiram.
    d. the Lord punished Solomon for dealing with Hiram.
    e. all of the above.

17. Which of the following is *not* associated with the Phoenicians?
    a. agriculture.
    b. alphabetic script.
    c. Astarte.
    d. city-states.
    e. shipbuilding.

18. Who first deduced the existence of an Indo-European culture?
    a. nineteenth-century linguists.
    b. twentieth-century archeologists.
    c. Jewish scholars.
    d. cuneiform translators.
    e. none of the above.

19. The key element in the expansion of the Indo-Europeans from their homeland was
    a. iron weapons.
    b. monotheism.
    c. trade.
    d. horses.
    e. writing.

20. Which of the following was *not* an area to which the Indo-Europeans migrated?
    a. east and southeast Asia.
    b. western Europe and the British Isles.
    c. India and Iran.
    d. Anatolia (modern Turkey).
    e. All of the above are places they migrated.

MATCHING

Match these peoples with the statements that follow.

A.	Hittites	F.	Aryans
B.	Chaldeans	G.	Phoenicians
C.	Jews	H.	Sumerians
D.	Hebrews	I.	Assyrians
E.	Akkadians		

1. ___ Indo-Europeans who built an empire with the technologies of chariots and iron weapons.

2. ___ Independent city-states that influenced other societies through their trade and industry.

3. ___ The earliest urban-based society in Mesopotamia, they developed cuneiform writing.

4. ___ Northern Mesopotamians who built an empire by first conquering Sumer.

5. ___ Semitic pastoral polytheists who settled the region of Palestine about 1850 B.C.E.

6. ___ Empire under King Nebuchadnezzar who lavished wealth and resources on his capital.

7. ___ Wave of Indo-Europeans who migrated into India and built powerful states.

8. ___ Group, exiled by New Babylonian conquerors, who eventually returned to Judea.

9. ___ Powerful and intimidating army that built far-flung empire including Mesopotamia, Palestine, and much of Egypt.

SEQUENCING

Place the following clusters of events in chronological order. Consider carefully how one event leads to another, and try to determine the internal logic of each sequence.

A.

_____ King Hammurabi has laws codified.

_____ Sargon overthrows king of Kish, then wages war on other city-states.

_____ King Nebuchadnezzar commissions the hanging gardens of Babylon.

_____ Legendary reign of King Gilgamesh.

_____ Assyrians conquer entire region of Mesopotamia.

B.

_____ Hebrews adapt principle of *lex talionis* and flood story from Mesopotamians.

_____ Federation of twelve tribes carves out territory for themselves in region of Palestine.

_____ Some Hebrews make their way into Egypt.

_____ Israelites divide into two kingdoms: Israel and Judea.

_____ Hebrews migrate from Sumer into Palestine.

_____ Moses announces the Ten Commandments to the Israelites.

_____ Exiles return to Judea, organize several small states, and build religious community.

_____ City of Jerusalem destroyed by the New Babylonian empire.

QUOTATIONS

For each of the following quotes, identify the speaker, if known, or the point of view. What is the significance of each passage?

1. "And behold, I plan to build a house in the name of the Lord, my God . . . Now therefore command thou that they hew me cedar trees out of Lebanon, and my servants shall be with thy servants."

2. "So the gods in their hearts were moved to let loose the deluge; but my lord Ea warned me in a dream…'tear down your house and build a boat.' For six days and six night the winds blew, torrent and tempest and flood overwhelmed the world."

3. "If a seignior wishes to divorce his wife who did not bear him children, he shall give her money to the full amount of her marriage price and . . . the dowry . . . and then he may divorce her."

23

4. "You shall have no other gods before me. You shall not make yourself a graven image . . . Remember the Sabbath day, to keep it holy . . . Honor your father and your mother."

MAP EXERCISES

1. Study the map on page 56 in the textbook (map 2.4) and then go to the Internet and find a map that shows the distribution of modern Indo-European languages. What modern languages are Indo-European? According to the map in the textbook, when is it likely that each language began developing independently? How does studying the relationships among modern languages shed light on historical migration?

2. On the outline map of Europe, north Africa and southwest Asia below, combine the information contained in maps 2.1, 2.2, and 2.3 in the textbook. Include the following, using different colors for different millennia: Sumer, Akkad, Assur, Uruk, Ur, Anatolia, Ninevah, Babylon, Tigris, Euphrates, Persian Gulf, Egypt, Israel, Judea, Jerusalem, Tyre, Carthage, Panermo, Gadir. Identify which location goes with which culture or cultures.

CONNECTIONS

In fifty words or less explain the relationship between each of the following pairs. How does one lead to or foster the other? Be specific in your response. (May be done individually or in small groups.)

*   Cuneiform and Gilgamesh
*   Hammurabi and Hebrews
*   Phoenicians and bronze
*   Chariots and empire
*   Indo-Europeans and iron

GROUP ACTIVITIES

1. As a group brainstorm the differences between neolithic villages (discussed in chapter 1) and early urban societies. How many differences can you come up with? Then agree on the five most significant differences and make a model on another page of how they are related to each other. You can use shapes, arrows, page placement, or other aids to visually display how they are connected to each other.

2. Study the list of Indo-European vocabulary words on page 54 of the textbook. Just by examining those words, which languages do you think are the most closely related? Look for patterns of similarities in the sounds, especially the consonant sounds, for pairs of languages. Which ones are the most different from the others? Now look at the map on page 56 (map 2.4). Can you detect any patterns in how closely related languages are and when and how migrations occurred?

CHAPTER 3
EARLY AFRICAN SOCIETIES AND THE BANTU MIGRATIONS

INTRODUCTION

Cultivation and domestication of animals transformed African cultures, like cultures in southwest Asia, into distinctive societies with more formal states, specialized labor, and more elaborate cultural traditions. The region around the Nile River, Egypt to the north and Nubia to the south, supported the fastest growing and most complex societies in Africa. These societies were noted for their

- Centralized political authority embodied in the absolute ruler the pharaoh in Egypt and the person of the King in the region of Kush (Nubia)
- Imperialist expansion in the second millennium B.C.E. as the Egyptian army pushed into Palestine, Syria, and north Africa and south into Nubia and as the Kushites later conquered Egypt and expanded their influence to the south
- Highly stratified and patriarchal societies based on an agricultural economy
- Development of industries, transportation, and trade networks that facilitated economic growth and the intermingling of cultural traditions
- Writing systems: hieroglyphic, hieratic, demotic, and Coptic scripts in Egypt and the yet-to-be-translated Meroitic inscriptions in Nubia
- Organized religious traditions that include worship of Amon and Re, sun gods, the cult of Osiris, pyramid building, and in Egypt, mummification of the dead

At the same time that Egypt and Nubia were becoming increasingly complex societies, the Bantu-speaking peoples to the south were undertaking gradual migrations from their homeland in west central Africa and displacing or intermingling with the foraging peoples of the forests. These migrations, and others, helped to spread both agricultural technology and, after 1000 B.C.E., iron metallurgy throughout sub-Saharan Africa.

OUTLINE

I. Early agricultural society in Africa

    A. Climatic change and the development of agriculture in Africa

        1. Sahara region used to be grassy steppe lands with water (10,000 B.C.E.)

            a. Abundant hunting, fishing, wild grains

            b. Eastern Sudan begins to herd cattle and collect grains (9000 B.C.E.)

            c. Permanent settlements and the growing of sorghum and yams (7500 B.C.E.)

            d. Small states with semidivine rulers (5000 B.C.E.)

        2. Climate becomes hotter and drier after 5000 B.C.E.

            a. People are driven into river regions—Nile

            b. Annual flooding makes rich soil for agriculture

    B. Egypt and Nubia: "gifts of the Nile"

1. Egypt—lower third of Nile River; Nubia—middle third of Nile

2. After 5000 B.C.E. peoples cultivate gourds and watermelons, domesticate donkeys and cattle (from Sudan), and grow wheat and barley (from Mesopotamia)

3. Agriculture easy in Egypt (due to Nile flooding) but more work in Nubia

4. States begin to emerge by 4000 B.C.E., small kingdoms by 3300 B.C.E.

C. The unification of Egypt

1. Strong Nubian realm, Ta Seti (3400-3200 B.C.E.)

2. Egypt, large and prosperous state by 3100 B.C.E.

    a. Menes at Memphis unites Upper and Lower Egypt

    b. Pharaoh, absolute ruler and owns all land

3. Archaic Period (3100–2660 B.C.E.) and Old Kingdom (2660–2160 B.C.E.)

    a. Great pyramids of Giza built during this period; Khufu the largest

    b. Violence between Egypt and Nubia (Egypt dominates from 3000–2400 B.C.E.)

    c. Nubia later develops into Kingdom of Kush

    d. Interaction through diplomacy, Nubian mercenaries, and intermarriage

D. Turmoil and empire

1. Period of upheaval after Old Kingdom (2160–2040 B.C.E.)

2. Middle Kingdom (2040–1640 B.C.E.)

3. Nomadic horsemen, Hyksos, invade Egypt

    a. Using bronze weapons and chariots (Egypt does not have)

    b. Captures Memphis in 1674 B.C.E.

    c. Causes revolts in Upper Egypt

4. New Kingdom (1550–1070 B.C.E.)

    a. Pharaoh gains power, huge army, large bureaucracy

    b. Building projects: temples, palaces, statues

    c. Tuthmosis III (1479–1425 B.C.E.) built empire including Palestine, Syrian, Nubia

    d. Then Egypt falls into a long period of decline

5. Egyptians driven out of Nubia in 1100 B.C.E.

    a. Nubian Kingdom of Kush; capital is Napata

    b. King Kashta conquers Thebes (in Egypt) in 760 B.C.E.

6. Assyrians with iron weapons invade from the north

7. After sixth century B.C.E. series of foreign conquests

II. The formation of complex societies and sophisticated cultural traditions

A. The emergence of cities and stratified societies

1. Cities are not as prominent in Egypt as in Mesopotamia (agricultural villages)
   a. Memphis, head of the delta
   b. Thebes, administrative center of Upper Egypt
   c. Heliopolis, center of sun god cult
   d. Tanis, important sea port on Mediterannean
2. Nubian cities
   a. Kerma, dominates trade routes
   b. Napata, most prosperous city after Nubian conquest of Egypt
   c. Meroë, most influential city after Assyrian invasion because it is farther south
3. Social classes
   a. Egypt: peasants and slaves (agriculture), pharaoh, professional military and administrators
   b. Nubia: complex and hierarchical society (can tell from tombs)
4. Patriarchy in both but women have more influence than in Mesopotamia
   a. Women act as regents, like female pharaoh Hatshepsut
   b. Nubia: women serve as queens, priestesses, and scribes

B. Economic specialization and trade
1. Bronze important but copper and tin rare and expensive
2. Iron metallurgy develops independently in Sudan
3. Transportation: sailboats, carts, and donkey caravans
4. Trade networks
   a. Egypt and Nubia: exotic goods from Nubia (ebony, gold, gems, slaves) and pottery, wine, linen, decorative items from Egypt
   b. Egypt and the north: especially wood, like cedar from Lebanon
   c. Egypt with Africa: Punt (east Africa)

C. Early writing in the Nile valley
1. Hieroglyphics found on monuments and papyrus by 3200 B.C.E.
2. Hieratic script, everyday writing 2600–600 B.C.E.
3. Demotic and Coptic scripts adapt Greek writing
4. Scribes live very privileged lives
5. Nubia adapts Egyptian writing until Meroitic in fifth century B.C.E. (untranslated)

D. The development of organized religious traditions
1. Principal gods: sun gods Amon and Re
2. Brief period of monotheism: Aten

     a.   Pharaoh Akhenaten's idea of a new capital at Akhetaten

     b.   Orders all other gods' names chiseled out; their names die with him

  3. Mummification

     a.   At first only pharaohs are mummified (Old Kingdom)

     b.   Later ruling classes and wealthy can afford it

     c.   Eventually commoners have it too (Middle and New Kingdom)

  4. Cult of Osiris

     a.   Brother Seth murders Osiris and scatters his body

     b.   Wife Isis gathers him up and gods restore him to life in underworld

     c.   Becomes associated with Nile, crops, life/death, immortality

     d.   Osiris judges the heart of the dead against the feather of truth

  5. Nubians combine Egyptian religions with their own

III.   Bantu migrations and early agricultural societies of sub-Saharan Africa

  A. The dynamics of Bantu expansion

    1. Bantu—language group from west central Africa

       a.   Live along banks of rivers; use canoes

       b.   Cultivate yams and oil palms

       c.   Live in clan-based villages

       d.   Trade with hunting/gathering forest people

    2. Early migrations of Bantu (3000–1000 B.C.E.)

       a.   Move south and west into the forest lands

       b.   Move south to Congo River and east to Great Lakes region

       c.   Absorb much of the population of hunter/gather/fisher people

       d.   By 1000 B.C.E. occupy most of Africa south of the equator

    3. Features of the Bantu

       a.   Use canoes and settle along banks of rivers; spread from there

       b.   Agricultural surplus causes them to move inland from rivers

       c.   Become involved in trade

    4. Bantu rate of migration increases after 1000 B.C.E. due to appearance of iron

       a.   Iron tools allow them to clear more land for agriculture

       b.   Iron weapons give them stronger position

  B. Early agricultural societies of sub-Saharan Africa

    1. Many other societies besides Bantu migrate

    2. Spread of agriculture to most of sub-Saharan Africa by 1000 B.C.E.

3. Mostly small communities led by chiefs with "age sets" and initiation rites

4. Religious differences by area

    a. Some worship single, impersonal divine force representing good and bad

    b. Many individuals pray to ancestors and local gods for intervention

5. Much mixing and intermingling of cultures

IDENTIFICATION: PEOPLE

What is the contribution of each of the following individuals to world history? (Identification should include answers to the questions *who, what, where, when, how,* and *why is this person important.*)

Menes

Khufu

Harkhuf

Tuthmosis III

King Kashta

Hatshepsut

Akhenaten

IDENTIFICATION: TERMS/CONCEPTS

State in your own words what each of the following terms means and why it is significant to a study of world history. (Those terms with an asterisk may be defined in the glossary.)

Sudan

Nile

Nubia

Memphis

Upper Egypt

Lower Egypt

Pharaoh

Horus

Amon

Archaic Period

Old Kingdom

Pyramids

Kush

Kerma

Middle Kingdom

Hyksos

New Kingdom

Napata

Patriarchy*

Thebes

Heliopolis

Tanis

Meroë

Bronze metallurgy

Iron metallurgy

Punt

Hieroglyphs

Papyrus

Hieratic script

Re

Aten

Tell el-Amarna

Mummification

Osiris

Apedemak

Sebiumeker

Bantu

Niger-Congo

Mande

Age sets

STUDY QUESTIONS

1. How did Egyptian religious beliefs reflect their society, lifestyle, and geographic location?

2. How did climatic change influence the early development of African cultures?

3. How did the institution of the pharaoh evolve, and what was the nature of the pharaoh's power through the Old Kingdom period?

4. Describe the early Kingdom of Kush. What was its relationship with Egypt like?

5. How did the invasion of the Hyksos influence the later development of Egypt?

6. In what ways was the New Kingdom period of Egypt different from the earlier ones? What were the relations with Kush like during this period?

7. What was society like in Egypt and Nubia in terms of both social classes and gender roles?

8. What kind of transportation systems did the Egyptians use, and how did their transportation influence the development of their trade networks?

9. What was the significance of the cult of Osiris?

10. How did the Bantu migrations influence the development of the societies of sub-Saharan Africa?

INQUIRY QUESTIONS

1. Compare and contrast Egyptian and Nubian society. Why is there so much more known about Egypt? Come up with at least five good reasons.

2. Herodotus said that Egypt was the "gift of the Nile." What does this mean? In what ways did the Nile affect Egyptian culture? Hint: think about more than just agriculture.

3. Agriculture spread through sub-Saharan Africa considerably later than it did through other parts of the world. Why do you think this is so? Come up with at least three possible explanations.

STUDENT QUIZ

1. The Greek historian Herodotus proclaimed Egypt "the gift of the Nile" because, in his account,
   a. the process of desiccation forced paleolithic human groups to migrate from the Sahara to the valley of the Nile.
   b. the Egyptians depended on the Nile for drinking water.
   c. the reliable rhythm of the Nile created fertile land, which supported a remarkably productive agricultural economy.
   d. Egyptian myth had their people emerging out of the river.
   e. all of the above.

2. Around 5000 B.C.E. the climate in northern Africa began to change by
   a. getting colder and wetter.
   b. getting colder and drier.
   c. getting hotter and wetter.
   d. getting hotter and drier.
   e. getting rainier.

3. Which of the following is true of the Nile?
   a. By worldwide standards it is a relatively short river.
   b. It is unusual in that it is navigable throughout its length.
   c. It used to flood very predictably.
   d. It flows from north to south.
   e. none of the above.

4. In contrast to Egypt, Nubian agriculture
   a. had to rely on rainfall.
   b. required extensive preparation of the soil.
   c. relied on a floodplain.
   d. was not an important factor in their economy.
   e. none of the above.

5. Unification of Egyptian rule came about through the conqueror
   a. Menes.
   b. Hatshepsut.
   c. Ta-Seti.
   d. Khufu.
   e. none of the above.

6. The Egyptian pyramids
   a. were built during the Old Kingdom.
   b. served as royal tombs.
   c. are testimony to the power of the pharaoh.
   d. stand at Giza.
   e. all of the above.

7. Mummification, pyramids, and funerary rituals in ancient Egypt were extremely costly and troublesome. The customs prevailed for several thousand years because
    a. the ruling elites perceived a need for demonstrating their power and wealth.
    b. Egyptians believed in an afterlife.
    c. the pharaohs tried to solve the problems of population pressure and unemployment.
    d. the pharaohs had slaves who could perform all these tasks.
    e. all of the above.

8. In ancient Egypt, the largest pyramid was that of
    a. Khufu.
    b. Menes.
    c. Horus.
    d. Tuthmosis III.
    e. Akhenaten.

9. After the Hyksos invasion
    a. the Middle Kingdom began.
    b. the Egyptians started using iron.
    c. the Nubians rose up and pushed them out.
    d. the Egyptians adopted horses and chariots in their military.
    e. all of the above.

10. After the tenth century, the Kingdom of Kush
    a. conquered Egypt.
    b. established a capital at Napata.
    c. claimed the title of pharaoh.
    d. warred with the Assyrians.
    e. all of the above.

11. Which of the following was *not* an important city in ancient Egypt?
    a. Meroë
    b. Tanis
    c. Heliopolis
    d. Thebes
    e. Memphis

12. Unlike Egypt, Nubian society
    a. was very egalitarian.
    b. did not include slaves.
    c. was patriarchal.
    d. saw many more women rulers.
    e. all of the above.

13. Technologically speaking, the Nile societies
    a. were slower to develop metallurgy than Mesopotamia was.
    b. learned iron metallurgy from sub-Saharan African cultures.
    c. developed systems of water transport like the sailboat.
    d. produced fine linen textiles.
    e. all of the above.

14. Which of the following is true of Egyptian writing?
    a. It has not been translated yet.
    b. Most writing was done on clay tablets.
    c. It was unintelligible to the Nubians.
    d. It included hieroglyphic, hieratic, demotic, and Coptic scripts.
    e. none of the above.

15. All of the following were important Egyptian gods *except*
    a. Osiris.
    b. Amon.
    c. Aten.
    d. Sepiumeker.
    e. Re.

16. A significant difference between Nubian and Egyptian religion was that
    a. Nubians did not build pyramids.
    b. Nubians did not recognize Egyptian sun gods.
    c. Nubians did not mummify their dead.
    d. Nubians did not have priests.
    e. all of the above.

17. The original Bantu people
    a. spoke a language in the Niger-Congo family.
    b. settled mostly on the banks of rivers.
    c. came from what is now Nigeria.
    d. cultivated yams and palm oils.
    e. all of the above.

18. With regard to the Bantu migrations,
    a. their suddenness suggested displacement by hunting/gathering people.
    b. they placed pressure on the forest dwellers by moving inland.
    c. they never migrated south of the equator.
    d. they gave up living along rivers for moving inland.
    e. all of the above.

19. Iron metallurgy
    a. was learned by the Africans from the Hittites.
    b. eventually was displaced by bronze metallurgy.
    c. never spread south of the Sahara.
    d. helped the Bantu expand their agricultural land.
    e. none of the above.

20. Which of the following is associated with agricultural societies south of the Sahara?
    a. cultivation of yams, oil palms, and sorghum.
    b. herding sheep, cattle, pigs.
    c. age sets and initiation rites.
    d. monotheistic religions.
    e. all of the above.

MATCHING

Match these figures with the statements that follow.

A. Khufu   E. Hatshepsut
B. Narmer   F. Amenhotep IV
C. Kashta   G. Herodotus
D. Tuthmosis III   H. Harkhuf

1. ___ Female Pharaoh during the New Kingdom.

2. ___ Imperialistic pharaoh of the New Kingdom.

3. ___ Ancient Greek historian who traveled to Egypt and wrote about the culture.

4. ___ King of Kush who conquered Egypt.

5. ___ Promoted first monotheistic religion on record.

6. ___ Name associated with legendary conqueror and unifier of Egypt.

7. ___ Royal official and governor of Upper Egypt who wrote autobiography.

8. ___ Pharaoh who had largest pyramid in Egypt built for his tomb.

SEQUENCING

Place the following clusters of events in chronological order. Consider carefully how one event leads to another, and try to determine the internal logic of each sequence.

A.

_____ Permanent settlements appear in eastern Sudan and sorghum is cultivated.

_____ Extended period of climatic change begins in north Africa.

_____ Cultivators and herders migrate to bodies of water.

_____ Peoples of north Africa adopt iron metallurgy.

_____ Peoples of Sudan hunt wild cattle on the grasslands and collect wild grains.

_____ Small kingdoms appear in Egypt and Nubia.

B.

_____ City of Memphis is founded.

_____ Assyrians conquer Egypt.

_____ King Kashta conquers Egypt.

_____ Hyksos invade Egypt.

_____ Great pyramids are built at Giza.

_____ Egypt conquers Palestine and Syria.

QUOTATIONS

For each of the following quotes, identify the speaker, if known, or the point of view or the subject. What is the significance of each passage?

1. "How many are your deeds, Though hidden from sight, O Sole God beside whom there is none! You made the earth as you wished you alone."

2. "How [the gods] rejoice: you have strengthened their offerings! How your [people] rejoice: you have made their frontiers! . . . How Egypt rejoices in your strength: you have protected its customs!"

3. "When you overflow, O Hapy, Sacrifice is made for you; Oxen are slaughtered for you, A great oblation is made to you. Fowl is fattened for you, desert game snared for you, As one repays your bounty."

4. "The majesty of [Pharaoh] Mernere, my lord, sent me together with my father . . . to . . . Yam to open the way to that country. I did it in seven months; I brought from it all kinds of beautiful and rare gifts, and was praised for it greatly."

MAP EXERCISES

1.   On the outline map of Africa below, color and write in the following locations: Sahara,
     Sudan, Egypt (Upper and Lower), Nubia, Red Sea, Nile (delta, first cataract, source),
     Memphis, Giza, Kush, Kerma, Napata, Thebes, Heliopolis, Tanis, Meroë, Punt, Tell el-
     Amarna, Aswan, Elephantine, Palestine, Syria, Bantu Homeland, Lake Chad, Congo River,
     Lake Victoria.

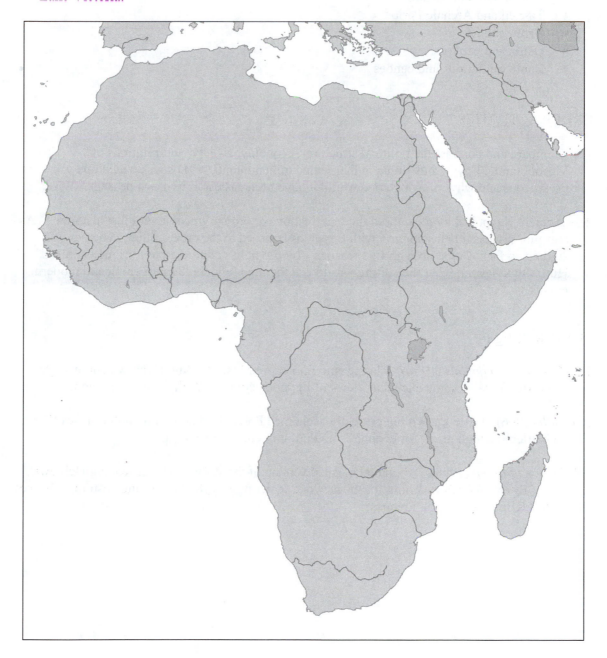

2.   Study the map of Bantu migrations on page 83. Then find a website that shows the
     distribution of Bantu-speaking peoples today. In what modern countries are they located?
     How many of those cultures could trace their migration back to the period studied in this
     chapter? How many must have migrated later?

CONNECTIONS

In fifty words or less explain the relationship between each of the following pairs. How does one lead to or foster the other? Be specific in your response. (May be done individually or in small groups.)

- Nile and mummification
- Ta-Seti and Archaic Period
- Bantu and iron
- Osiris and papyrus
- Bantu migrations and canoes

GROUP ACTIVITIES

1. Compare and contrast the political structures, economy, society, and religions of Mesopotamia, Egypt, and Nubia in the second millennium B.C.E. Discuss which one was most prosperous and why. In which one would it have been easiest to live as a peasant? Why?

2. Ancient Egypt has long captured the imaginations of ordinary people, not just historians. As a group, discuss this fascination with Egypt (as opposed to the other cultures you have studied so far). Come up with five reasons why Egypt has continued to intrigue people. Hint: think beyond what the culture was like at the time to include intervening and modern events.

FEATURE FILMS

The Ten Commandments (1956). Classic epic film about Moses leading Hebrews out of Egypt. First part contains some excellent views of Egyptian culture. With Charlton Heston.

Pharaoh (1966). Little-known but critically acclaimed Polish film about Pharaoh Ramses III as he battled the high priest for economic and military control of Egypt.

The Prince of Egypt (1998). Animated musical version of the story of Moses leading Hebrews out of Egypt. Worth watching for the artwork depicting Egyptian cities and costumes. Voices of Val Kilmer and Ralph Fiennes.

CHAPTER 4
EARLY SOCIETIES IN SOUTH ASIA

INTRODUCTION

An agricultural economy and its accompanying neolithic communities emerged on the Indian subcontinent some time after 7000 B.C.E. Eventually some of the neolithic villages further evolved into urban societies. The earliest such society was Dravidian and was known as the Harappan society. It flourished along the Indus River valley in the third millennium B.C.E. Coinciding with the decline of the Harappan society, large numbers of Indo-European migrants were moving into India from central Asia beginning around 1900 B.C.E. These peoples, known as Aryans, brought with them cultural traditions sharply different from the earlier societies. After a period of turmoil the Aryan and Dravidian cultures merged to generate a distinctive Indian society characterized by

- Regional states with kingship (*rajas*) as the most common form of government.
- The caste system, a complex social class system that served as a vehicle for imparting a powerful sense of group identity, as a stabilizing influence in Indian society and as a foundation for the religious belief system.
- A distinctive set of religious beliefs encompassing the doctrines of samsara and karma along with the notion of a universal soul, or Brahman.
- A rich literary religious tradition based on centuries of oral transmission that included such classics as the Vedas and the Upanishads.

OUTLINE

I. Harappan society

    A. Background

        1. Neolithic villages in Indus River valley by 3000 B.C.E.

        2. Earliest remains inaccessible because of silt deposits and rising water table

        3. Also little known because writing not yet translated

    B. Foundations of Harappan society

        1. The Indus River

            a. Runs through north India, with sources at Hindu Kush and the Himalayas

            b. Rich deposits but less predictable than the Nile

            c. Wheat and barley were cultivated in Indus valley

            d. Cultivated cotton before 5000 B.C.E.

            e. Complex society of Dravidians, 3000 B.C.E.

        2. No evidence about political system

        3. Harappa and Mohenjo-daro: two main cities

            a. Each city had a fortified citadel and a large granary

  b. Broad streets, marketplaces, temples, public buildings

  c. Standardized weights, measures, architectural styles, and brick sizes

 C. Harappan society and culture

  1. Social distinctions, as seen from living styles

  2. Religious beliefs strongly emphasized fertility

  3. Harappan society declined from 1900 B.C.E. onward

   a. Ecological degradation led to a subsistence crisis

   b. Another possibility: natural catastrophes such as floods or earthquakes

   c. Population began to abandon their cities by about 1700 B.C.E.

   d. Almost entirely collapsed by about 1500 B.C.E.

   e. Some Harappan cultural traditions maintained

II. The Indo-European migrations and early Aryan India

 A. The Aryans and India

  1. The early Aryans

   a. Depended heavily on a pastoral economy

   b. No writing system, but had orally transmitted works called the Vedas

   c. Sacred language (Sanskrit) and daily-use language (Prakit)

  2. The Vedic Age: 1500–500 B.C.E.

   a. A boisterous period; conflicts with indigenous peoples

   b. Called indigenous people *dasas*—"enemies" or "subject people"

   c. Indra, the Aryans' war god and military hero

   d. Aryan chiefdoms fought ferociously among themselves

   e. Most chiefdoms had leader *raja,* king

  3. Aryan migrations in India: first Punjab and by 500 B.C.E. in northern Deccan

   a. Used iron tools and developed agriculture

   b. Lost tribal organizations but established regional kingdoms

 B. Origins of the caste system

  1. Caste and *varna*

   a. The meaning of *caste*: hereditary, unchangeable social classes

   b. The Sanskrit word *varna,* "color," refers to social classes

  2. Social distinctions in the late Vedic Age

   a. Four main *varnas,* recognized after 1000 B.C.E.: *brahmins* (priests), *kshatriyas* (warriors and aristocrats), *vaishyas* (cultivators, artisans, and merchants), *shudras* (landless peasants and serfs)

      b. Later the category of the untouchables was added

   3. Subcaste, or *jati*

      a. Represented more elaborate scheme of social classification; developed after the sixth century B.C.E.

      b. *Jati*, or subcastes, were determined by occupations

      c. Elaborate rules of *jati* life: eating, communication, behavior

   4. In caste system, social mobility difficult but still possible

      a. Usually a result of group, not individual, effort

      b. Foreign peoples could find a place in society of the castes

C. Development of patriarchal society

   1. Patriarchal and patrilineal society

   2. *The Lawbook of Manu*

      a. Prepared by an anonymous sage, first century B.C.E.

      b. Dealt with moral behavior and social relationships

      c. Advised men to treat women with honor and respect

      d. Subjected women to the control and guidance of men

      e. Women's duties: to bear children and maintain the household

   3. *Sati,* social custom in which widow throws self on funeral pyre

III. Religion in the Vedic Age

A. Aryan religion

   1. Aryan gods

      a. War god, Indra

      b. Gods of the sun, the sky, the moon, fire, health, disease

      c. God Varuna: ethical concern, cosmic order

   2. Ritual sacrifices were more important than ethics

      a. Priests were specialists of the ritual sacrifices

      b. Ritual sacrifices for rewards from the divine power

      c. Sacrifices, chants, *soma*

   3. Spirituality underwent a shift after about 800 B.C.E.

      a. Thoughtful individuals retreated to forests as hermits

      b. Dravidian notions of transmigration and reincarnation were adapted

B. The blending of Aryan and Dravidian values

   1. The Upanishads, works of religious teachings (800–400 B.C.E.)

      a. The religious forums: dialogues between disciples and sages

b. Brahman: the universal soul

c. Highest goal: to escape reincarnation and join with Brahman

d. Samsara: an individual soul was born many times

e. Karma: specific incarnations that a soul experienced

f. *Moksha*: permanent liberation from physical incarnation

2. Religion and Vedic society

a. Samsara and karma reinforced caste and social hierarchy

b. Upanishads were also spiritual and intellectual contemplations

c. Taught to observe high ethical standards: discourage greed, envy, vice

d. Respect for all living things, a vegetarian diet

IDENTIFICATION: TERMS/CONCEPTS

State in your own words what each of the following terms means and why it is significant to a study of world history. (Those terms with an asterisk may be defined in the glossary.)

Indra

Aryans

Dravidians

Harappan society

Indus River

Harappa

Mohenjo-daro

Sanskrit

Pakrit

Vedas

Rig Veda

Raja

Punjab

Ganges River

Caste*

Varna

Brahmans

Kshatriyas

Vaishyas

Shudras

Jati

Patriarchy*

Lawbook of Manu

Sati

Varuna

Soma

Upanishads

Brahman

Samsara

Karma

Moksha

Yoga

STUDY QUESTIONS

1. Why is so little known about the Harappan society? What is it that we *do* know about the nature of that society?

2. How do historians and archeologists explain the decline of the Harappan culture?

3. How were the Indo-European migrants different from the cultures that already existed in India?

4. Trace the origins of the caste system, making sure to include a discussion of *varna* and *jati*.

5. Discuss the nature of patriarchy in early Indian societies. What is the *Lawbook of Manu* and how does it relate to gender roles?

6. What are the Vedas and what do they teach us about early Indian societies?

7. What are the fundamental religious teachings of the Upanishads?

8. How did the religious beliefs as expressed in the Upanishads dovetail with the social order during the Vedic age?

9. In what ways did the religion of the Upanishads include an ethical system?

10. How did the Dravidian and Aryan cultures blend during this period?

INQUIRY QUESTIONS

1. There are very few names of prominent individuals included in this chapter. Why is this so? What is it about the nature of the society and the available historical sources that makes it difficult to discern individuals?

2. What were the advantages of the caste system to the development of Indian societies during this time period? Why do you believe this system managed to persist for millennia?

3. The religious beliefs of this period emerged as a result of the blending of Aryan and Dravidian traditions and significant developments in the later Vedic age. These beliefs were the underpinnings of the Hindu religion, which is still the most prevalent religion of the Indian subcontinent. What aspects of this belief system make it so appealing to people? How did it both reflect and support other social institutions?

STUDENT QUIZ

1. Our understanding of Harappan society depends entirely on
    a. written records uncovered in Harappa and other Dravidian cities.
    b. archaeological discoveries of Harappan physical remains below the water table.
    c. archaeological discoveries of Harappan physical remains above the water table.
    d. the Vedas and the Upanishads.
    e. all of the above.

2. The inhabitants of Harappan society enjoyed a rich variety of diet. Their food included
    a. wheat, barley, chicken, cattle, sheep, goats.
    b. soybeans, sorghum, rice, pigs, fish.
    c. sweet potatoes, tomatoes, maize, cacao beans.
    d. millet, yams, legumes, no meat.
    e. none of the above.

3. In the sites of Harappa and Mohenjo-daro, archeologists have found a high degree of standardization of weights, measures, architectural styles, and even brick sizes. Such standardization may suggest that
    a. the Harappan state was very oppressive, forcing different racial groups to adopt the same standards.
    b. there might have been a central authority powerful enough to reach all corners of society.
    c. there was a high degree of commercialization in the economy.
    d. these cultures actually migrated from Mesopotamia.
    e. none of the above.

4. Archaeologists claim that there were sharp social distinctions in Harappan society, which can be illustrated by the people's
    a. gold, gems, and decorative items.
    b. bathrooms, showers, and toilets.
    c. foods, clothes, and hairstyles.
    d. houses, ovens, and wells.
    e. all of the above.

5. Harappan religion reflected a strong concern for fertility. We know this because
    a. it was very common for the peoples in other early agricultural societies to honor fertility gods or goddesses.
    b. the bronze figurine of a dancing girl discovered at Mohenjo-daro reveals this point.
    c. of the similarities between the images of Harappan deities and the images of Hindu fertility deities.
    d. there is written documentation to support it.
    e. none of the above.

6. By about 1700 B.C.E., the residents of Harappa and Mohenjo-daro began to abandon their cities because
    a. frequent epidemics made city living impossible.
    b. deforestation of the Indus River valley brought about ecological degradation.
    c. the horse-riding Aryans began to invade the cities.
    d. the Indus River dried up.
    e. all of the above.

7. The Aryans
    a. forcibly drove the Harappans out of their cities.
    b. came suddenly, in a massive migration.
    c. entered the Indus valley at the height of the Harappan society.
    d. refused to intermingle with the Dravidians.
    e. none of the above.

8. The Indo-Europeans who migrated to the Indian subcontinent
    a. were primarily herders.
    b. utilized horses for transportation.
    c. judged wealth by the number of cattle.
    d. called themselves Aryans.
    e. all of the above.

9. The period of Indian history from 1500 to 500 B.C.E. is called the Vedic Age. It is so called because
    a. this was how the Aryans referred to this period.
    b. the four earliest religious texts were compiled in this period.
    c. this was the period in which the Indians were particularly religious.
    d. the major god was Vedas.
    e. none of the above.

10. The Aryans' term for their four original castes was
    a. *jati.*
    b. brahmans.
    c. *varnas.*
    d. *shudras.*
    e. none of the above.

11. The Indian caste system
    a. was a central institution that served to promote social stability.
    b. was incapable of accommodating social changes.
    c. was actually not much of a restriction on the upward mobility of individuals.
    d. did not persist beyond the Vedic age.
    e. none of the above.

12. One of the hymns in the *Rig Veda* offered a brief account of the origins of the four *varnas* (castes). It was said that
    a. the four castes were created according to the wills of Indra and Agni (the god of fire).
    b. Purusha, a primeval being, sacrificed himself in order to create the four castes.
    c. the brahman priests created the four castes with themselves at the top.
    d. the four castes emanated from the four parts of Purusha when the gods sacrificed him.
    e. none of the above.

13. Which of the following was evidence of the subordination of women to men in Aryan society?
    a. patrilineal descent
    b. the *Lawbook of Manu.*
    c. the practice of *sati.*
    d. women had no responsibilities for religious rituals.
    e. all of the above.

14. Aryan religion during the early Vedic Age was relatively unconcerned with ethics, but concerned itself more with
    a. ritual sacrifices and the god of war.
    b. fertility and immortality.
    c. spirituality and meditation.
    d. building religious buildings.
    e. all of the above.

15. The Upanishads can be best characterized as
    a. the spiritual longing of the Aryans.
    b. the further development of the religious tradition of the Dravidians.
    c. a how-to book of religious ritual.
    d. the blending of Aryan and Dravidian values.
    e. none of the above.

16. According to the teachings of the Upanishads, the highest goal of the individual soul was
    a. to attain the state of samsara.
    b. to attain the state of *moksha*.
    c. to avoid one's karma.
    d. to separate from Brahman.
    e. to practice yoga.

17. According to the Upanishads,
    a. each person is part of a larger cosmic order..
    b. the highest goal of the individual is to escape the cycle of birth and rebirth.
    c. individuals who live virtuous lives and do their duty can expect rebirth into a purer form.
    d. ascetism and meditation are vehicles for escaping the cycle of birth and rebirth.
    e. all of the above.

18. In the *Chandogya Upanishad*, a man explained to his son how
    a. bees made honey.
    b. to remove salt from water.
    c. the subtle essence of Brahman pervades everything.
    d. individuals were separate in universal reality.
    e. none of the above.

19. According to the teachings of the Upanishads, an individual should
    a. be attached to the material world as closely as possible.
    b. ignore ethical standards, since these standards were not the ultimate reality.
    c. observe high ethical standards like honesty, self-control, and charity.
    d. avoid any inclinations to gain self-knowledge.
    e. none of the above.

20. Believers in the Upanishads
    a. often are vegetarians.
    b. believe you should respect all living things, even animals and insects.
    c. believe that animals might be holding incarnations of unfortunate souls.
    d. humans should have compassion for the suffering of the souls in animals.
    e. all of the above.

MATCHING

Match these terms with the statements that follow.

A.	*Soma*	G.	Karma
B.	*Moksha*	H.	Upanishad
C.	Samsara	I.	*Jati*
D.	*Sati*	J.	*Dasas*
E.	*Rig Veda*	K.	*Varna*
F.	Brahman	L.	*Kshatriyas*

1. ____ The Indian custom in which a widow throws herself on her husband's funeral pyre to join him in death.

2. ____ Aryan term for the Sanskrit word meaning "color"; refers to the major social classes.

3. ____ A hallucinogenic drink used in religious ceremonies.

4. ____ A universal soul: permanent, unchanging and eternal.

5. ____ Aryan term for the indigenous people of India; technically it means "enemies" or "subject peoples."

6. ____ The warrior and aristocratic class of the Vedic age.

7. ____ The doctrine that held that after death individual souls go to the World of the Fathers and then return to earth in a new incarnation.

8. ____ "A sitting in front of"; it refers to the practice of disciples gathering before a sage.

9. ____ A collection of over 1,000 hymns addressed to the Aryan gods.

10. ____ The doctrine that accounted for the specific incarnations of the soul based on deeds in previous incarnations.

11. ____ A state like deep, dreamless sleep that comes with permanent liberation from physical incarnation.

12. ____ A subcaste usually based on occupation.

SEQUENCING

Place the following clusters of events in chronological order. Consider carefully how one event leads to another, and try to determine the internal logic of each sequence.

A.

_____   Harappan society covers a territory larger than Mesopotamia.

_____   Inhabitants abandon Mohenjo-daro.

_____   Regional kingdoms replace chiefdoms in most parts of northern India.

_____   Aryan priests begin to compile the *Rig Veda*.

_____   Indo-Europeans migrate into Indus valley.

_____   Indus valley inhabitants begin cultivating cotton.

QUOTATIONS

For each of the following quotes, identify the speaker, if known, or the point of view or the subject. What is the significance of each passage?

1. "So mighty is his greatness; yea, greater than this is Purusha. All creatures are one-fourth of him, [the other] three-fourths [of him are] eternal life in heaven."

2. "Women are to be honored and adorned by their fathers, brothers, husbands and brothers-in-law, who desire much prosperity . . . Houses, cursed by women and not honored, perish utterly as if destroyed by magic."

3. "Now as a man is like this or like that, according as he acts and according as he behaves, so will he be: a man of good acts will become good, a man of bad acts, bad. He becomes pure by pure deeds, bad by bad deeds."

4. "Believe it, my son. That which is the subtle essence, in it all that exists has its self. It is the True. It is the Self, and you, Svetaketu, are it."

MAP EXERCISES

1. Examine map 2.4 (page 56) and map 4.1 (page 92) showing the Indo-European migrations and the Harappan society. What kinds of contact might the Harappan people have had with the Indo-Europeans before the Indo-Europeans began migrating into the Indus valley? Where did their paths cross? What routes did the Indo-Europeans take into India? Explain the progress of their migrations over a fifteen-hundred-year period.

CONNECTIONS

In fifty words or less explain the relationship between each of the following pairs. How does one lead to or foster the other? Be specific in your response. (May be done individually or in small groups.)

- Caste and Upanishads
- Harappan society and cattle
- The Vedas and the *Lawbook of Manu*
- Karma and vegetarianism
- Aryans and *rajas*

GROUP ACTIVITIES

1. Imagine that you are a group of archeologists who are about to begin excavating a site on the Indus River that you believe dates back to about 2000 B.C.E. Make a list of the sorts of artifacts you expect to find there. What sorts of evidence might you be looking for to find answers to as-yet-unanswered questions about this society?

CHAPTER 5
EARLY SOCIETY IN EAST ASIA

INTRODUCTION

The cultures of east Asia had relatively little direct contact with the complex societies to the west; nevertheless, powerful states (the Xia, Shang, and Zhou dynasties), sophisticated technologies, and highly stratified societies developed along the banks of the Yellow and Yangzi rivers in China. These early societies were built on a foundation that would endure for millennia, some of the significant components of which include

- The belief in the principle that the emperor was granted the power to rule through "the mandate of heaven." Thus the emperor, known as the son of heaven, served as a crucial link between the heavenly powers and the people on earth.
- The extended family as the primary institution of society. The patriarchal head of the family wielded tremendous power and shouldered great responsibilities. It was his job to see that appropriate religious rituals were observed in the worship of the family's departed ancestors. Those ancestors were believed to have control over the living family's well-being.
- A writing system that spread widely throughout China and still persists in its basic form, although modified through time. Consequently Chinese society has experienced a virtually uninterrupted literary tradition.
- Sharp distinctions and clearly defined roles within the society based on class, gender, and age.

OUTLINE

I. Political organization in early China

    A. Early agricultural society and the Xia dynasty

        1. The Yellow River

            a. Water source at high plateau of Tibet

            b. Loess soil carried by the river's water, hence "yellow"

            c. "China's Sorrow"—extensive flooding

            d. Loess provided rich soil, soft and easy to work

        2. Neolithic societies after 5000 B.C.E.

            a. Yangshao society, 5000–3000 B.C.E.

            b. Excavations at Banpo village: fine pottery, bone tools

        3. The Xia dynasty

            a. Archeological discovery of the Xia is still in its early stages

            b. Established about 2200 B.C.E.

            c. Legendary King Yu, the dynasty founder, a hero of flood control

        d.   Erlitou: possibly the capital city of the Xia

B. The Shang dynasty: 1766–1122 B.C.E.

    1. Arose in the southern and eastern areas of the Xia realm

    2. Many written records and material remains discovered

    3. Bronze metallurgy, monopolized by ruling elite

    4. Horses and chariots traveled with Indo-European migrants to China

    5. Agricultural surpluses supported large troops

    6. A vast network of walled towns

    7. The Shang capital moved six times

    8. Lavish tombs of Shang kings with thousands of objects

    9. Other states besides Shang, for example, Sanxingdui

C. The Zhou dynasty: 1122–256 B.C.E.

    1. Zhou gradually eclipsed Shang

    2. Mandate of heaven, the right to rule

        a. The Zhou needed to justify the overthrow

        b. Ruler as "the son of heaven"

        c. Mandate of heaven only given to virtuous rulers

    3. Political organization: decentralized administration

        a. Used princes and relatives to rule regions

        b. Consequence: weak central government and rise of regional powers

    4. Iron metallurgy spread through China in first millennium B.C.E.

    5. The fall of the Zhou

        a. Nomadic invasion sacked Zhou capital in 711 B.C.E.

        b. Territorial princes became more independent

        c. The Warring States (403–221 B.C.E.)

        d. The last king of the Zhou abdicated his position in 256 B.C.E.

II. Society and family in ancient China

A. The social order

    1. The ruling elites with their lavish consumption of bronze

        a. Hereditary aristocrats with extensive landholding

        b. Administrative and military offices

        c. Manuals of etiquette

    2. Free artisans and craftsmen mostly worked for elites

    3. Merchants and trade were important

      a.   Trade networks linked China with west and south

      b.   Oar-propelled boats traded with Korea and offshore islands

   4. Peasants, the majority of population

      a.   Landless peasants provided labor

      b.   Lived in small subterranean houses

      c.   Women's work: wine making, weaving, silkworm raising

      d.   Wood, bone, stone tools before iron was spread in the sixth century B.C.E.

   5. Slaves, mostly war prisoners

B. Family and patriarchy

   1. Early dynasties ruled through family and kinship groups

   2. Veneration of ancestors

      a.   Belief in ancestors' presence and their continuing influence

      b.   Burial of material goods with the dead

      c.   Offering sacrifices at the graves

      d.   Family heads presided over rites of honoring ancestors' spirits

   3. Patriarchal society evolved out of matrilineal one

      a.   The rise of large states brought focus on men's contribution

      b.   After the Shang, females devalued

III. Early Chinese writing and cultural development

A. The secular cultural tradition

   1. Absence of organized religion and priestly class

   2. Believed in the impersonal heavenly power—*tian*

   3. Oracle bones used by fortune-tellers

      a.   Inscribed question, subjected to heat, read cracks

      b.   Discovery of the "dragon bones" in 1890s

   4. Early Chinese writing, from pictograph to ideograph

      a.   More than two thousand characters identified on oracle bones

      b.   Modern Chinese writing is direct descendant of Shang writing

B. Thought and literature

   1. Zhou literature—many kinds of books

      a.   *The Book of Change*, a manual of diviners

      b.   *The Book of History*, the history of the Zhou

      c.   *The Book of Rites*, the rules of etiquette and rituals for aristocrats

      d.   *The Book of Songs,* a collection of verses—most notable work

2. Most Zhou writings have perished

IV. Ancient China and the larger world

    A. Chinese cultivators and nomadic peoples of central Asia

        1. Nomadic peoples of the steppe lands—herders

            a. Exchange of products between nomads and Chinese farmers

            b. Nomads frequently invaded rich agricultural society

            c. Nomads did not imitate Chinese ways

            d. Nomads relied on grains and manufactured goods of the Chinese

    B. The southern expansion of Chinese society

        1. The Yangzi valley; dependable river; two crops of rice per year

        2. The indigenous peoples of southern China

            a. Many were assimilated into Chinese agricultural society

            b. Some were pushed to hills and mountains

            c. Some migrated to Taiwan, Vietnam, Thailand

        3. The state of Chu in the central region of Yanzi

            a. Challenged the Zhou for supremacy

            b. Adopted Chinese political and social traditions and writing

IDENTIFICATION: PEOPLE

What is the contribution of each of the following individuals to world history? (Identification should include answers to the questions *who, what, where, when, how,* and *why is this person important.*)

Yao

Shun

Yu

IDENTIFICATION: TERMS/CONCEPTS

State in your own words what each of the following terms means and why it is significant to a study of world history. (Those terms with an asterisk may be defined in the glossary.)

Xia dynasty

Huang He

Yangzi

Loess

Ao

Yin

Shang dynasty

Sanxingdui

Bronze metallurgy

Mandate of heaven

Zhou dynasty

Iron metallurgy

Period of the Warring States

Ancestor worship*

Book of Songs

Oracle bones

Book of Changes

Chu

Steppe lands

STUDY QUESTIONS

1. What do the legends of the three sage-kings tell us about the matters of greatest importance to the people of the early east Asian societies?

2. How did the physical features of the land and waters in east Asia influence the development of the culture?

3. What does the term *mandate of heaven* mean? How did it influence political developments in early east Asia?

4. What were the causes of the decline and eventual fall of the Zhou dynasty?

5. Describe the different social orders that developed during the first three dynasties.

6. What is the relationship between patriarchy and ancestor worship in early China?

7. What was the purpose of oracle bones during the Shang? What do they tell us about life at that time?

8. What do we know about writing and literature during the Zhou? Why is our knowledge so limited?

9. Describe the relationship between the Chinese society under the dynasties and the people of the steppe lands. How did these cultures differ? How did they influence each other?

10. What was the relationship between the culture of the Yellow River and that of the Yangzi Valley?

INQUIRY QUESTIONS

1. Many of the institutions and customs that emerged in east Asia during this era persisted until the twentieth century or even the present. Why do you think this is so? Why does there seem to be more continuity in east Asian history than in other parts of the world?

2. What are the advantages and disadvantages of a form of writing that is pictographic and ideographic (like Chinese) versus one that is alphabetic?

3. How do early east Asian religious beliefs and practices differ from those of the other early cultures you have studied so far? What do these differences imply about the societies' structures and their most important values?

STUDENT QUIZ

1. By exalting the legendary sage kings (Yao, Shun, and Yu) as exemplars of virtue, Chinese moralists promoted the values of
   a. hunting and gathering.
   b. military aggression and masculinity.
   c. social harmony, selflessness, hard work.
   d. matriarchy and the home.
   e. none of the above.

2. The Yellow River earned its nickname "China's Sorrow" because
   a. it was a turbulent river.
   b. its frequent floods were very destructive to agricultural society.
   c. it carried a heavy load of loess.
   d. it was a common place for people to commit suicide.
   e. none of the above.

3. In Yangshao society (5000–3000 B.C.E.), the people
   a. had fine pottery and used bone tools.
   b. cultivated rice through irrigation.
   c. began to use bronze tools.
   d. formed the first dynasty in Chinese history.
   e. none of the above.

4. Many scholars believe that the dynasty of China, Xia, was not a mere legend but a real state, because
    a. Erlitou, the capital of Xia, has been excavated.
    b. the oracle bones of Shang mentioned the Xia kings.
    c. Chinese writing has been traced back that far.
    d. the Chinese legends associated the founder of Xia with flood control.
    e. all of the above.

5. The Shang rulers monopolized bronze technology for the purpose of
    a. making superior weapons against potential competitors.
    b. distributing bronze tools among the farmers.
    c. preventing proliferation of weapons.
    d. making works of art.
    e. all of the above.

6. Which of the following were *not* found in the Shang tomb of Fu Hao?
    a. thousands of cowrie shells.
    b. sacrificial humans and dogs.
    c. jade figurines of servants.
    d. iron weapons.
    e. bronzes and bone carvings.

7. According to Zhou political theory, the Zhou king overthrew the Shang dynasty because
    a. the Shang lost the mandate of heaven.
    b. the subjects of Shang shifted their loyalty to Zhou.
    c. the last Shang king was a criminal fool.
    d. the Zhou was a much larger state than the Shang.
    e. none of the above.

8. The Chinese king was called the "son of heaven" and served as
    a. a ruler who could not be challenged.
    b. a link between heaven and earth.
    c. a divine king.
    d. the living son of the first emperor.
    e. none of the above.

9. To rule an extensive territory without advanced transportation and communication technology, Zhou rulers relied on decentralized administration, which meant that
    a. they entrusted power to locally elected authorities.
    b. they entrusted their relatives to rule the regions of their kingdom.
    c. they divided powers into three parts: legislative, judicial, and administrative.
    d. the local authorities did not have to collect taxes or tribute.
    e. none of the above.

10. The Zhou central government was unable to monopolize the production of iron because
    a. iron ore was too cheap and abundant.
    b. iron weapons were of such poor quality that no one really wanted them.
    c. the Zhou rulers spent too much money on bronze weaponry.
    d. the production of iron was kept a secret.
    e. none of the above.

11. All of the following were social classes of Xia, Shang, and Zhou, except
    a. hereditary aristocrats.
    b. scholars and bureaucrats.
    c. craftsmen and merchants.
    d. peasants and slaves.
    e. priests and monks.

12. The tradition of venerating ancestors was firmly established during the Xia, Shang, and Zhou dynasties. According to this tradition,
    a. one must treat the ancestors as gods or deities.
    b. one worshipped the departed ancestors for protection and good fortune.
    c. one only venerated those ancestors who performed good deeds for the family.
    d. one worshipped the emperor as the incarnation of one's ancestors.
    e. all of the above.

13. In practice, the veneration of ancestors reinforced the authority of the patriarchal head of the family because
    a. only male ancestors were the subjects of worship.
    b. female members of the family did not participate in honoring ancestors.
    c. it was the patriarch who presided at the rites honoring ancestors.
    d. only male ancestors were reincarnated.
    e. all of the above.

14. During the Xia, Shang, and Zhou dynasties China experienced the shift from a matrilineal society to a patrilineal society. This shift was caused by
    a. settled agriculture.
    b. the rise of large states.
    c. bronze metallurgy.
    d. the appearance of writing.
    e. none of the above.

15. During the early dynasties, Chinese diviners used oracle bones
    a. as objects of art.
    b. as drugs to cure people's diseases.
    c. to record manuals of etiquette.
    d. to predict the future and answer questions.
    e. none of the above.

16. From Shang times until today, Chinese writing is primarily
    a. ideographic.
    b. pictographic.
    c. phonetic.
    d. untranslated.
    e. none of the above.

16. All but one of the following were part of Zhou literature:
    a. poetry
    b. manuals of divination and ritual
    c. books of etiquette
    d. books of religious teaching
    e. political histories

17. The nomadic peoples to the north and west of China did not imitate Chinese ways because
    a. they did not speak Chinese.
    b. the grassy steppe lands were not suitable for agriculture or permanent settlement.
    c. the Chinese were their enemies.
    d. they had little exposure to the Chinese society.
    e. none of the above.

18. During the Zhou dynasty China expanded into the Yangzi River valley primarily through
    a. military conquest and colonization.
    b. migration and assimilation.
    c. interracial marriage.
    d. sending missionaries to convert them.
    e. all of the above.

19. The state of Chu
    a. was an autonomous state to the south of the Zhou state.
    b. refused to accept Chinese traditions and writing system.
    c. established a society radically different from that of north China.
    d. conquered the Zhou, ending the dynasty.
    e. none of the above.

MATCHING

Match these figures, terms, or dynasties with the statements that follow.

A. Sanxingdui   E. Yu
B. Shang   F. Xia
C. Banpo   G. Yao
D. Zhou   H. Luoyang

1. ___ State in the Sichuan province that existed at the same time as the Shang.

2. ___ Capital of Zhou dynasty after royal court was forced to move further east because of nomadic invasions from the west.

3. ___ Legendary sage-king who brought harmony to his family and all the states of China.

4. ___ Important archeological excavation of neolithic village in Yellow River valley.

5. ___ Traditionally considered the first of the Chinese dynasties; it established the precedent for hereditary monarchies.

6. ___ Legendary sage-king who was believed responsible for teaching flood control techniques in the earliest dynasty.

7. ___ Dynasty most associated with the production of oracle bones and bronze metallurgy.

8 ___ Dynasty that contributed some of the earliest literary works to Chinese history, even though many have deteriorated or been destroyed.

SEQUENCING

Place the following clusters of events in chronological order. Consider carefully how one event leads to another, and try to determine the internal logic of each sequence.

A.

_____ The dynasty's founder is traditionally believed to have been responsible for instituting flood control measures on the Yellow River.

_____ Dynastic rulers are noted for establishing a monopoly on the technologies and materials necessary to make weapons out of bronze. This weaponry allowed them to maintain their military superiority for more than five centuries.

_____ The agriculture-based Yangshao society flourishes in the Yellow River valley and creates fine pottery and bone tools.

_____ The development of the technology of iron metallurgy contributes to the decline of the Zhou. The rulers cannot maintain a monopoly on the manufacture of iron weaponry, making them vulnerable to challenges by their subordinates.

_____ A dynasty from northwestern China eventually overshadows the previous one by being more effective in winning allies. It rules, at least nominally, for more than eight hundred years.

QUOTATIONS

For each of the following quotes, identify the speaker, if known, or the point of view or the subject. What is the significance of each passage?

1. "When brothers are in urgent difficulties, friends, though they may be good will only heave long sighs."

2. "China's sorrow"

3. "Will the season's harvest be abundant or poor?"

4. "The peach tree is young and elegant; brilliant are its flowers. This young lady is going to her future home, and will order well her chamber and house."

MAP EXERCISES

1. On the outline map below, label the Yellow River and Yangzi River. Then draw the
    successive boundaries of the Xia, Shang, and Zhou dynasties. Shade in the areas where the
    nomadic herders had contact with the early Chinese and the area where the southern
    cultivation took place. What does this map tell you about the progress of east Asian history
    from about 2200 B.C.E. to 221 B.C.E.?

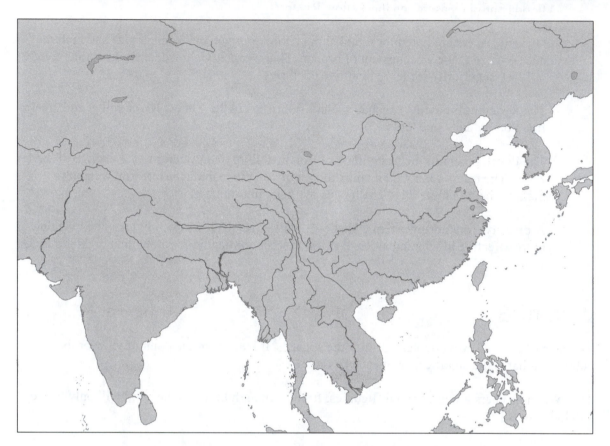

2. Examine the examples of the development of writing on page 94 in the textbook. Go to a
    website on Chinese writing and practice writing some words. Based on this limited sample,
    why do you think the Chinese consider calligraphy a high art form?

CONNECTIONS

In fifty words or less explain the relationship between each of the following pairs. How does one lead to or foster the other? Be specific in your response. (May be done individually or in small groups.)

- Bronze metallurgy and Shang dynasty
- Ancestor worship and patriarchy
- Oracle bones and *Book of Songs*
- Yu and mandate of heaven
- Iron metallurgy and Period of Warring States

GROUP ACTIVITIES

1. How would the structure of our lives differ today if we were all believers in the veneration of ancestors, as the early east Asians were? How would modern American rituals and ceremonies change? How would societal roles be different? How would values change?

2. Make a list of what you think would be the most likely questions a Shang ruler would want answered from a reading of the oracle bones. How might a diviner read the cracks and respond to the questions?

3. Compare and contrast early east Asian societies with early south Asian, Mesopotamian, and Egyptian societies. Find at least one important similarity and one important difference (if possible) in religion, government, social structure, economy, arts, literature.

FEATURE FILMS

The Emperor and the Assassin (1999). Chinese film set in the period of the Warring States: battles, blood, intrigue, and romance. Directed by Kaige Chen.

CHAPTER 6
EARLY SOCIETIES IN THE AMERICAS AND OCEANIA

INTRODUCTION

The cultures of the Americas and Oceania developed in relative isolation to the other early complex societies. Nevertheless, they too developed an agricultural base sufficient to support growing populations, specialized labor, political institutions, diverse societies, and long-distance trading networks. Less is known of these cultures than those in other parts of the world primarily because either writing systems did not develop or written documents perished or were destroyed. The fragments of writing and archeological findings indicate that these societies were complex and developed rich cultural traditions.

The early societies in the Americas

- Built elaborate ceremonial centers that reflected both a complex religion and a powerful political authority
- Left a rich artistic legacy that included pottery, sculpture, metalwork, and painting
- Developed sophisticated knowledge of astronomy and mathematics

The early societies of Oceania

- Saw the gradual dissemination of agricultural technology spread by Austronesian seafarers who traded and settled throughout the Pacific
- Formed a well-integrated society known as Lapita that stretched from New Guinea to Tonga

OUTLINE

I. **Early societies of Mesoamerica**

   A. The Olmecs

      1. Migration to Mesoamerica

         a. Large wave of humans traveled from Siberia to Alaska around 13,000 B.C.E.

         b. By 9500 B.C.E., humans reached the southernmost part of South America

         c. As hunting became difficult, agriculture began (7500 B.C.E.)

      2. Early agriculture: beans, squashes, chilis; later, maize became the staple (5000 B.C.E.)

         a. Agricultural villages appeared after 3000 B.C.E.

         b. No large domesticated animals, no wheeled vehicles

      3. Ceremonial centers by the end of the second millennium B.C.E.

      4. Olmecs, the "rubber people," lived near the Gulf of Mexico (1200 B.C.E.)

         a. Elaborate complexes built

         b. The colossal human heads—possibly likenesses of rulers

      c. Rulers' power shown in construction of huge pyramids

      d. Trade in jade and obsidian

      e. Decline of Olmecs: systematically destroyed ceremonial centers by 400 B.C.E.

  5. Influence of Olmec: maize, ceremonial centers, calendar, human sacrifice, ball game

B. Heirs of the Olmecs: the Maya

  1. The Maya lived in the highlands of Guatemala

      a. Besides maize, they also cultivated cotton and cacao

      b. Tikal was the most important Maya political center, 300 to 900 C.E.

      c. Maya warfare: warriors had prestige; captives were slaves or victims

      d. Chichén Itzá, power by the ninth century; loose empire in Yucatan

      e. Maya decline began in 800 C.E.; many Mayans deserted their cities

C. Maya society and religion

  1. Maya society was hierarchical

      a. Kings, priests, and hereditary nobility at the top

      b. Merchants were from the ruling class; they served also as ambassadors

      c. Professional architects and artisans were important

      d. Peasants and slaves were majority of population

  2. The Maya calendar had both solar and ritual years interwoven

  3. Maya writing was ideographic and syllabic; only four books survive

  4. Religious thought

      a. *Popol Vuh*, a Maya creation myth, taught that gods created humans out of maize and water

      b. Gods maintained agricultural cycles in exchange for honors and sacrifices

      c. Bloodletting rituals honored gods for rains

  5. The Maya ball game: sporting, gambling, and religious significance

D. Heirs of the Olmecs: Teotihuacan

  1. The city of Teotihuacan in the highlands of Mexico

      a. Colossal pyramids of sun and moon

      b. High point between 400 and 600 C.E.; two hundred thousand inhabitants

      c. Paintings and murals reflect the importance of priests

  2. Teotihuacan society

      a. Rulers and priests dominated society

      b. Two-thirds of the city inhabitants worked in fields during daytime

      c. Artisans were famous for their obsidian tools and orange pottery

          d.   Professional merchants traded extensively throughout Mesoamerica

          e.   No sign of military organization or conquest

     3. Cultural traditions: ball game, calendar, writing, sacrifices

     4. Decline of Teotihuacan from about 650 C.E.; was sacked and destroyed mid-eighth century

II. Early societies of South America

  A. Early Andean society and the Chavín cult

     1. Early migration to Peru and Bolivia region

          a. By 12,000 B.C.E. hunting and gathering peoples reached South America

          b. By 8000 B.C.E. they began to experiment with agriculture

          c. Complex societies appeared in central Andean region after 1000 B.C.E.

          d. Andean societies were located in modern-day Peru and Bolivia

     2. Early agriculture in South America

          a. Main crops: beans, peanuts, sweet potatoes, cotton

          b. Fishing supplemented agricultural harvests

          c. By 1800 B.C.E. the people produced pottery, built temples and pyramids

     3. The Chavín Cult, from about 900 to 300 B.C.E.

          a. Complexity of Andean society increases during Chavín

          b. Devised techniques of producing cotton textiles and fishing nets

          c. Discovered gold, silver, and copper metallurgy

          d. Cities began to appear shortly after Chavín cult

          e. Early Andeans did not make use of writing

  B. Early Andean states: Mochica (300–700 C.E.) in northern Peru

     1. Irrigation, trade, military, no writing

     2. Artistic legacy: painting on pottery, ceramics

III. Early societies of Oceania

  A. Early societies in Australia and New Guinea

     1. Human migrants arrived in Australia and New Guinea at least sixty thousand years ago

          a. By the mid-centuries of the first millennium C.E., human communities in all habitable islands of the Pacific Ocean

          b. About ten thousand years ago, rising seas separated Australia and New Guinea

          c. Australia: hunting and gathering until the nineteenth and twentieth centuries C.E.

          d. New Guinea: Turned to agriculture about 3000 B.C.E.

2. Austronesian peoples from southeast Asia were seafarers to New Guinea, 3000 B.C.E.

3. Early agriculture in New Guinea: root crops and herding animals

B. The peopling of the Pacific Islands

1. Austronesian migration to Polynesia

   a. Outrigger canoes enabled them to sail safely

   b. Agriculture and domesticated animals

2. Austronesian migrations to Micronesia and Madagascar

3. Lapita Society from New Guinea to Tonga (1500–500 B.C.E.)

   a. Agricultural villages

   b. Pottery with geometric designs

   c. Networks of trade/communication: pottery, obsidian, shells, tools traded

   d. After 500 B.C.E. trade network declined; cultures developed independently

   e. Hierarchical chiefdoms; tension led to migration

   f. Divine or semidivine chiefs: led public rituals, oversaw irrigation

IDENTIFICATION: TERMS/CONCEPTS

State in your own words what each of the following terms means and why it is significant to a study of world history.

Land bridges

Olmecs

Maya

Tikal

Chichén Itzá

Popol Vuh

Ball game

Teotihuacan

Chavín

Mochica

Austronesians

Lapita

70

STUDY QUESTIONS

1. How did humans come to settle in all parts of the Americas and in Oceania?

2. What traditions begun by the Olmecs were later adopted by other Mesoamerican societies?

3. How did the religion of the Maya reflect and reinforce their economy and governmental structure?

4. What role did human sacrifice play in early American societies?

5. For what were the people of the Teotihuacan culture most noted?

6. How did the geography of South America influence the development of the early complex societies there?

7. Compare and contrast the societies that existed under the Chavín cult and the Mochica State.

8. Where and how did agriculture spread in Oceania?

9. Describe the origins and development and the decline of the Lapita society.

10. In general, how did political structures evolve on the islands of Oceania?

INQUIRY QUESTIONS

1. Consider the meaning of bloodletting and human sacrifice to the Mesoamericans. How do these practices make sense in the context of their belief systems? How did their societies evolve to support these beliefs and these practices? What sorts of practices evolved out of different belief systems in other parts of the world?

2. How did the geography of the Americas and Oceania contribute to their unique development? What are the similarities in their patterns of development in spite of the geographical differences?

3. The paucity of written documentation for these cultures makes for large gaps in our understanding of them. What sorts of information can we obtain about cultures such as these without written texts, and what will we never know?

STUDENT QUIZ

1. By cutting slits onto his penis in a public ritual, the Maya prince Chan Bahlum intended to
    a. test his potency and power of fertility.
    b. please the goddess.
    c. imitate the gods' sacrifice.
    d. be circumcised.
    e. none of the above.

2. The low sea levels during ice ages
    a. prohibited human migrations from Siberia to North America.
    b. exposed land bridges that linked Siberia with Alaska and Australia with New Guinea.
    c. enabled humans to migrate via floating glaciers.
    d. made it impossible for indigenous Americans to fish.
    e. all of the above.

3. All but one of the following is true regarding migrations to the Americas:
    a. A large migration came about 13,000 B.C.E.
    b. By 9500 B.C.E. the migrants had reached the tip of South America.
    c. The migrants were hunters and gatherers.
    d. Most of the migrants arrived by boat.
    e. Most of the migrations to the Americas took place during the last ice age.

4. As for early agriculture in Mesoamerica, we can say that
    a. the settlers developed food crops brought from Siberia.
    b. horses and oxen played important roles in transportation and farming.
    c. the settlers developed maize as their staple food around 5000 B.C.E.
    d. the settlers supplemented their diets with meat from cattle.
    e. all of the above.

5. The Olmecs
    a. established the first complex society in Mesoamerica.
    b. built ceremonial centers with pyramids and temples.
    c. lived in an area where rubber trees flourished.
    d. constructed elaborate drainage systems.
    e. all of the above.

6. The Olmec society produced
    a. paintings that depicted the daily lives of the ruling elite.
    b. books on astronomy.
    c. huge sculptures of human heads.
    d. colorful murals on walls of temples.
    e. all of the above.

7. The decline of Olmec society might have been caused by
    a. civil conflicts.
    b. human sacrifice.
    c. calendrical miscalculation.
    d. epidemics.
    e. none of the above.

8. For the Olmecs, the ceremonial center at San Lorenzo was like
    a. Tikal to the Maya.
    b. Chichén Itzá to the Tikal.
    c. La Venta to the Tikal.
    d. Teotihuacan to the Maya.
    e. none of the above.

9. A traveler in Tikal might have seen
    a. pyramids, plazas, and palaces.
    b. stone-paved courts for ball games.
    c. the Temple of the Giant Jaguar.
    d. kings, priests, nobles, merchants, slaves, and war captives.
    e. all of the above.

10. The Maya calendar
    a. contained a lunar year and a solar year.
    b. contained a twelve-year cycle.
    c. was devised by the kings.
    d. was used to determine the fortune of activities on a given day.
    e. none of the above.

11. The *Popul Vah* concerned
    a. the Maya calendar.
    b. the hunt for jaguars.
    c. the rules for the ball game.
    d. the creation of the world.
    e. none of the above.

12. Which of the following would *not* have been seen at Teotihuacan?
    a. the Pyramid of the Sun.
    b. the Pyramid of the Moon.
    c. a large quantity of books.
    d. iron tools.
    e. orange pottery.

13. After about 650 C.E., the city of Teotihuacan, another of the successor societies of the Olmecs, began to decline. The reasons for the downfall of Teotihuacan are
    a. military pressure and invasion from surrounding peoples.
    b. epidemic diseases, population pressure, and ecological destruction.
    c. multiple civil wars.
    d. a series of natural disasters.
    e. still unknown.

14. The heartland of early Andean society was
    a. the region now occupied by the states of Peru and Bolivia.
    b. the region now occupied by the states of Mexico, Honduras, and El Salvador.
    c. the islands of the Pacific ocean.
    d. the region of the Amazon basin.
    e. all of the above.

15. During the period of the Chavín cult,
    a. large temple complexes were built.
    b. carvings of wild animals were created.
    c. weavers produced cotton textiles.
    d. gold, silver, and copper jewelry was made.
    e. all of the above.

16. Mochica was
    a. one of several large states of Andean society.
    b. one of several large ceremonial centers of Andean society.
    c. one of several large cults of the Andean region.
    d. one of several gods of the Andean region.
    e. none of the above.

17. Which of the following is true of the story of the voyage of Ru?
    a. It was written down in the early centuries C.E.
    b. It told of contact between the Austronesians and the coastal Americans.
    c. It told of crossing the land bridge from southeast Asia to New Guinea.
    d. It told of a migration from Hawai'i to an uninhabited island.
    e. It told of the creation of the world.

18. The Lapita peoples
    a. were named after the language they spoke.
    b. used items made of copper and iron as items of exchange.
    c. spread throughout Australia.
    d. lived in large urban centers throughout Oceania.
    e. developed sea trading and communications networks.

19. The developments of early societies in Australia and New Guinea took different paths because
    a. the environments of the two islands were very different.
    b. the Austronesians introduced root crops and domesticated animals to New Guinea.
    c. the aboriginal peoples of Australia relied on kangaroo meat, which made agriculture unnecessary.
    d. the people of Australia converted to agriculture much earlier.
    e. none of the above.

20. All of the following conditions helped the Austronesians to people the islands of the Pacific except
    a. their skills of navigation and boat building.
    b. their knowledge of agriculture and raising domestic animals.
    c. population pressure and internal conflicts.
    d. their chiefly political organizations.
    e. the trade network of the Lapita.

MATCHING

Match these terms with the statements that follow.

A. Maya   E. Teotihuacan
B. Chavín   F. Austronesians
C. Olmec   G. Tikal
D. Mochica   H. Lapita

1. ___ Religious cult of the central Andes; followers built large temple complexes and created elaborate stone carvings.

2. ___ Large city of Mesoamerica that contained huge pyramids of the sun and the moon.

3. ___ Well-integrated society of the south Pacific islands.

4. ___ Mesoamerican culture responsible for sophisticated calendar and writings on the creation of humans.

5. ___ City that flourished in Mesoamerica from 300 to 900 C.E.; it contained the Temple of the Jaguar.

6. ___ Early Andean state noted for its paintings on pottery.

7. ___ People who used navigational and agricultural skills to establish settlements on Pacific Islands.

8. ___ Earliest known society with ceremonial centers in Mesoamerica.

SEQUENCING

Place the following clusters of events in chronological order. Consider carefully how one event leads to another and try to determine the internal logic of each sequence.

A.
___ Teotihuacan is home to almost two hundred thousand inhabitants.

___ Colossal heads carved out of basalt rock are created.

___ Chichén Itzá organizes an empire, bringing stability to the Yucatan.

___ People of Mesoamerica begin experimenting with the cultivation of maize.

B.
___ Humans migrate to Australia.

___ Austronesian mariners arrive in Hawai'i.

___ Cultivation of root crops and animal herding begins on New Guinea.

___ Lapita peoples build states based on chiefdoms that eventually develop a divine or semidivine status.

MAP EXERCISES

1. On the outline map below, trace the movement of peoples from Asia to the Americas and to Oceania. Use different colored pencils to represent the different groups of people who migrated.

CONNECTIONS

In fifty words or less explain the relationship between each of the following pairs. How does one lead to or foster the other? Be specific in your response. (May be done individually or in small groups.)

- Maya and cacao
- Maya calendar and *Popol Vuh*
- Bloodletting and ball game
- Outrigger canoes and agriculture
- New Guinea and Madagascar

GROUP ACTIVITIES

1. You are a group of archeologists who have just discovered a settlement site about two thousand years old on an island in the South Pacific. Your hypothesis is that it was peopled by Austronesians migrating from Samoa. Make a list of the artifacts and remains you would expect to encounter in this dig if your hypothesis was supported.

2. Your group works for a tour company, and you are asked to design a tour of Mexico and Guatemala that focuses on early complex societies. Design a tour itinerary (using maps and avoiding much backtracking) that hits the highlights of the early societies in roughly chronological order.

CHAPTER 7
THE EMPIRES OF PERSIA

<u>INTRODUCTION</u>

This chapter describes the series of empires that arose in Persia (modern-day Iran) and controlled much of the territory between the Mediterranean Sea and India for over one thousand years, from about 550 B.C.E. through 650 C.E. The first empire, founded by Cyrus the Achaemenid, expanded under him and his successors until it became the largest empire the world had ever seen. The four Persian dynasties of this era (Achaemenid, Seleucid, Parthian, and Sasanid) were noted for several important developments.

- Tightly governed administration with networks of educated bureaucrats, tax collectors, and spies to maintain the order and the authority of the emperor
- The development of *qanats*, underground canals, to support the economic foundation of the empires: agriculture
- Sophisticated policies promoting long-distance trade such as standardized coinage, road building, a courier service, accessible marketplaces, and banks and investment companies
- The emergence and elaboration of Zoroastrianism, a popular and influential religion whose teachings demanded high moral and ethical standards

<u>OUTLINE</u>

I. **The rise and fall of the Persian Empires**

A. The Achaemenid Empire

1. Medes and Persians migrated from central Asia to Persia before 1000 B.C.E.

    a. Indo-European speakers, sharing cultural traits with Aryans

    b. Challenged the Assyrian and Babylonian empires

2. Cyrus the Achaemenid (the Shepherd) (reigned 558–530 B.C.E.)

    a. Became king of Persian tribes in 558 B.C.E.

    b. All of Iran under his control by 548 B.C.E.

    c. Established a vast empire from India to borders of Egypt

3. Cyrus's son, Cambyses (reigned 530–522 B.C.E.), conquered Egypt in 525

4. Darius (reigned 521–486 B.C.E.); largest extent of empire; population thirty-five million

    a. Diverse empire, seventy ethnic groups

    b. New capital at Persepolis, 520 B.C.E.

5. Achaemenid administration

    a. Twenty-three satrapies (Persian governors), appointed by central government

    b. Local officials were from local population

  c. Satraps' power was checked by military officers and "imperial spies"

  d. Replaced irregular tribute payments with formal taxes

  e. Standardization of coins and laws

  f. Communication systems: Persian Royal Road and postal stations

B. Decline and fall of the Achaemenid Empire

 1. Commonwealth: law, justice, administration led to political stability and public works

 2. Xerxes (reigned 486–465 B.C.E.)

  a. Retreated from the policy of cultural toleration

  b. Caused ill will and rebellions among the peoples in Mesopotamia and Egypt

 3. The Persian Wars (500–479 B.C.E.)

  a. Rebellion of Ionian Greeks

  b. Persian rulers failed to put down the rebellion, sparred for 150 years

 4. Alexander of Macedon invaded Persia in 334 B.C.E.

  a. Battle of Gaugamela, the end of Achaemenid empire, in 331 B.C.E.

  b. Alexander burned the city of Persepolis

C. The Seleucid, Parthian, and Sasanid Empires

 1. Seleucus inherited most of Achaemenid when Alexander died

  a. Retained the Achaemenid system of administration

  b. Opposition from native Persians; lost control over northern India and Iran

 2. The Parthians, based in Iran, extend to Mesopotamia

  a. Power of Parthian was heavy cavalry

  b. Mithradates I established a empire through conquests from 171–155 B.C.E.

  c. Parthian government followed the example of Achaemenid administration

 3. The Sasanids, from Persia, toppled Parthians; ruled 224–651 C.E.

  a. Merchants brought in various crops from India and China

  b. Shapur I (239–272 C.E.); buffer states with Romans; standoff with Kushan

  c. In 651 C.E., empire incorporated into Islamic empire

II. Imperial society and economy

A. Social development in classical Persia

 1. Nomadic society; importance of family and clan relationships

 2. Imperial bureaucrats

  a. Imperial administration called for educated bureaucrats

  b. Shared power and influence with warriors and clan leaders

3. Free classes were bulk of Persian society

    a. In the city: artisans, craftsmen, merchants, civil servants

    b. In the countryside: peasants, some of whom were building underground canals (*qanat*)

4. Large class of slaves who were prisoners of war and debtors

B. Economic foundations of classical Persia

1. Agriculture was the economic foundation

2. Trade from India to Egypt

    a. Standardized coins, good trade routes, markets, banks

    b. Specialization of production in different regions

III. Religions of salvation in classical Persian society

A. Zarathustra and his faith

1. Zoroastrianism

    a. Emerged from the teachings of Zarathustra

    b. Visions; supreme god (Ahura Mazda) made Zarathustra prophet

    c. The *Gathas,* Zarathustra's hymns in honor of deities

    d. Teachings preserved later in writing, by *magi*

    e. Compilation of the holy scriptures, Avesta, under Sasanid dynasty

2. Zoroastrian teachings

    a. Ahura Mazda as a supreme deity, with six lesser deities

    b. Cosmic conflict between Ahura Mazda (good) and Angra Mainyu (evil)

    c. Heavenly paradise and hellish realm as reward and punishment

    d. The material world as a blessing

    e. Moral formula: good words, good thoughts, good deeds

3. Popularity of Zoroastrianism grows from sixth century B.C.E.

    a. Attracted Persian aristocrats and ruling elites

    b. Darius regarded Ahura Mazda as supreme God

    c. Most popular in Iran; followings in Mesopotamia, Anatolia, Egypt, and more

B. Religions of salvation in a cosmopolitan society

1. Suffering of Zoroastrian community during Alexander's invasion

2. Officially sponsored Zoroastrianism during the Sasanid empire

3. The Zoroastrians' difficulties

    a. Islamic conquerors toppled the Sasanid empire, seventh century C.E.

    b. Some Zoroastrians fled to India (Parsis)

　　　　c.　Most Zoroastrians in Persia converted to Islam

　　　　d.　Some Zoroastrians still exist in modern-day Iran

　　4.　Zoroastrianism influenced Judaism, Christianity, and later, Islam

　　5.　Buddhism, Christianity, Manichaeism, Judaism also in Persia

IDENTIFICATION: PEOPLE

What is the contribution of each of the following individuals to world history? (Identification should include answers to the questions *who, what, where, when, how,* and *why is this person important.*)

Cyrus

Croesus

Darius

Xerxes

Seleucis

Mithradates I

Shapur I

Zarathustra

IDENTIFICATION: TERMS/CONCEPTS

State in your own words what each of the following terms means and why it is significant to a study of world history. (Those terms with an asterisk may be defined in the glossary.)

Achaemenids

Persepolis

Satrapy

Royal Road

Persian Wars

Seleucids

Parthians

Qanat

Zoroastrianism*

Ahura Mazda

Magi

Gathas

Avesta

STUDY QUESTIONS

1. How did Cyrus manage to expand the Persian holdings so dramatically during his lifetime?

2. Why does the book say that Darius was "more important as an administrator than as a conqueror"?

3. Describe the administrative structure of the Achaemenid Empire.

4. In what ways did Darius, and his successors, promote communication and commerce throughout the empire?

5. In what ways did Alexander of Macedon both destroy and preserve elements of the Achaemenid Empire?

6. How did the Parthians come to control the Persian Empire?

7. What was the role of the imperial bureaucrats in Persian society? How did they fit in with the other social classes?

8. What agricultural technologies and techniques did the Persians use to produce the large surpluses they needed to feed their huge population of nonfood producers?

9. The Persian Empires were noted for being part of a trade route critical to the economy of the classical world. What did the rulers do to facilitate trade? Why was Persia geographically so important?

10. What were the basic teachings of Zoroastrianism? Why is it considered a highly moralistic religion? How did Zoroastrianism influence other religions?

INQUIRY QUESTIONS

1. What aspects of Zoroastrianism seem like modern religions? How do you think the teachings of Zarathustra would influence the believers' behavior and attitudes at the time?

2. The authors refer to the Persian Empires as "cosmopolitan." What does this mean? In what ways did the rulers promote this cosmopolitanism?

3. The authors suggest that classical societies were more complex and more sophisticated than the early societies discussed in part 1. What evidence do you see of this in the development of the Persian Empires?

STUDENT QUIZ

1. The Medes and the Persians were
   a. Sumerians who migrated from Mesopotamia to Persia.
   b. Babylonians who migrated from Mesopotamia to Persia.
   c. Indo-Europeans who migrated from Anatolia to Iran.
   d. Indo-Europeans who migrated from central Asia to Persia.
   e. none of the above.

2. All but one of the following sets of characteristics were true with regard to the Medes and Persians from the tenth to the sixth century B.C.E. :
   a. expert agriculturalists, good at irrigation and rice cultivation.
   b. expert archers, frequently raided the wealthy lands of Mesopotamia.
   c. descendants of nomadic peoples, pastoralists culturally close to the Aryans.
   d. rulers of the largest empire the world had ever seen.
   e. descendants of the Greeks, related to Alexander of Macedon.

3. Which of the following is true of Cyrus?
   a. His contemporaries called him "the Shepherd" because of the region he came from.
   b. His conquests laid the foundation of the first Persian empire.
   c. He conquered Babylon in a swift campaign.
   d. He ruled from his palace in Pasargadae.
   e. All of the above.

4. Egypt was conquered by
   a. Cyrus.
   b. Cambyses.
   c. Darius.
   d. Xerxes.
   e. Zarathustra.

5. To govern a far-flung empire consisting of more than seventy distinct ethnic groups, the Achaemenid rulers
   a. established lines of communication and centralized administration.
   b. forced the peoples to speak only Persian and believe only in the Persian religion.
   c. used imperial spies to control the conquered masses.
   d. decentralized their administration.
   e. all of the above.

6. The Persian Royal Road stretched some 2,575 kilometers (1,600 miles) from Sardis in Lydia to Susa in Iran. To travel from one end to the other, it would take
    a. six months for caravans.
    b. ninety days for caravans.
    c. two weeks for Marathon runners.
    d. one week for imperial couriers.
    e. one year for merchants.

7. The Persian Wars (500–479 B.C.E.) referred to
    a. the rebellions of Mesopotamia and Egypt against the Achaemenid overlord.
    b. the rebellions of the Greek city-states, fighting for their independence.
    c. the wars between Alexander of Macedon and the Achaemenid empire.
    d. the series of civil wars that occurred within the Achaemenid empire.
    e. none of the above.

8. Alexander's invasion of the Achaemenid empire met with great success because
    a. his army outnumbered the Persian army.
    b. he proclaimed himself the heir to the Achaemenid rulers.
    c. his army was well disciplined, was well armed, and used sophisticated tactics.
    d. he was popular with the people of the empire.
    e. all of the above.

9. The rulers of the Seleucid empire could not control the empire effectively primarily because
    a. they abandoned the Achaemenid systems of administration and communication.
    b. as foreigners, they were opposed by native Persians.
    c. they were challenged by the Greeks.
    d. they were not able to resist the military pressure of the Islamic empire.
    e. none of the above.

10. All of the following were true about the Parthians except that
    a. they had a centralized government.
    b. they were seminomadic people.
    c. they had well-trained forces of heavily armed cavalry.
    d. they portrayed themselves as restorers of Persian traditions.
    e. they were pressured by the Roman empire.

11. The Parthian empire was toppled by
    a. the Roman army.
    b. the Islamic army.
    c. the Sasanid army.
    d. a revolt from within the empire.
    e. none of the above.

13. The administration of the Persian empires called for a new class of bureaucrats who
    a. undermined the position of the old warrior elite.
    b. came to share power and influence with warriors and clan leaders.
    c. were well educated.
    d. included a corps of translators.
    e. all of the above.

13. The construction of numerous underground canals (known as *qanat*) was undertaken because
    a. a scarcity of land meant that there was no room for normal irrigation techniques.
    b. there was an overabundance of slave labor that needed to be utilized.
    c. water was scarce and underground canals could keep water from evaporating.
    d. it was the least labor-intensive way to irrigate.
    e. there was no agriculture surplus in the empire.

14. In classical Persia, slaves
    a. often came from the ranks of the free who went into debt.
    b. could not marry another slave at will.
    c. were often prisoners of war or people who had rebelled against imperial authorities.
    d. provided much of the manual labor on construction projects.
    e. all of the above.

15. The economic foundation of classical Persian society was
    a. long-distance trade.
    b. herding domestic animals.
    c. manufactured goods.
    d. slavery.
    e. agriculture.

16. The growth of trade was promoted by
    a. linking the lands from India to Egypt into a vast commercial zone.
    b. standardizing coinage.
    c. cities establishing banks to facilitate commercial activities.
    d. relative political stability.
    e. all of the above.

17. Zarathustra was
    a. an emperor.
    b. a prophet.
    c. a *magi*.
    d. a monotheist.
    e. none of the above.

18. Which of the following was *not* a Zoroastrian teaching?
    a. the cosmic conflict between Ahura Mazda and Angra Mainyu.
    b. individual souls would undergo future judgment.
    c. ascetic renunciation of the world in favor of a future heavenly existence.
    d. the forces of good would ultimately prevail.
    e. a belief in six lesser deities.

19. From the mid-seventh century, Zoroastrianism lost its popularity because
    a. Zoroastrians were converting to Islam.
    b. it was outlawed by the Persian government.
    c. it was outlawed by the Islamic conquerors.
    d. more and more people turned to belief in Christianity.
    e. none of the above.

20. Which of the following religions did *not* attract large numbers of converts in the Persian empires?
    a. Buddhism
    b. Christianity
    c. Manicheism
    d. Hinduism
    e. Zoroastrianism

MATCHING

Match these figures with the statements that follow.

A.	Zarathustra	E.	Ahura Mazda
B.	Darius	F.	Shapur I
C.	Croesus	G.	Xerxes
D.	Seleucis	H.	Cyrus

1. ____ First great conqueror of the Achaemenid Dynasty, he expanded his holdings until they stretched from Egypt to India.

2. ____ This supreme god and benevolent creator was described in the Zoroastrian religion.

3. ____ This Lydian king's defeat at the hands of the Persians was predicted by the oracle at Delphi.

4. ____ This Sasanid ruler consolidated the empire's holdings and created buffer states between the Persians and the Romans.

5. ____ This prophet of the Zoroastrian religion had a series of visions that included a revelation about the cosmic conflict between good and evil.

6. ____ Former commander for Alexander of Macedon, this man founded the dynasty that created the second Persian Empire.

7. ____ This intolerant Achaemenid emperor spent years trying to subjugate the Greek city-states but to no avail.

8. ____ This emperor ruled over an empire larger than the world had ever known and had the great classical city of Persepolis completed.

SEQUENCING

Place the following clusters of events in chronological order. Consider carefully how one event leads to another, and try to determine the internal logic of each sequence.

A.

_____ Arabs overrun Persia and incorporate it into the rapidly growing Islamic empire.

_____ Alexander of Macedon conquers the empire easily and burns the capital city to the ground.

_____ Seleucids establish non-Persian rule over the realm but preserve many of the Persian administrative and economic practices.

_____ Ruler of the Persian tribes initiates a rebellion against the Median overlords.

_____ The dynasty preserves older Persian customs while infusing into the culture some of the customs and traditions of nomads from the Central Asian steppes.

B.

_____ Traditional Persian religion centers on nature cults, including ritual sacrifices and the use of hallucinogens.

_____ Zoroastrians flee their homeland in the wake of Islamic conquest and settle in India.

_____ Zoroastrian scholars collect the traditional holy texts and compile them in the Avesta.

_____ Zarathustra leaves his home in search of knowledge and has a series of religious visions.

_____ *Magi* keep Zarathustra's teachings alive by transmitting them orally in the form of *Gathas,* hymns to the deities.

QUOTATIONS

For each of the following quotes, identify the speaker, if known, or the point of view or the subject. What is the significance of each passage?

1. "Long punishment for the evil-doer, and bliss for the follower of the Truth, the joy of salvation for the Righteous ever afterwards!"

2. "The Great King, King of Kings, King in Persia, King of Countries."

3. "Good words, good thoughts, good deeds."

4. "If you would cross the Halys, you would destroy a great kingdom."

MAP EXERCISES

1. Draw in the approximate boundaries of the Persian Empires on the outline map. Locate the significant cultures to the east and west. Explain why the Persian Empires were in a critical geographic position to exploit trade and commerce.

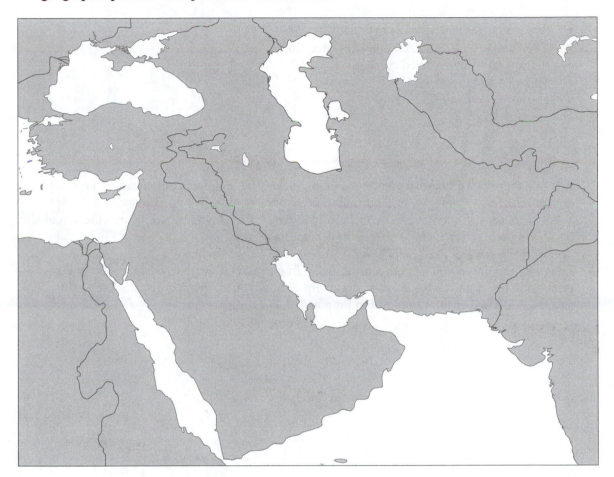

In fifty words or less explain the relationship between each of the following pairs. How does one lead to or foster the other? Be specific in your response. (May be done individually or in small groups.)

- Persian Royal Road and Zoroastrianism
- The Persian Wars and Alexander of Macedon
- Satraps and standardized coinage
- Shapur I and the Avesta
- *Qanats* and slavery

GROUP ACTIVITIES

1. Imagine that your group is a committee of engineers and architects organized by Darius to design his great capital city of Persepolis. What ancient cities would you use as models? What structures would have to be included and why? Check your plans against the actual site by visiting one of the many websites on Persepolis.

2. Imagine that one of you is a bureaucrat, one a free peasant, one a merchant trader, one a priest, and one a slave. Recreate an argument of how you are most indispensable to the success and prosperity of the Persian Empire.

CHAPTER 8
THE UNIFICATION OF CHINA

<u>INTRODUCTION</u>

This chapter explores the unification and expansion of China during the Qin and Han dynasties (221 B.C.E. to 220 C.E.). A rich tradition of the social and political philosophies of Confucians, Daoists, and Legalists was the foundation on which these and later dynasties rested. Some of the significant elements contributing to the unification of China in this period were

- The building of a centralized bureaucracy staffed with professionals educated in Confucian thought and values
- A prosperous economy based on technological and industrial development and long-distance trade
- The standardization of the written language

<u>OUTLINE</u>

I. **In search of political and social order**

    A. Confucius (551–479 B.C.E.) and his school

        1. Confucius

            a. Educator and political advisor

            b. Sayings were compiled in the *Analects* by his disciples

        2. Confucian ideas

            a. Fundamentally moral and ethical in character

            b. Thoroughly practical: how to restore political and social order

            c. Concentrated on formation of *junzi*—"superior individuals"

            d. Edited and compiled the Zhou classics for his disciples to study

        3. Key Confucian values

            a) *Ren*—a sense of humanity, kindness, benevolence

            b) *Li*—a sense of propriety, courtesy, respect, deference to elders

            c) *Xiao*—filial piety, familial obligation

            d) Cultivate personal morality and *junzi* for bringing order to China

        4. Mencius (372–289 B.C.E.), spokesman for the Confucian school

            a. Believed in the goodness of human nature (*ren*)

            b. Advocated government by benevolence and humanity

         5. Xunzi (298–238 B.C.E.) had a less positive view of human nature

            a. Believed that humans selfishly pursue own interests

      b.   Preferred harsh social discipline to bring order to society

      c.   Advocated moral education and good public behavior

B. Daoism featured prominent critics of Confucian activism

    1. Preferred philosophical reflection and introspection, a life in harmony with nature

    2. Laozi, founder of Daoism, allegedly wrote the Daodejing (*Classic of the Way and of Virtue*)

    3. *Zhuangzi* (compendium of Daoist philosophy)

    4. The *Dao*—the way of nature, the way of the cosmos

      a.   Elusive concept: an eternal principle governing all the workings of the world

      b.   *Dao* is passive and yielding, does nothing yet accomplishes everything

      c.   Humans should tailor their behavior to the passive and yielding nature of the *Dao*

      d.   Ambition and activism had only brought the world to chaos

      e.   Doctrine of *wuwei:* disengagement from worldly affairs, simple life

      f.   Advocated small, self-sufficient communities

    5. Political implications: served as counterbalance to Confucian activism

C. Legalism

    1. The doctrine of practical and efficient statecraft

      a.   No concern with ethics and morality

      b.   No concern with the principles governing nature

    2. Shang Yang (ca. 390–338 B.C.E.), chief minister of Qin and Legalist writer

    3. Han Feizi (ca. 280–233 B.C.E.) synthesized Legalist ideas in essays

    4. Legalist doctrine

      a.   The state's strength was in agriculture and military force

      b.   Discouraged commerce, education, and the arts

      c.   Harnessing self-interest of the people for the needs of the state

      d.   Called for harsh penalties even for minor infractions

      e.   Advocated collective responsibility before the law

      f.   Not popular among Chinese, but practical; put end to Period of Warring States

II. The Unification of China

A. The Qin dynasty

    1. Qin, Located in west China, adopted Legalist policies

      a.   Encouraged agriculture, resulted in strong economy

      b.   Organized a powerful army equipped with iron weapons

      c.   Conquered other states and unified China in 221 B.C.E.

2. The first emperor was Qin Shihuangdi (221 B.C.E.)

    a. Established centralized imperial rule

    b. Project of connecting and extending the Great Wall

    c. Buried 460 scholars alive because of their criticism against the Qin

    d. Burned all books except some with utilitarian value

3. Policies of centralization

    a. Standardization of laws, currencies, weights, measures

    b. Standardization of scripts

4. Tomb of the First Emperor, who died 210 B.C.E.

    a. Tomb was underground palace with army of life-size terra-cotta figures

    b. Excavation of the tomb since 1974

5. The collapse of the Qin dynasty

    a. Massive public works generated tremendous ill will among the people

    b. Waves of rebels overwhelmed the Qin court in 207 B.C.E.

    c. Short-lived dynasty, but left deep marks in Chinese history

B. The early Han dynasty

1. Liu Bang; persistent and methodical; by 206 B.C.E. restored order

2. Early Han policies

    a. Sought a middle way between Zhou decentralization and Qin overcentralization

    b. Han Wudi, the Martial Emperor (reigned 141–87 B.C.E.), emphasized centralization and expansion

3. Han centralization; adopted Legalist policies

    a. Built an enormous bureaucracy to rule the empire

    b. Continued to build roads and canals

    c. Levied taxes on agriculture, trade, and craft industries

    d. Imperial monopolies on production of iron and salt

    e. Established Confucian educational system for training bureaucrats

4. Han imperial expansion

    a. Invaded and colonized northern Vietnam and Korea

    b. Han organized vast armies to invade Xiongnu territory (nomads from steppes)

    c. Han enjoyed uncontested hegemony in east and central Asia

III. **From economic prosperity to social disorder**

A. Productivity and prosperity during the Former Han

1. Patriarchal social structure

    a. Women's subordination; Ban Zhao's *Admonitions for Women*

    b. Children obey and honor parents

  2. Vast majority of population were cultivators

  3. Iron metallurgy: farming tools, utensils, and weapons

  4. Silk textiles; sericulture spread all over China during the Han

  5. Paper production; replaced silk and bamboo as writing material

  6. Population growth: twenty million to sixty million from 220 B.C.E. to 9 C.E.

B. Economic and social difficulties

  1. Expeditions consumed the empire's surplus

    a. Raised taxes and confiscated land of some wealthy individuals

    b. Taxes and land confiscations discouraged investment in manufacture and trade

  2. Social tensions, caused by stratification between the poor and rich

  3. Problems of land distribution

  4. The reign of Wang Mang (9–23 C.E.)

    a. Land reforms by the "socialist emperor"

    b. Overthrown by revolts, 23 C.E.

C. The later Han dynasty (25–220 C.E.)

  1. Yellow Turban Uprising: revolt due to problems of land distribution

  2. Collapse of the Han

    a. Factions at court paralyzed the central government

    b. Han empire dissolved; China was divided into regional kingdoms

IDENTIFICATION: PEOPLE

What is the contribution of each of the following individuals to world history? (Identification should include answers to the questions *who, what, where, when, how,* and *why is this person important.*)

Sima Qian

Confucius (Kong Fuzi)

Mencius

Xunzi

Laozi

Shang Yang

Han Feizi

Qin Shihuangdi

Liu Bang

Han Wudi

Wang Mang

IDENTIFICATION: TERMS/CONCEPTS

State in your own words what each of the following terms means and why it is significant to a study of world history. (Those terms with an asterisk may be defined in the glossary.)

Confucianism*

Ren

Li

Xiao

Daoism*

Wuwei

Legalism*

Qin dynasty

Han dynasty

Xiongnu

Sericulture

Yellow Turban Uprising

STUDY QUESTIONS

1. What are the fundamental ideas and values of Confucianism? Make sure to include the concepts of *ren, li,* and *xiao* in your answer.

2. How does Daoism contrast with Confucianism?

3. What were the fundamental principles of Legalism, and how does it differ from Confucianism and Daoism?

4. Why does your book call Qin Shihuangdi "one of the most important figures in Chinese history"?

5. How did the early Han contribute to the unification of China?

6. Discuss the role of the Xiongnu in the history of China during the Han.

7. What were the most significant technological developments during this period of Chinese history?

8. How did the issue of uneven distribution of wealth contribute to the collapse of the Han?

9. How did the educational system develop in China during this period?

10. What was the role of the family in classical China?

INQUIRY QUESTIONS

1. What factors during the Qin and the Han worked against political stability and economic prosperity? How did these factors eventually contribute to the collapse of the Han?

2. Which aspects of Chinese culture during this period were most influenced by Confucianism? By Daoism? By Legalism? Explain your responses.

3. What did the discovery of the Tomb of the First Emperor tell us about China during the Qin?

STUDENT QUIZ

1. In 99 B.C.E. the great historian of China, Sima Qian, suffered from castration because
   a. he was blamed for distorting history.
   b. he inflicted this pain on himself in order to be a eunuch.
   c. his view contradicted the emperor's judgment.
   d. he was a Legalist.
   e. none of the above.

2. Confucius left an enduring mark on Chinese society as
   a. an educator and political advisor.
   b. a man involved in the practice of statecraft as an ambitious official.
   c. a great traveler and writer of deep philosophical treatises.
   d. a powerful and wise emperor.
   e. none of the above.

3. By *junzi*, or "superior individuals," Confucius meant
   a. wealthy men of the ruling elite.
   b. strong and brave warriors.
   c. individuals who withdraw from society and live in harmony with nature.
   d. well-educated and conscientious individuals to fill state offices.
   e. writers of important philosophical tracts.

4. Which of the following key Confucian concepts is incorrectly described?
    a. *Ren*: filial piety, or unconditional obligation to respect parents and grandparents.
    b. *Li*: a sense of propriety.
    c. *Xiao*: respecting and taking care of parents and grandparents when they are still alive and worshipping them after they have died.
    d. *Junzi*: people who don't let personal interest influence their judgments.
    e. All of the above are incorrect.

5. Mencius, the principal spokesman for the Confucian school, advocated that
    a. the evil nature of human beings could be improved by moral education.
    b. government should be organized through benevolence and humane action.
    c. government should be run by laws.
    d. people should strive to live in harmony with nature.
    e. all of the above.

6. The concept *dao* means
    a. natural laws such as those defined by modern physics.
    b. the original force of the cosmos, an eternal and unchanging principle that governs all the workings of the world.
    c. passive and yielding forces that exist only in water and empty spaces.
    d. living according to *ren, li,* and *xia.*
    e. all of the above.

7. An individual who practiced the Daoist virtue of *wuwei* would
    a. motivate himself or herself to change the world.
    b. follow high ethical standards and strive for success.
    c. try to govern the state according to benevolent paternalism.
    d. go with the flow of the cosmos and live in harmony with nature.
    e. all of the above.

8. Individuals in traditional China could live as Confucians by day and Daoists by night. This refers to the notion that
    a. the difference between Confucianism and Daoism was as clear-cut as day and night.
    b. Confucianism and Daoism were not mutually exclusive but, in many people's eyes, complemented each other.
    c. the Chinese, like other peoples, were active in daytime and became passive at night.
    d. Daoism was associated with darkness and evil and Confucianism with light and good.
    e. People often pretended to be Confucians to others but were secretly practicing Daoism.

9. To make a strong and powerful state, Legalist ministers
    a. encouraged commerce, entrepreneurial activity, and education.
    b. won the people's support by providing them with legal rights.
    c. sought to rule according to principles of benevolence.
    d. encouraged agricultural cultivation and military service.
    e. all of the above.

10. The First Emperor Qin Shihuangdi
    a. ordered the burning of most books.
    b. ordered workers to link defensive walls into one barrier.
    c. sentenced scholars to be buried alive.
    d. standardized the written script.
    e. all of the above.

11. The excavation site of the First Emperor's tomb nearby Xi'an is a great tourist attraction. When you visit the tomb, you can see
    a. a great terra-cotta army of Qin soldiers and cavalry.
    b. sacrificed slaves, concubines, and craftsmen who designed and built the tomb.
    c. a map of the emperor's realm on the ceiling.
    d. an underground palace lined with bronze.
    e. all of the above.

12. The great Qin empire only lasted a few years. It was ended by
    a. a military coup.
    b. waves of revolts.
    c. deadly epidemics.
    d. violence of court factions.
    e. invasions by nomadic people.

13. Liu Bang
    a. was the last of the Qin emperors.
    b. was a brilliant and charismatic leader who relied on no one.
    c. constructed the most highly decentralized state in China's history up to that point.
    d. was captured and killed by nomadic Xiongnu warriors.
    e. none of the above.

14. Han Wudi, the greatest and most energetic emperor of the Han dynasty, was remembered by later generations
    a. as the "First Emperor."
    b. as the "Martial Emperor."
    c. as a "socialist emperor."
    d. for his successful conquest of central Asia.
    e. none of the above.

15. In preparing governmental officials, the imperial university of the Later Han enrolled more than three thousand students, with its curriculum primarily based on
    a. the statecraft policies of Legalism.
    b. political science and the study of law.
    c. Daoism.
    d. Confucianism.
    e. none of the above.

16. Han Wudi decided to go on the offensive against the Xiongnu primarily because
    a. he intended to invade the Persian empire from central Asia.
    b. other methods were not effective to pacify the Xiongnu and stop their raids.
    c. the powerful Xiongnu leader, Maodun, killed his father.
    d. he wanted to capture the wealthy Xiongnu cities.
    e. all of the above.

17. Which of the following is NOT true with regard to Chinese silk?
    a. Sericulture was first discovered by the Chinese during the Han dynasty.
    b. Chinese silk was finer than others because of advanced sericulture techniques.
    c. During Han times, Chinese silk became a prized commodity in India, Persia, Mesopotamia, and the Roman empire.
    d. During the Han, sericulture expanded from the Yellow River valley to most of China.
    e. Chinese silk thread was made from unraveling silkworm cocoons.

18. After 100 C.E. most Chinese writing was on
    a. bamboo strips.
    b. silk.
    c. paper.
    d. papyrus.
    e. parchment.

19. After Wang Mang usurped the throne of the Han, he attempted
    a. restore land that had been taken from the royal family.
    b. to solve the problem of court factions.
    c. to redistribute land more equitably.
    d. to conquer the Xiongnu.
    e. all of the above.

20. An event leading to the collapse of the Han dynasty was
    a. the Yellow Turban Uprising.
    b. the invasion of the Xiongnu.
    c. the rise of the "socialist emperor."
    d. moving the capital to Luoyang.
    e. all of the above.

MATCHING

Match these figures with the statements that follow.

A. Maodun   E. Kong Fuzi
B. Shang Yang   F. Qin Shihuangdi
C. Laozi   G. Wang Mang
D. Mencius   H. Liu Bang

1. ___ Sage who contributed to the *Daodejing*.

2. ___ Confucian who emphasized the virtue of *ren*.

3. ___ Unifier and founder of the Han dynasty.

4. ___ Powerful First Emperor who built a lavish tomb.

5. ___ Radical minister who seized the throne and attempted a program of land reform.

6. ___ Successful military leader of the Xiongnu.

7. ___ Powerful administrator who based his policies on Legalist philosophy.

8. ___ Important philosopher who wrote the *Analects*.

SEQUENCING

Place the following clusters of events in chronological order. Consider carefully how one event leads to another, and try to determine the internal logic of each sequence.

A.

___ Legalist philosophy is embraced by Qin state.

___ Liu Bang restores order to China.

___ The emperor orders workers to link existing walls together to defend against nomadic invasions.

___ Political chaos reigns during the Period of the Warring States.

___ Qin Shihuangdi is buried along with an army of life-size terra-cotta figures.

B.

___ Fighting factions at the imperial court bring government to a standstill.

___ Han Wudi raises taxes and confiscates land from the wealthy.

___ Yellow Turbans stage violent revolt that spreads throughout China.

___ Wang Mang undertakes a land redistribution program.

QUOTATIONS

For each of the following quotes, identify the speaker, if known, or the point of view or the subject. What is the significance of each passage?

1. "He who exercises government by means of his virtue may be compared to the north polar star, which keeps its place, while all the stars turn toward it."

2. "How virtuous must a man be before he can become a true King? He becomes a true King by bringing peace to the people. This is something no one can stop."

3. "In a strict household there are no unruly slaves, but the children of a kindly mother often turn out bad. From this I know that power and authority can prevent violence, but kindness and generosity are insufficient to put an end to disorder."

4. "In governing men and in serving heaven, there is nothing like moderation . . . The soft overcomes the hard; the weak overcomes the strong."

5. "No one is glad when a girl is born: by *her* the family sets no store. When she grows up, she hides in her room afraid to look a man in the face."

MAP EXERCISES

1. Referring back also to Chapter 5, draw on the outline map below the successive boundaries of the Xia, Shang, Zhou, Qin, and Han dynasties. What does this exercise tell you about the expansion and unification of China? Now add the Xiongnu confederation and the wall of China. Why did the emperors have the walls built where they did?

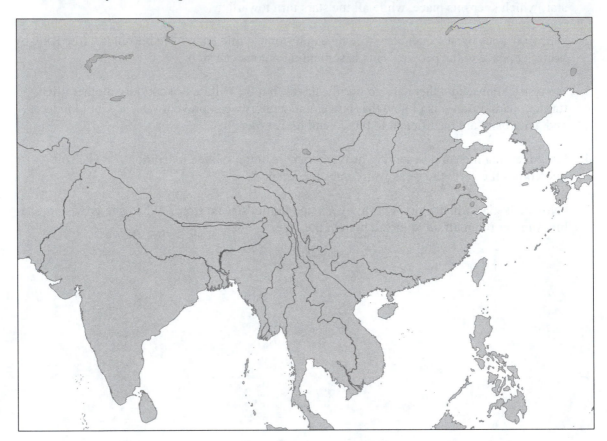

<u>CONNECTIONS</u>

In fifty words or less explain the relationship between each of the following pairs. How does one lead to or foster the other? Be specific in your response. (May be done individually or in small groups.)

- Legalism and Qin
- Confucianism and bureaucracy
- Wang Mang and Yellow Turbans
- Sericulture and Han Wudi

<u>GROUP ACTIVITIES</u>

1. Either singly or in pairs, outline the structure of the ideal government from the point of view of a Confucian, a Daoist, or a Legalist. Then come back together and present your outlines, arguing for your positions. Can you imagine a government where all three of these philosophies are represented?

CHAPTER 9
STATE, SOCIETY, AND THE QUEST FOR SALVATION IN INDIA

<u>INTRODUCTION</u>

This chapter addresses the significant developments in classical India between about 520 B.C.E. and 550 C.E. during which two influential empires emerged in northern India: the Maurya and the Gupta. Although these two state systems were not permanent, they contributed to the growth of long-distance trading networks, the consolidation of cultural traditions, and the promotion of several significant religions. More specifically, India, during this period of one thousand years or so, witnessed the following important developments.

- A high volume of manufacture and trade with regions as far east as China and as far west as the Mediterranean basin.
- The consolidation of the social traditions of patriarchal families and caste distinctions, the latter becoming more elaborated with the appearance of subcastes called *jati* usually based on occupation.
- The emergence and spread of salvation-based religions: Jainism, Buddhism, and popular Hinduism.

<u>OUTLINE</u>

I. The fortunes of empire in classical India

    A. The Mauryan dynasty and the temporary unification of India

        1. Magadha kingdom filled power vacuum left by withdrawal of Alexander of Macedon

        2. Chandragupta Maurya began conquest in 320s B.C.E.

            a. Founded Maurya dynasty stretching from Bactria to Ganges

            b. Kautala's advice manual, *Arthashastra*, outlined administrative methods

        3. Ashoka Maurya (reigned 268–232 B.C.E.)—peak of empire

            a. Conquered the kingdom of Kalinga, 260 B.C.E.

            b. Ruled through tightly organized bureaucracy

            c. Established capital at Pataliputra

            d. Policies were written on rocks or pillars

            e. Empire declined after his death because of financial problems

    B. The revival of empire under the Guptas

        1. Greek-speaking Bactrians ruled in northwest India for two centuries

        2. Kushans (nomads from Central Asia) conquered and ruled, 1–300 C.E.

            a. High point was Emperor Kashika, 78–103 C.E.

            b. Crucial role in Silk Road trading network

3. The Gupta dynasty, founded by Chandra Gupta (375–415 C.E.)

    a. Smaller and more decentralized than Maurya

    b. Invasion of White Huns weakened the empire

    c. After the fifth century C.E., Gupta dynasty continued in name only

    d. Large regional kingdoms dominated political life in India

II. Economic development and social distinctions

A. Towns and trade

    1. Towns dotted the India countryside after 600 B.C.E.

       a. Towns provided manufactured products and luxury goods

       b. Active marketplaces, especially along Ganges

    2. Trade with Persia, China, Indian Ocean basin, Indonesia, southeast Asia, Mediterranean basin

B. Family life and the caste system

    1. Gender relations: patriarchal families, female subordination, child marriage

    2. Development of caste system

       a. With trade and commerce new social groups of artisans, craftsmen, and merchants appeared

       b. These social groups functioned as subcastes, or *jati*

       c. *Vaishyas* and *shudras* saw unprecedented wealth

       d. Old beliefs and values of early Aryan society became increasingly irrelevant

III. Religions of salvation in classical India

A. Jainism and the challenge to the established cultural order

    1. Vardhamana Mahavira (*Jina*) founded Jain religion in 5th century B.C.E.

    2. Jainist doctrine and ethics

       a. Inspired by the Upanishads: everything in universe has a soul

       b. Striving to purify one's selfish behavior to attain a state of bliss

       c. Principle of *ahimsa*, nonviolence toward all living things

       d. Too demanding, not a practical alternative to the cult of the *brahmans*

    3. Appeal of Jainism

       a. Social implication: individual souls equally participated in ultimate reality

       b. Jains did not recognize social hierarchies of caste and *jati*

B. Early Buddhism

    1. Siddhartha Gautama (563–483 B.C.E.) became the Buddha

       a. Gave up his comfortable life to search for cause of suffering

      b.   Received enlightenment under the bo tree

      c.   First sermon about 528 B.C.E. at the Deer Park of Sarnath

      d.   Organized followers into a community of monks

  2. Buddhist doctrine: the dharma

      a.   The Four Noble Truths and the Noble Eightfold Path are the way to end suffering

      b.   Suffering is caused by desire

      c.   Religious goal: personal salvation, or nirvana, a state of perfect spiritual independence

  3. Appeal of Buddhism

      a.   Appealed strongly to members of lower castes because it did not recognize social hierarchies of castes and *jati*

      b.   Was less demanding than Jainism, which made it more popular

      c.   Used vernacular tongues, not Sanskrit

      d.   Holy sites venerated by pilgrims

      e.   The monastic organizations—extremely efficient at spreading the Buddhist message and winning converts to the faith

  4. Ashoka converted and became important patron of Buddhism

C. Mahayana Buddhism

  1. Early Buddhism made heavy demands on individuals

  2. Development of Buddhism between 3rd century B.C.E. and 1st century C.E.

      a.   Buddha became a god

      b.   The notion of *boddhisatva*—"an enlightened being"

      c.   Monasteries began to accept gifts from wealthy individuals

      d.   These changes became known as Mahayana Buddhism

      e.   Educational institutions (like Nalanda) promoted new faith

D. The emergence of popular Hinduism

  1. The epics

      a.   *Mahabharata*, a secular poem revised by brahman scholars to honor the god Vishnu, the preserver of the world

      b.   *Ramayana*, a secular story of Rama and Sita, was changed into a Hindu story

  2. The *Bhagavad Gita*

      a.   A short poetic work: dialogue between Vishnu and warrior

      b.   Illustrated expectations of Hinduism and promise of salvation

  3. Hindu ethics

      a.   Achieve salvation through meeting caste responsibilities

      b.   Lead honorable lives in the world

  4.   Hinduism gradually replaced Buddhism in India

IDENTIFICATION: PEOPLE

What is the contribution of each of the following individuals to world history? (Identification should include answers to the questions *who, what, where, when, how*, and *why is this person important*.)

Chandragupta Maurya

Kautalya

Ashoka

Kashika

Chandra Gupta

Vardhamana Mahavira

Siddhartha Gautama

IDENTIFICATION: TERMS/CONCEPTS

State in your own words what each of the following terms means and why it is significant to a study of world history. (Those terms with an asterisk may be defined in the glossary.)

Kingdom of Magadha

Maurya empire

Bactria

Kushan empire

Gupta dynasty

White Huns

Caste*

Jainism

Buddhism*

Nalanda

Hinduism*

<u>STUDY QUESTIONS</u>

1. How did the Persian conquest set the stage for the emergence of the Maurya empire?

2. What were five major accomplishments of the emperor Ashoka?

3. How did the Gupta administrative practices differ from the Maurya?

4. How did India fit in to the trade along the Silk Road?

5. In what ways did the development of trade and manufacturing impact the caste system?

6. What are the fundamental beliefs of Jainism? What has been its long-term impact? Why did it never become as popular as other major world religions?

7. What was the popular appeal of Buddhism? How does it compare and contrast to Hinduism?

8. How did early Buddhism evolve into Mahayana Buddhism? How did that help spread the religion?

9. How did Hinduism evolve in India during this period?

10. Why did Buddhism eventually lose popularity in India?

<u>INQUIRY QUESTIONS</u>

1. Even though the Maurya and Gupta empires were highly influential, Indian history largely is characterized by small regional kingdoms. Why do you think large empires did not "take hold" in India as they did in other parts of the world we have studied? What is unusual or different about Indian culture in this respect?

2. How did the social customs of India—especially family patriarchy and caste—and classical Hinduism mesh? How did the practices and beliefs reinforce each other?

3. Jainism, Buddhism, and Hinduism all emerged in India in this period. How did each one appeal to people? Did each one appeal to different groups of people? Why? How did their popularity develop through this period?

STUDENT QUIZ

1. Which of the following was *not* conveyed by the author of the *Indika*?
    a. Indian ants were as big as foxes and could mine gold from the earth.
    b. Large Indian armies used elephants as war animals.
    c. The Indians were suffering from poverty and all kinds of miseries.
    d. The capital of Patalputra had 570 towers.
    e. There were two prominent belief systems that were exempt from taxes.

2. In contrast to Persia and China, classical India
    a. was isolated from the outside world by formidable geographical barriers.
    b. did not have well-developed religions.
    c. lacked a strong and continuing imperial tradition.
    d. was a backward country in terms of economy and culture.
    e. all of the above.

3. The invasions of Darius and Alexander played an important role in Indian politics and history because
    a. the conquests brought India, Persia, and Mesopotamia together as one country.
    b. foreign religions began to take root in Indian society.
    c. the Greeks dominated Indian history for centuries.
    d. the intrusions destroyed many petty kingdoms and created a political vacuum.
    e. all of the above.

4. The man who founded the first Indian empire was
    a. Chandragupta Maurya
    b. Chandra Gupta
    c. Ashoka Maurya
    d. Alexander of Macedon
    e. Siddhartha Gautama

5. Ashoka, the great emperor of the Mauryan empire,
    a. was the only emperor who extended India beyond the subcontinent.
    b. wrote a handbook on the principles of government
    c. converted to Buddhism after his bloody war against Kalinga.
    d. abdicated his throne and led a life so ascetic that he starved himself to death.
    e. none of the above

6. Which of the following caused the Maurya empire to decline and collapse?
    a. financial difficulties caused by maintaining the army and bureaucracy.
    b. peasant rebellions and factional violence among members of the imperial court.
    c. foreign invasion by White Huns.
    d. too many converts to Jainism refused to fight wars.
    e. all of the above.

7. The Kushan empire
    a. originated from nomadic conquerors from central Asia.
    b. pacified large areas of present-day Pakistan, Afghanistan, and north India.
    c. peaked under the rule of Kashika.
    d. played a crucial role in the Silk Road trading network.
    e. all of the above.

8. Compared with the Mauryan empire, the Gupta empire was
    a. smaller in size.
    b. less powerful and stable.
    c. less centralized.
    d. longer-lived.
    e. all of the above.

9. The White Huns occupied Bactria and prepared to cross the Hindu Kush into India during the fourth and fifth centuries. Their invasions
    a. reduced the Gupta empire into an empty name.
    b. galvanized local kingdoms to unify themselves for self-defense.
    c. met fierce resistance from the Gupta empire.
    d. introduced Buddhism to India.
    e. none of the above.

10. Which of the following is true with respect to marriage in classical India?
    a. Child marriage was common.
    b. Intercaste marriage was forbidden by law.
    c. An ideal wife was weak-willed, faithful, and loyal to her husband.
    d. Sita was the model of the ideal wife.
    e. All of the above.

11. In classical India, *jati*
    a. were economically self-sufficient and politically autonomous.
    b. had their own courts to control crimes and solve disputes.
    c. were not much different from guilds of other societies.
    d. were based on religious affiliation.
    e. all of the above.

12. Your textbook states that "economic development and social change in classical India had profound implications for the established cultural as well as social order." By this the authors meant that
    a. social distinctions based on castes and *jati* were practically out of date.
    b. asceticism became unnecessary when more and more people became wealthy.
    c. Aryan rituals and beliefs became more popular.
    d. new religions emerged to meet the needs of changing times.
    e. none of the above.

13. Among the principles of Jainist ethics, the most important was
    a. *ahimsa.*
    b. *kshatriya.*
    c. *Jina.*
    d. *kama.*
    e. *Boddhisatva.*

14. According to legend, Siddhartha Gautama, the first Buddha, abandoned his family and comfortable life to lead the existence of a holy man because of his concern with
    a. suffering.
    b. the souls of everything in the universe.
    c. social responsibility associated with his caste.
    d. his guilt over his behavior in battle.
    e. his children.

15. The religious goal of early Buddhism was
    a. "Turning of the Wheel of the Law."
    b. the Four Noble Truths.
    c. the Noble Eightfold path.
    d. *nirvana.*
    e. reincarnation.

16. According to the authors of the textbook, Jainism and Buddhism appealed especially to members of lower castes because both religions
    a. practiced asceticism, which poor people could afford to do.
    b. did not recognize social distinctions based on caste or *jati.*
    c. organized monastic orders that provided the poor with shelters and a meaningful lifestyle as monks.
    d. appealed to the brahmans.
    e. all of the above.

17. Which of the following statements do *not* apply to Ashoka's support of Buddhism?
    a. He banned animal sacrifices and hunting.
    b. He became a vegetarian.
    c. He built monasteries and stupas and made pilgrimages to Buddhist holy sites.
    d. He sent Buddhist missionaries to foreign countries.
    e. He abdicated his throne, abandoned his imperial family, lived in a Buddhist monastery, and finally attained *nirvana.*

18. One of the differences between early Buddhism and Mahayana Buddhism was that
    a. Mahayana theologians invented the notion of the *boddhisatva.*
    b. Mahayana theologians revised the Four Noble Truths.
    c. Mahayana Buddhists did not honor the Buddha as a god.
    d. Mahayana Buddhists did not embrace the notion of *dharma.*
    e. Mahayana Buddhism was dominant in Ceylon.

19. Buddhism gradually lost its popularity in India because
    a. it did not promise to make life easy for its adherents.
    b. brahmans, the dominant class of classical India, no longer tolerated Buddhism.
    c. Buddhist monasteries were abolished in India by royal decree.
    d. it grew increasingly remote from the population at large.
    e. all of the above.

20. Which of the following is *not* true with regard to Hinduism?
    a. It restricted sexual activities.
    b. It became the most popular religion of classical India.
    c. It did not have a single founder like Siddhartha Gautama for Buddhism.
    d. It supported the caste system.
    e. It included a belief in reincarnation.

MATCHING

Match these figures, terms, or dynasties with the statements that follow.

A.	*Jati*	F.	*Arthashastra*
B.	*Nirvana*	G.	*Ahimsa*
C.	*Ramayana*	H.	*Mahayana*
D.	*Dharma*	I.	*Bhagavad Gita*
E.	*Brahmans*	J.	*Boddhisatva*

1. ___ Jainist principle meaning nonviolence toward other living things or their souls.

2. ___ Political handbook containing advice from Kautalya and others to the Gupta dynasty regarding principles of government.

3. ___ "Song of the Lord," a short poetic work of India that clearly illustrated both the expectations and promise of Hinduism for its believers.

4. ___ "The enlightened being," a Buddhist concept referring to inspirational individuals who had reached spiritual perfection but who intentionally delayed their salvation to help others.

5. ___ Basic Buddhist doctrine that including the teachings of the Four Noble Truths and the Noble Eightfold Path.

6. ___ One of the great Indian epics; it was originally a love and adventure story and later revised by scholars to bear Hindu values.

7. ___ Subcastes that evolved out of occupational guilds; they assumed much of the responsibility for maintaining social order.

8. ___ Highest, priestly caste that was increasingly challenged by popular new religious beliefs.

9. ___ "The greater vehicle" branch of Buddhism that included the worship of the Buddha as a god.

10. ___ The state of perfect spiritual independence achieved through the escape from the cycle of incarnation.

SEQUENCING

Place the following clusters of events in chronological order. Consider carefully how one event leads to another, and try to determine the internal logic of each sequence.

A.

_____ Ashoka converts to Buddhism and becomes one of its greatest patrons.

_____ Chandragupta Maurya gradually conquers the Magadha kingdom.

_____ Ashoka conquers Kalinga in a bloody military campaign.

_____ The Guptas are weakened by expending resources to repel the invasions of the White Huns.

_____ Nomadic conquerors from central Asia establish the Kushan empire.

_____ Conquest of northern section of India by Alexander of Macedon.

B.

_____ Ashoka sends missionaries to Bactria and Ceylon.

_____ The Buddha delivers a sermon at the Deer Park of Sarnath.

_____ Mahayana spreads to China, Japan, and Korea.

_____ Buddhism noticeably declines in India and Hinduism grows in popularity.

_____ Siddhartha Gautama receives enlightenment under a bo tree.

QUOTATIONS

For each of the following quotes, identify the speaker, if known, or the point of view or the subject. What is the significance of each passage?

1. "I shall also tell thee, O Bharata, what the duties are of a Kshatriya. A Kshatriya, O king, should give but not beg . . . He should protect the people, he should put forth his prowess in battle."

2. "You, sir, look at the caste (*jati*) and not at the inherent qualities of the monks. Haughty, deluded, and obsessed with caste, you harm yourself and others."

3. "Union with women who are of lower caste, or who are excommunicated, or with those once married and later deserted or widowed, or with courtesans, is neither commended nor condemned, since this relationship is entered into for mere pleasure."

4. "though hurt by the grass, he should not wear clothes . . . the wise monk will not lament his lost comfort. He must bear it all to wear out his karma . . . Until his body breaks up, he should bear the filth upon it."

5. "So he pours out his love and compassion upon all those beings, and attends to them, thinking, I shall become the savior of all beings, and set them free from their sufferings."

6. "As a man, casting off old clothes, puts on others and new ones, so the embodied self, casting off old bodies, goes to others and new ones."

MAP EXERCISE

Fill in the following information on the map below.
- Regions: Magadha, Deccan Plateau, Gandhara, Kushan, Punjab, Bactria, Burma, Ceylon
- Cities: Pataliputra, Sarnath, Bodh Gaya, Taxila, Nalanda
- Mountains: Himalayas, Hindu Kush
- Bodies of water: Ganges River, Indus River, Bay of Bengal, Persian Gulf, Arabian Sea

Look on a current map and identify the modern names for the locations of Ceylon, Bactria, Indus River, Kushan, Magadha.

Why do you think the most important cities of this period were grouped so closely together?

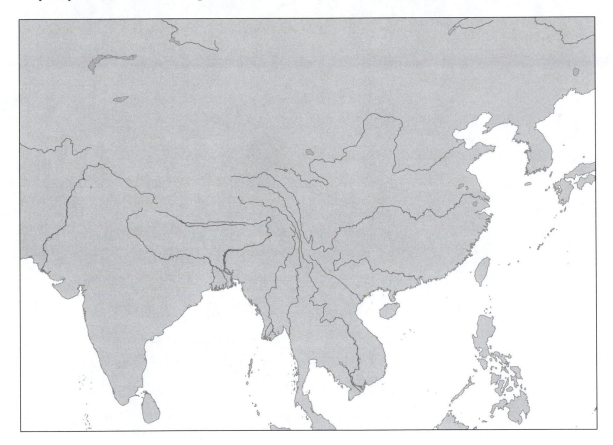

CONNECTIONS

In fifty words or less explain the relationship between each of the following pairs. How does one lead to or foster the other? Be specific in your response. (May be done individually or in small groups.)

- Darius of Persia and Chandragupta Maurya
- *Jati* and Silk Road
- Ashoka and Buddhism
- "Turning of the Wheel of the Law" and *Bhagavad Gita*

FEATURE FILMS

"*Asoka*" (2001). Half fact, half fiction account of the life of one of the greatest Indian emperors. Directed by Satosh Sivan and with Shah Rukh Khan and Kareena Kapoor.

CHAPTER 10
MEDITERRANEAN SOCIETY: THE GREEK PHASE

<u>INTRODUCTION</u>

Although the Greeks did not build a centralized state until the short reign of Alexander of Macedon, they did serve to link the Mediterranean and Black Sea regions through colonization, commerce, and cultural interaction. Through their unprecedented abilities as sea traders, and later through the unification provided by the Hellenistic empires, the Greeks left a rich cultural legacy of politics, philosophy, art, literature, and science that would go on to shape the European and Islamic worlds for centuries. Some of the enduring innovations for which the classical Greek cultures are best known include

- The earliest of form of democracy, the best realization of which was found in Athens under the leadership of the statesman Pericles.
- The establishment of hundreds of cities throughout the Mediterranean basin and southwest Asia.
- Unique contributions to literature in the forms of mythology, poetry, drama, and essays.
- The contributions of the rational philosophical thought of Socrates, Plato, and Aristotle and later the Epicureans, the Skeptics, and the Stoics.

<u>OUTLINE</u>

I.   Early development of Greek society

  A. Minoan and Mycenaean Societies

   1.   Minoan society arose on the island of Crete, late 3 third millennium B.C.E.

      a.   Between 2200 and 1450 B.C.E., was the center of Mediterranean commerce

      b.   Received early influences from Phoenicia and Egypt

      c.   Untranslated form of writing, Linear A, was used

      d.   By 1100 B.C.E., Crete fell under foreign domination

   2.   Mycenaean society: named after important city, Mycenae

      a.   Indo-European immigrants settled in Greece, 2000 B.C.E.

      b.   Adapted Minoan Linear A into their script, Linear B

      c.   Stone fortresses in the Peloponnesus (southern Greece) protected agricultural settlements

      d.   Overpowered Minoan society and expanded to Anatolia, Sicily, and Italy

   3.   Chaos in the eastern Mediterranean after Trojan War (1200 B.C.E.)

  B. The world of the polis gradually emerged in Greece

   1.   Sparta began to extend control during eighth and seventh centuries B.C.E.

      a.   Reduced the neighboring peoples to the status of helots, or semi-free servants

117

      b.   Maintained domination by a powerful military machine

  2. Spartan society

      a.   Discouraged social distinction, observed austere lifestyle

      b.   Distinction was drawn by prowess, discipline, and military talent

  3. Athens gradually broadened base of political participation

      a.   Solon sought to negotiate order by democratic principles

      b.   Citizenship was open to free adult males, not to foreigners, slaves, and women

  4. Athenian society

      a.   Maritime trade brought about prosperity to Attica, the region of Athens

      b.   Aristocratic landowners were primary beneficiaries

      c.   Class tension became intensified in the sixth century B.C.E.

  5. Pericles (ca. 443–429 B.C.E.), most popular democratic leader of Athens

II. Greece and the larger world

  A. Greek colonization

    1. Greeks founded more than four hundred colonies

      a.   Facilitated trade among Mediterranean lands and people

      b.   Spread of Greek language and cultural traditions

      c.   Stimulated development of surrounding areas

  B. Conflict with Persia and its results

    1. The Persian War (500–479 B.C.E.)

      a.   Greek cities on Ionian coast revolted against Persia, 500 B.C.E.

      b.   Battle of Marathon, 490 B.C.E., is decisive victory for Athens

      c.   Xerxes tried again to seize Athens; his navy lost battle of Salamis (480 B.C.E.)

      d.   Persian army retreated back to Anatolia (479 B.C.E.)

    2. The Delian League

      a.   Military and financial alliance among Greek poleis against Persian threat

      b.   When Persian threat subsided, poleis, other than Athens, no longer wanted to make contributions

    3. The Peloponnesian War (431–404 B.C.E.)

      a.   Tensions led to two armed camps, under leadership of Athens and Sparta

      b.   Unconditional surrender of Athens, 404 B.C.E.

  C. The Macedonians and the coming of empire

    1. The kingdom of Macedon, a frontier state north of peninsular Greece

    2. Philip of Macedon (reigned 359–336 B.C.E.) brought Greece under control

3. Alexander of Macedon succeeds Philip at age twenty and begins conquests

    a. By 331 B.C.E., controlled Syria, Egypt, Mesopotamia

    b. Invaded Persian homeland and burned Persepolis, 331 B.C.E.

    c. Crossed Indus River by 327 B.C.E., army refused to go farther

    d. Died in 323 B.C.E. at age of thirty-three

D. Hellenistic Empires: Alexander's realm was divided into Antigonid, Ptolemaic, Seleucid

    1. Antigonid empire: Greece and Macedon

        a. Continuous tension between the Antigonid rulers and Greek cities

        b. Economy of Athens and Corinth flourished again through trade

    2. The Ptolemaic empire: Egypt—the wealthiest

        a. The rulers did not interfere in Egyptian society

        b. Alexandria, capital at mouth of the Nile

        c. Cultural center: the famous Alexandria Museum and Alexandria Library

    3. The Seleucid empire: largest, from Bactria to Anatolia

        a. Greek and Macedonian colonists flocked to Greek cities of the former Persia

        b. Colonists created a Mediterranean-style urban society

        c. Bactria withdrew from Seleucids and established independent Greek kingdom

III. The fruits of trade: Greek economy and society

A. Trade and the integration of the Mediterranean Basin

    1. Trade and commerce flourished resulting in population growth and more colonies

        a. Production of olive oil and wine, in exchange for grain and other items

        b. Led to broader sense of Greek community

    2. Panhellenic festivals (like Olympic Games) became popular

B. Family and society

    1. Greek society in Homer's works

        a. Heroic warriors and outspoken wives in Homer's world

        b. Strong-willed human beings clashed constantly

    2. Patriarchal society was the norm

        a. Women could not own landed property but could operate small businesses

        b. Priestess was the only public position for women

        c. Spartan women enjoyed higher status than women of other poleis

    3. Sappho: Talented female poet wrote poems of attraction to women

        a. Instructed young women in music and literature at home

        b. Critics charged her with homosexual activity (not acceptable for women)

4. Slavery: private chattel, property of their owners

    a. Worked as cultivators, domestic servants

    b. Educated or skilled slaves worked as craftsmen and business managers

IV. The cultural life of classical Greece

A. Rational thought and philosophy

1. The formation of Greek cultural traditions: philosophy based on human reason

2. Socrates (470–399 B.C.E.): "An unexamined life is not worth living"

    a. Encouraged reflection on questions of ethics and morality

    b. Was condemned to death on charge of corrupting Athenian youths

3. Plato (430–347 B.C.E.): A zealous disciple of Socrates

    a. The theory of Forms or Ideas—world of ideal qualities

    b. This world is imperfect reflection of world of Forms

    c. His *Republic* expressed the ideal of philosophical kings

4. Aristotle (384–322 B.C.E.): Plato's student, but distrusted theory of Forms

    a. Devised rules of logic to construct powerful arguments

    b. Philosophers should rely on senses to provide accurate information

5. Legacy of Greek philosophy

    a. Intellectual authorities for European philosophers until seventeenth century

    b. Intellectual inspiration for Christian and Islamic theologians

B. Popular religion and Greek drama

1. Greek deities: Zeus and scores of subordinate deities

2. Various types of religious cults; Cult of Dionysus most popular

3. Drama was performed at annual theatrical festivals

    a. Great tragedians explored the possibilities and limitations of human action

    b. Comic drama took delight in lampooning the public figures

C. Hellenistic philosophy and religion

1. The Hellenistic philosophers: search for personal tranquility

    a. Epicureans: identified pleasure as the greatest good

    b. Skeptics: doubted certainty of knowledge, sought equanimity

    c. Stoics: taught individuals duty to aid others and lead virtuous lives

2. Religions of salvation spread through trade routes

    a. Mystery religions promised eternal bliss for believers; like Cult of Osiris

    b. Speculation about a single, universal god emerged

IDENTIFICATION: PEOPLE

What is the contribution of each of the following individuals to world history? (Identification should include answers to the questions *who, what, where, when, how*, and *why is this person important*.)

Homer

Solon

Pericles

Philip of Macedon

Alexander of Macedon

King Menander

Sappho

Socrates

Plato

Aristotle

Euripides

Aristophanes

IDENTIFICATION: TERMS/CONCEPTS

State in your own words what each of the following terms means and why it is significant to a study of world history. (Those terms with an asterisk may be defined in the Glossary.)

Minoan society

Knossos

Linear A

Mycenaean society

Linear B

Trojan War

Polis

Sparta

Athens

Persian Wars

Delian League

Peloponnesian War

Macedon

Hellenistic Age*

Antigonid empire

Ptolemaic empire

Seleucid empire

Ai Khanum

Olympic games

Forms or Ideas

Cult of Dionysus

Stoicism*

STUDY QUESTIONS

1. Compare and contrast the Minoan and the Mycenaean societies.

2. What was Greece like during the "Dark Ages," from about 1200 to 800 B.C.E.?

3. What is a polis? How did having the polis as the central political institution of classical Greece shape the history of Greece during this period?

4. Compare and contrast Sparta and Athens.

5. What was the significance to the history of the Mediterranean region of Greek colonization?

6. How did the Persian and Peloponnesian Wars influence the development of the Greek city-states?

7. How do you explain Alexander of Macedon's success as a conqueror in such a short period of time?

8. What was the legacy of the empire of Alexander?

9. Trace the development of Greek philosophical thought from Socrates through the Hellenistic philosophers.

10. How did Greek religion and drama influence each other?

INQUIRY QUESTIONS

1. Many of the contributions made by Athens during the classical age have continued to influence European and American society up to the present day. First, what are the enduring contributions? Where can you observe them in modern American culture? What was it about Athens at the time that nurtured these developments? Why were these contributions so enormously influential?

2. Even though classical Greece seemed to be an enlightened culture, it still supported slavery and the oppression of women. How do you reconcile this dichotomy?

3. Alexander of Macedon created one of the largest empires in the world in less than thirteen years. What was the significance of the feat? Have you studied any other conquerors who were as successful?

STUDENT QUIZ

1. In Homer's *Iliad* and *Odyssey*, the ancient Greeks were portrayed as
   a. expert and fearless seafarers.
   b. professional pirates.
   c. warriors with human heads and horse bodies.
   d. rational philosophers.
   e. drunken homosexuals.

2. Which of the following is true with regard to Minoan and Mycenaean societies?
   a. Both societies used Linear A.
   b. Both societies built palaces.
   c. Both societies were established by Indo-European immigrants.
   d. Both societies fought in the Trojan War.
   e. Both were centered on Crete.

3. By "tyrants" the Greeks meant
   a. oppressive despots with no popular support.
   b. ambitious politicians who gained power by irregular means.
   c. extremely popular leaders of poleis.
   d. democratic rulers of Athens.
   e. none of the above.

4. Which of the following was part of Spartan life?
    a. Boys were taken away from their mothers for military training.
    b. Young married women did not live with their husbands.
    c. The helots were unfree servants of the Spartan state.
    d. Vigorous physical exercise for girls was encouraged, in hopes that they would bear strong children.
    e. All of the above.

5. Which of the following was an Athenian political leader?
    a. Sophocles
    b. Sappho
    c. Pericles
    d. Homer
    e. Darius

6. How democratic was the Athenian democracy? Choose the best description.
    a. Citizenship was open to all residents.
    b. Slavery was abolished through Solon's reform.
    c. All citizens were qualified to join the city councils.
    d. Men and women could hold political office.
    e. None of the above.

7. Between the mid-eighth and the late sixth centuries B.C.E., the Greeks founded more than four hundred colonies along the shores of the Mediterranean and the Black Sea. The driving force behind such a movement was primarily
    a. population pressure.
    b. an abundance of agricultural land in Greece.
    c. earthquakes and volcanic eruptions on the Greek peninsula.
    d. a sense of pride associated with military conquests of other peoples.
    e. fleeing from the Persians.

8. Which of the following was *not* a consequence of Greek colonization?
    a. It quickened the social development of the peoples living in the western Mediterranean and Black Sea regions.
    b. It led to direct conflict between the Greeks and the Persians.
    c. It made Greeks weak and isolated from one another.
    d. It disrupted trade and commerce.
    e. It led to the gradual decline in the economy of the Peloponnese.

9. The Delian League was created to
    a. conduct democratic reforms in Athens.
    b. discourage further Persian invasions.
    c. maintain peace within the Greek world.
    d. bring greater wealth to Sparta and its allies.
    e. all of the above.

10. The Peloponnesian War was fought between
    a. two groups of Greek adversaries under the leadership of Athens and Sparta.
    b. Thebes and Corinth.
    c. Anatolian Greeks and peninsular Greeks.
    d. the Persian Empire and Athens.
    e. none of the above.

11. The freedom and independence of the Greek poleis finally fell under
    a. Xerxes by 480 B.C.E.
    b. Pericles by 429 B.C.E.
    c. Philip II by 338 B.C.E.
    d. Alexander by 336 B.C.E.
    e. Plato by 400 B.C.E.

12. By 327 B.C.E. Alexander's troops refused to go any further from home after they reached
    a. Egypt.
    b. Bactria.
    c. China.
    d. Mesopotamia.
    e. India.

13. Which of the following is *not* true with regard to Alexandria of Egypt?
    a. It had one of the largest libraries in the ancient world.
    b. It was the commercial center of the Mediterranean.
    c. It was the cultural capital of the Hellenistic world.
    d. It was originally a colony of Athens.
    e. It was the administrative center of the Ptolemaic empire.

14. The Greek peninsula was
    a. known for its fertile valleys and copious rainfall.
    b. especially good for travel and communication.
    c. ideal for cultivating olives and grapes.
    d. the homeland of Alexander.
    e. all of the above.

15. Which of the following would you have been *likely* to have witnessed in classical Greece?
    a. A woman accused her husband of abandoning her newborn baby, but the court rejected her petition.
    b. After her husband's death, a woman managed the family shop by herself.
    c. After a woman's homosexuality was exposed, even the homosexual men of her community condemned her.
    d. A Spartan woman took up arms to defend the polis.
    e. All of the above.

16. Greek philosophy is often characterized as "rational" because
    a. it was based purely on human reason.
    b. its reasoning was based purely on experiment.
    c. it transformed the Greek myths into philosophical speculation.
    d. it encouraged personal emotional response to the gods.
    e. all of the above.

17. Which of the following was *not* one of Plato's ideas?
    a. the belief that our display of virtue or other qualities in the world was merely an imperfect reflection of the true reality.
    b. the belief that there was another world of ideal qualities called Forms.
    c. the belief that the ideal state was one ruled by a philosophical elite.
    d. the belief that only democracy could make the philosopher-king possible.
    e. the belief that the ideal state would allow people to work at jobs where their talents lie.

18. The most respected and influential of the Hellenistic philosophers were
    a. the Aristotelians.
    b. the Epicureans.
    c. the Stoics.
    d. the Platonists.
    e. the Skeptics.

19. According to Plato, Socrates' view of death was that
    a. death is an eternity of nothingness.
    b. no evil can happen to a good man either in life or after death.
    c. all men know life is better than death.
    d. death is a good thing.
    e. none of the above.

20. Which of the following was true of the religions of salvation in Hellenistic society?
    a. They promised the possibility of eternal bliss.
    b. The cult of Osiris became one of the most popular.
    c. Many included the belief in a savior who dies and is resurrected.
    d. Faith in them spread along the trade routes.
    e. All of the above.

MATCHING

Match these figures or terms with the statements that follow.

A. *Iliad*   F. Massalia
B. *Odyssey*   G. Epicurean
C. Helots   H. *The Republic*
D. Poleis   I. Akrotiri
E. Bacchae   J. Parthenon

1. ___ Semi-free agricultural laborers for Sparta.

2. ___ Hellenistic philosophy that argued for the pursuit of pleasure as the greatest good.

3. ___ Greek colony on the southern coast of what is present-day France.

4. ___ Marble temple dedicated to the goddess Athena.

5. ___ Greek city that was destroyed during the volcanic eruption of 1628 B.C.E.

6. ___ Plato's work in which he advocates states ruled by philosopher-kings.

7. ___ Greek epic that recounts the war between Greek warriors and the city of Troy.

8. ___ Commercial cities and their surrounding regions that were the principle centers of Greek society.

9. ___ The celebrants of the festival of the cult of Dionysus.

10. ___ Greek epic that recounts a hero's journey home from the Trojan War.

SEQUENCING

Place the following clusters of events in chronological order. Consider carefully how one event leads to another, and try to determine the internal logic of each sequence.

A.

____ Philip II takes advantage of the disarray of the Greek city-states and conquers them.

____ Band of Greek warriors engage in war with the city of Troy in Anatolia.

____ Solon promulgates a series of reforms to the Athenian government and economy.

____ Antigonus takes over the rule of Greece and Macedon.

____ Greek city-states begin establishing colonies in the Mediterranean basin.

____ Athenians have spectacular victory on the plains of Marathon.

For each of the following quotes, identify the speaker, if known, or the point of view or the subject. What is the significance of each passage?

1. "never in all the world was there another like him, and therefore I cannot but feel that some power more than human was concerned in his birth."

2. "When my sons grow up . . . vex them in the same way that I have vexed you if they seem to you to care for riches or for anything other than virtue."

3. "To sum up: I say that Athens is the school of Hellas, and that the individual Athenian in his own person seems to have the power of adapting himself to the most varied forms of action with the utmost versatility and grace."

4. "But how can I help? What am I capable of doing? It is on you that everything depends. My duty, my mother said, is to be well behaved."

5. "When, therefore, we maintain that pleasure is the end, we do not mean the pleasures of profligates and those that consist in sensuality . . . but freedom from pain in the body and from trouble in the mind."

6. His "career was the motive force for the spread of Hellenism throughout the western Mediterranean and the Near East, and his achievement thus provided the matrix in which the Roman Empire, Christianity and other important aspects of western civilisation could take root."

MAP EXERCISES

1. Using the map on page 247 (Map 10.2) and a more modern map of the region, identify what modern cities were originally Greek colonies.

2. Using the map, follow the course of Alexander's conquest. Using what you have learned in previous chapters, figure out which states he would have had to conquer along this route. Figure out what was his logic was for taking the route that he did? What did he hope to gain? Why did he not proceed into India?

CONNECTIONS

In fifty words or less explain the relationship between each of the following pairs. How does one lead to or foster the other? Be specific in your response. (May be done individually or in small groups.)

- Mycenae and the *Iliad*
- Sparta and the Peloponnesian War
- Pericles and Socrates
- Colonization and the Olympic Games
- The Poleis and the Hellenistic Empires

GROUP ACTIVITY

Imagine that one of you is a follower of Plato, one is a follower of Aristotle, one is Epicurean, one is a Skeptic, and one is a Stoic. From those perspectives, have a discussion in which you argue over the following questions.

- How can a person achieve happiness?
- How can we learn what is true?
- What are the most important virtues a person can possess?

FEATURE FILMS

The Odyssey (1997). Best literal version of Homer's epic available. With Armand Assante and Isabella Rossellini.

CHAPTER 11
MEDITERRANEAN SOCIETY: THE ROMAN PHASE

INTRODUCTION

This chapter traces the growth and development of Rome from its humble beginnings on the banks of the Tiber River through its republican phase and its transformation into a sprawling, cosmopolitan empire encompassing much of Europe and northern Africa. A tight administrative structure and organized trade network promoted the movement of people, goods, and ideas throughout the empire. The Romans had a significant impact on later Mediterranean, European, and southwest Asian cultures. These influences include, but are not limited to,

- The concept of a republican form of government governed by a constitution and a fixed body of law that guaranteed the rights of citizens.
- Elaborate transportation and communications networks with sophisticated roads, sea lanes linking port cities, and an imperial postal system.
- Economically specialized regions, either in the development of cash crops for export or in localized industries.
- New cities built throughout the empire with unprecedented levels of sanitation, comfort, and entertainment opportunities.
- Widespread dissemination of philosophical beliefs and values, like Stoicism, and religions of salvation, like Christianity.

OUTLINE

I. From kingdom to republic

A. The Etruscans and Rome

1. Romulus and Remus: legendary twins rescued by a she-wolf; founded Rome in 753 B.C.E.

2. The Etruscans dominated Italy eighth to fifth centuries B.C.E.

3. The kingdom of Rome was on the Tiber River

B. The Roman republic and its constitution

1. Establishment of the republic

a. Rome nobility deposed the last Etruscan king in 509 B.C.E.

b. Republican constitution included two consuls: civil and military

c. Consuls were elected by an assembly dominated by the patricians

d. Senate advised the consuls and ratified major decisions

e. Both Senate and consuls represented the interests of the patricians

2. Conflicts between patricians and plebeians

a. Patricians granted plebeians the tribunes

b. Tribunes' power to intervene and veto decisions

      c.   Plebeians' tribunes dominated Roman politics, early third century B.C.E.

  C. The expansion of the republic

      a.   Rome consolidated its position in Italy, fifth and fourth centuries B.C.E.

      b.   Conflict with Carthage (Punic Wars) and Hellenistic realms

      c.   Rome became preeminent power in eastern and western Mediterranean

II. From republic to empire

  A. Imperial expansion and domestic problems

     1. The Gracchi brothers supported land redistribution; both were assassinated

     2. Military commanders recruited rural and urban poor—intensely loyal armies

        a.   Gaius Marius: general who advocated land redistribution

        b.   Conservative aristocratic class supported general Lucius Cornelius Sulla

     3. Civil war

  B. The foundation of empire

     1. Julius Caesar: very popular social reformer and conqueror (Gaul)

        a.   Seized Rome in 49 B.C.E.

        b.   Claimed the title "dictator for life," 46 B.C.E.

        c.   Social reforms and centralized control

        d.   Assassinated in 44 B.C.E.

     2. Octavion brought civil conflict to an end

        a.   Senate bestowed title "Augustus", 27 B.C.E.

        b.   Monarchy disguised as a republic

        c.   Created a new standing army under his control

        d.   The imperial institutions began to take root

  C. Continuing expansion and integration of the empire

     1. Roman expansion into Mediterranean basin, western Europe, down Nile to Kush

     2. *Pax romana*, Roman Peace, for two and a half centuries

     3. Well-engineered Roman roads; postal system

     4. Roman law—tradition: twelve tables (450 B.C.E.)

III. Economy and society in the Roman Mediterranean

  A. Trade and urbanization

     1. Owners of *latifundia* focused on specialized production for export

     2. Mediterranean trade

        a.   Sea lanes linked ports of the Mediterranean

        b.   Roman navy kept the seas largely free of pirates

      c.   The Mediterranean became a Roman lake

   3. The city of Rome

      a.   Wealth of the city fueled its urban development

      b.   Statues, pools, fountains, arches, temples, stadiums

      c.   First use of concrete as construction material

      d.   Rome attracted numerous immigrants

      e.   Attractions: baths, pools, gymnasia, circuses, stadiums, amphitheaters

B. Family and society in Roman times

   1. The *pater familias*—eldest male of the family ruled

      a.   Women wielded considerable influence within their families

      b.   Many women supervised family business and wealthy estates

   2. Wealth and social change

      a.   Newly rich classes built palatial houses and threw lavish banquets

      b.   Cultivators and urban masses lived at subsistence level

      c.   Poor classes became a serious problem in Rome and other cities

      d.   No urban policy developed, only "bread and circuses"

   3. Slavery—one-third of the population

      a.   Spartacus's uprising in 73 B.C.E.

      b.   Urban slaves saw better conditions and possibility of manumission

IV. The cosmopolitan Mediterranean

A. Greek philosophy and religions of salvation

   1. Roman deities: gods, goddesses, and household gods

   2. Greek influence—Stoicism

      a.   Appealed to Roman intellectuals

      b.   Cicero (106–43 B.C.E.) persuasive orator and writer on Stoicism

   3. Religions of salvation gave sense of purpose and promised afterlife

      a.   Roman roads served as highways for religious spread

      b.   Mithraism was popular with Roman soldiers—men only

      c.   Cult of Isis very popular

B. Judaism and early Christianity

   1. Monotheistic Jews considered state cults to be blasphemy

   2. The Essenes, sect of Judaism; Dead Sea Scrolls

   3. Jesus of Nazareth

      a.   Charismatic Jewish teacher, taught devotion to God and love for human beings

      b.   Attracted large crowds through his wisdom and miraculous powers

      c.   The teaching "the kingdom of God is at hand" alarmed the Romans

      d.   Crucifixion in early 30s C.E.

      e.   Became "Christ," or "the anointed one"

5. The New Testament and the Old Testament became the holy book of Christianity

6. Paul of Tarsus was principle figure in spread of Christianity

7. Rapid growth of early Christianity

      a.   Strong appeal to lower classes, urban population, and women

      b.   Became the most influential faith in the Mediterranean by the third century C.E.

IDENTIFICATION: PEOPLE

What is the contribution of each of the following individuals to world history?
(Identification should include answers to the questions *who, what, where, when, how*, and *why is this person important*.)

Romulus

Gracchi brothers

Marius

Sulla

Julius Caesar

Augustus Caesar

Cicero

Jesus

Paul of Tarsus

IDENTIFICATION: TERMS/CONCEPTS

State in your own words what each of the following terms means and why it is significant to a study of world history. (Those terms with an asterisk may be defined in the Glossary.)

Etruscans

Roman Senate

Punic Wars

Twelve tables

Roman roads

Coloseum

Patricians

Plebeians

Stoicism*

Mithraism*

Cult of Isis

Essenes

Judaism*

Christianity*

New Testament

Sermon on the Mount

LATIN TERMS

Itendify what each of the following Latin terms means and its significance in the context of Roman history.

Latifundia

Pax Romana

Mare nostrum

Pater familias

STUDY QUESTIONS

1. What contributions did the Etruscans and the early Roman monarchy make to the Roman republic?

2. How did the republican constitution set the stage for conflict between the patricians and the plebeians?

3. What was the significance of the Punic Wars to the later development of Rome?

4. In general, how did the Romans deal with the people and lands that they conquered?

5. What inherent weaknesses in the political and economic institutions of Rome did the Gracchi brothers' conflicts highlight?

6. Describe the transition from republic to empire in the 1st century B.C.E.

7. How did the Romans promote trade throughout the empire?

8. What was the status of women during the empire?

9. How did Jesus' message threaten the Roman administration? How did they respond?

10. What was the appeal of the early Christian teachings? What sorts of people were most attracted to it?

INQUIRY QUESTIONS

1. How were the Romans so successful in conquering and holding such a vast territory?

2. Why did Christianity spread so much more rapidly than other religions of salvation?

3. The book refers to Augustus's government as "a monarchy disguised as a republic." What does this phrase mean? Does this disguise continue throughout the empire period?

STUDENT QUIZ

1. About 55 C.E., Paul of Tarsus traveled from a port in Palestine to Rome to
   a. seek converts.
   b. appeal his case.
   c. apply for Roman citizenship.
   d. seek his fortune.
   e. none of the above

2. According to the ancient legends, the kingdom of Rome was established in 753 B.C.E. by
   a. Remus.
   b. a she-wolf.
   c. Aeneas.
   d. Romulus.
   e. none of the above.

3. The society of the Etruscans was ruled by
   a. city-states.
   b. a republican government.
   c. powerful kings.
   d. two consuls.
   e. tribunes.

4. The Roman republic was dominated by
    a. patricians.
    b. plebeians.
    c. democratic leaders.
    d. merchants.
    e. priests.

5. Which of the following was *not* done by the Romans after they defeated the Carthaginians in the Punic Wars?
    a. They spread salt on Carthaginian lands.
    b. They forced many survivors into slavery.
    c. They confiscated Carthaginian possessions in north Africa and Iberia.
    d. They exempted Carthaginians from taxation.
    e. They used Carthaginian resources to finance future expansion.

6. The Gracchi brothers were known as
    a. owners of *latifundia*.
    b. reformers.
    c. powerful generals.
    d. emperors.
    e. none of the above.

7. The rise of private armies directly threatened the existence of the Roman republic. Which of the following men did *not* command private armies?
    a. Gaius Marius.
    b. the Gracchi brothers.
    c. Lucius Cornelius Sulla.
    d. Julius Caesar.
    e. Mark Antony.

8. Which of the following was done by Caesar after he seized power in 49 B.C.E.?
    a. He started large-scale building projects.
    b. He centralized the military under his control.
    c. He named himself dictator for life.
    d. He distributed property to the veterans of his armies.
    e. All of the above.

9. Augustus's government was
    a. a republic disguised as a monarchy.
    b. a monarchy disguised as a republic.
    c. an oligarchy disguised as democracy.
    d. a democracy disguised as an empire.
    e. an empire disguised as a democracy.

10. Who wrote on the corruption in the early Roman empire?
    a. Juvenal.
    b. Cicero.
    c. Livy.
    d. Tacitus.
    e. None of the above.

11. By Roman law,
    a. a defendant was assumed innocent until proven guilty.
    b. defendants had a right to challenge their accusers before a judge.
    c. the judge enjoyed great discretion in applying laws.
    d. judges could set aside laws.
    e. all of the above.

12. Which of the following were not attractions of the city of Rome?
    a. public baths, swimming pools, gymnasia.
    b. the Pantheon's dome.
    c. statues, monumental arches, temples, aqueducts.
    d. public beaches on the Mediterranean.
    e. chariot races in the Circus Maximus.

13. Which of the following is true of the Roman family?
    a. It meant an entire household, including slaves, servants, and relatives.
    b. It included the *pater familias*, who was the authority.
    c. Women supervised the domestic affairs.
    d. Children could be sold into slavery.
    e. All of the above.

14. Which of the following does *not* describe Roman slaves?
    a. They were often chained together to work on *latifundia*.
    b. In cities, they were often freed when they reached thirty years of age.
    c. They had the right to elect their own tribunes.
    d. Female slaves usually worked as domestic servants.
    e. Some slaves were highly educated.

15. One of the most popular religions in the Roman empire prior to Christianity was
    a. Judaism.
    b. the cult of Isis.
    c. stoicism.
    d. the cult of Cybele.
    e. Islam.

16. Mithraism was especially popular among
    a. soldiers.
    b. women.
    c. slaves.
    d. the wealthy.
    e. intellectuals.

17. The Jewish people could not get along well with a number of imperial regimes because
    a. they declined to pay taxes.
    b. they did not respect any secular authorities.
    c. they had difficulty recognizing emperors as divine.
    d. they were converting to Mithraism.
    e. all of the above.

18. The Essenes
    a. were an early Christian sect.
    b. were a sect of Mithraism.
    c. was another term for the Dead Sea scrolls.
    d. followed their own savior.
    e. none of the above.

19. After Jesus' crucifixion, his followers called him "Christ," meaning
    a. "the anointed one."
    b. "the son of God."
    c. "the enlightened one."
    d. "the sacrificer."
    e. none of the above.

20. The remarkable growth of early Christianity reflected the new faith's appeal particularly to
    a. Roman emperors.
    b. high-ranking officials and the wealthy elite.
    c. Roman soldiers and military officers.
    d. the lower classes, urban populations, and women.
    e. all of the above.

MATCHING

Match these figures with the statements that follow.

A. Sulla   E. Julius Caesar
B. Tiberius Gracchus   F. Romulus
C. Paul of Tarsus   G. Mithras
D. Cicero   H. Spartacus

1. ____ Legendary founder of Rome, along with his twin brother Remus.

2. ____ Led most serious slave uprising in Roman history in 73 B.C.E.

3. ____ Ruthless general who seized Rome in 83 B.C.E., slaughtered thousands of his enemies, and strengthened the political power of the wealthy at the expense of the lower classes.

4. ____ General who conquered Gaul, then went on to march on Rome and make himself dictator for life until he was assassinated in the forum.

5. ____ Follower of Jesus who was largely responsible for the rapid spread of Christianity through the Roman Empire.

6. ____ Important god in Zoroastrian mythology who was popular among the Roman soldiers because he became associated with military virtues such as strength, discipline, and courage.

7. ____ Popular Roman tribune who advocated limiting the amount of conquered land that anyone could hold.

8. ____ Persuasive orator and writer who contributed to making Stoicism one of the most prominent philosophies in Rome.

139

SEQUENCING

Place the following clusters of events in chronological order. Consider carefully how one event leads to another, and try to determine the internal logic of each sequence.

A.

_____   Senate confers the title of Augustus on Octavion.

_____   Julius Caesar marches his army into Rome.

_____   Civil war erupts in Rome as ambitious generals vie for power and threaten political and social stability.

_____   Octavion defeats Mark Antony in naval battle at Actium.

_____   Group of wealthy, powerful Romans plot to have Julius Caesar assassinated.

B.

_____   Romans consolidate their power on the Italian peninsula.

_____   Julius Caesar and his army conquer Gaul.

_____   Roman holdings expand to include Egypt, last ruled by Ptolemaic heir Cleopatra.

_____   Romans fight a series of wars against Carthage.

QUOTATIONS

For each of the following quotes, identify the speaker, if known, or the point of view. What is the significance of each passage?

1. "But I say unto you, love your enemies, bless them that curse you, do good to them that hate you . . . that ye may be the children of your Father which is in heaven."

2. "I pursued my studies of every kind . . . I lodged and boarded at my own house Diodotus the Stoic; whom I employed as my preceptor in various other parts of learning, but particularly in logic."

3. "Therefore do I obey the command of my master, carefully and diligently do I observe it; and in such manner do I pay obedience, as I think is for the interest of my back."

4. "The new reign's first crime was the assassination of Agrippa Postumus . . . Meanwhile at Rome consuls, senate, knights, precipitately became servile."

5. "Let Christ Jesus himself be the armor that you wear; give no more thought to satisfying the bodily appetites."

6. "If . . . there are any matters of state which require the authorization of the people, it is their business to see to them, to summon the popular meetings, to bring the proposals before them and to carry out the decrees of the majority."

140

1. Use the outline map of Europe and north Africa below to illustrate the expansion of Rome from the fourth century B.C.E., century by century, until the end of the third century C.E. Use a different color for each century.

2. Examine the major Roman roads illustrated on the map on page 279. What would be the political and/or economic rationale for each major stretch of road? How would each part benefit the Roman empire?

CONNECTIONS

In fifty words or less explain the relationship between each of the following pairs. How does one lead to or foster the other? Be specific in your response. (May be done individually or in small groups.)

- The Gracchi brothers and Sulla
- Mithraism and Christianity
- *Latifundia* and the Senate
- Paul of Tarsus and urbanization
- Julius Caesar and the Republic

GROUP ACTIVITIES

1. As a group, brainstorm the contributions of Rome to later European cultures. Narrow it down to the three most significant contributions. Why these three? How are these contributions more far-reaching or important than the others you came up with?

2. Imagine that you are living in the Roman Empire in the second century C.E. and each one of your group members (or in pairs if your group is bigger) believes in a different ideology: Stoicism, Mithraism, Christianity, Judaism. First, describe the profile of the person you would be most likely to be, based on which groups were attracted to each belief system. Then argue why your belief system has more to offer than the others.

3. Imagine that you are average citizens living in Rome; your group is a group of friends who have the day off. Discuss and try to come to agreement on how you should spend your day. Try to persuade your friends to do what you want to do.

FEATURE FILMS

Ben Hur (1959). Older epic starring Charlton Heston as a Jew in the time of Jesus who chafes under Roman domination. Contains famous chariot-racing scene.

Spartacus (1960). Directed by Stanley Kubrick, this film depicts the events surrounding the great Roman slave rebellion of 73 B.C.E.

Cleopatra (1963). Costly spectacle starring Elizabeth Taylor and Richard Burton that presents the events surrounding the rise and fall of Julius Caesar and the ultimate triumph of Octavion.

The Greatest Story Ever Told (1965). The life of Jesus. With Max Von Sydow and Charlton Heston.

Gladiator (2000). Recent Academy Award–winning film directed by Ridley Scott that utilizes the latest special effects technology to re-create Rome in the second century C.E. Starring Russell Crowe.

CHAPTER 12
CROSS-CULTURAL EXCHANGES ON THE SILK ROADS

INTRODUCTION

The classical era witnessed the growth and consolidation of vast empires such as Rome, China, and Parthia. The relative political stability, economic prosperity, and close proximity of their borders encouraged an unprecedented growth in long-distance trade. Regular land and sea trading routes, collectively known as the silk roads, became established thoroughfares for the spread of goods from the coast of China to Western Europe. This extensive trading network had several consequences, both intended and unintended.

- Regions began to specialize in certain products that were particularly valuable as trade goods.
- Merchants, traders, mariners, and bankers became much more wealthy and influential than they had ever been before.
- Merchants, travelers, and missionaries carried popular religious beliefs to distant lands via the silk roads. Christianity, Buddhism, Hinduism, and Mithraism in particular became much more widespread.
- Disease pathogens were carried to populations that had no immunities to them, causing widespread epidemics throughout Eurasia. Inadvertently these epidemics contributed to the downfall of the Han and Roman Empires.

OUTLINE

I. Long-distance trade and the silk roads network

    A. Zhang Qian's mission to the west

        1. Held by Xiongnu for years

        2. Told Han Wudi of possibility of establishing trade relations to Bactria

        3. Han Wudi subdued Xiongnu, opening up region to safe trade routes

    B. Trade networks of the Hellenistic era

        1. Important developments of the classical era that reduced risks

            a. Rulers invested in constructing roads and bridges

            b. Large empires expanded until borders were closer

        2. Trade networks of the Hellenistic world

            a. Exchanges between India/Bactria in east and Mediterranean basin in west

            b. Ptolemies learned about the monsoon system in Indian Ocean

            c. Maritime trade included East Africa—Rhapta

    C. The silk roads

        1. Trade routes

a. Overland trade routes linked China to Roman empire

b. Sea lanes joined Asia, Africa, and Mediterranean basin into one network

2. Trade goods

a. Silk and spices traveled west

b. Central Asia produced large horses and jade, sold in China

c. Roman empire provided glassware, jewelry, artworks, perfumes, textiles

3. The organization of long-distance trade

a. Merchants of different regions handled long-distance trade in stages

b. On the seas, long-distance trade was dominated by different empires

II. Cultural and biological exchanges along the silk roads

A. The spread of Buddhism and Hinduism

1. Buddhism in central Asia and China

a. First present in oasis towns of central Asia along silk roads

b. Further spread to steppe lands

c. Foreign merchants as Buddhists in China, first century B.C.E.

d. Popularity of monasteries and missionaries, fifth century C.E.

2. Buddhism and Hinduism in Southeast Asia

B. The spread of Christianity

1. Christianity in the Mediterranean basin

a. Missionaries, like Gregory the Wonderworker, attracted converts

b. Christian communities flourished in Mediterranean basin by late third century C.E.

2. Christianity in Southwest Asia follows the trade routes

a. Sizable communities in Mesopotamia and Iran, second century C.E.

b. Sizable number of converts in southwest Asia until the seventh century C.E.

c. Their ascetic practices influenced Christian practices in the Roman empire

d. Nestorians emphasized human nature of Jesus, fifth century C.E.

e. Nestorian communities in central Asia, India, and China by seventh century C.E.

C. The spread of Manichaeism; best example of religion spread on silk roads

1. Mani and Manichaeism

a. Prophet Mani, a Zoroastrian, drew influence from Christianity and Buddhism

b. Dualism: perceived a cosmic struggle between light and darkness, good and evil

c. Offered means to achieve personal salvation

d. Ascetic lifestyle and high ethical standards

  e. Differentiation between the "elect" and the "hearers"

 2. Spread of Manichaeism; appealed to merchants

  a. Attracted converts first in Mesopotamia and east Mediterranean region

  b. Appeared in all large cities of Roman empire, third century C.E.

 3. Persecuted by Sasanids and Romans but survived in central Asia

D. The spread of epidemic disease

 1. Epidemic diseases

  a. Common epidemics in Rome and China: smallpox, measles, bubonic plague

  b. Roman empire: population dropped by a quarter from the first to tenth century C.E.

  c. China: population dropped by a quarter from the first to seventh century C.E.

 2. Effects of epidemic diseases

  a. Both Chinese and Roman economies contracted

  b. Small regional economies emerged

  c. Epidemics weakened Han and Roman empires

III. China after the han dynasty

A. Internal decay of the Han state

 1. Problems of factions and land distribution led to rebellions

 2. Generals usurped political authority; the emperor became a puppet

  a. By 220 C.E., generals abolished the Han and divided the empire into three kingdoms

  b. Nomadic peoples came in; China became even more divided for 350 years

B. Cultural change in post-Han China

 1. Gradual sinicization of nomadic peoples

 2. Withering of Confucianism in light of political instability

 3. Popularity of Buddhism; nomadic rulers embraced it

IV. The fall of the Roman empire

A. Internal decay in the Roman empire

 1. The barracks emperors: series of generals seizing throne (235–284 C.E.)

 2. The emperor Diocletian (284–305 C.E.)

  a. Divided the empire into two administrative districts

  b. A co-emperor ruled each district with the aid of a powerful lieutenant

 3. The emperor Constantine and new capital Constantinople

B. Germanic invasions and the fall of the western Roman empire

1. Germanic migrations from northern Europe to eastern and northern part of Roman empire
    a. Visigoths—settled agriculturalists; adopted Roman law and Christianity
    b. Roman authorities kept Germanic peoples on the borders as a buffer
2. The Huns under Attila attacked Europe mid-fifth century C.E.
3. The collapse of the western Roman empire
    a. Under the Huns' pressure, Germanic peoples streamed into the Roman empire
    b. Established settlements in Italy, Gaul, Spain, Britain, and north Africa
    c. Germanic general Odovacer deposed the Roman emperor, 476 C.E.
    d. Imperial authority survived in the eastern half of the empire
C. Cultural change in the late Roman empire
    1. Christianity most prominent survivor of the collapse of the empire
        a. With Constantine's Edict of Milan, Christianity became a legitimate religion, 313 C.E.
        b. Emperor Theodosius proclaimed Christianity the official religion, 380 C.E.
        c. St. Augustine harmonized Christianity with Platonic thought
    2. The Church became increasingly institutionalized
        a. Conflicting doctrines and practices among early Christians
        b. Established standardized hierarchy of church officials
        c. The bishop of Rome, known as the pope, became spiritual leader
        d. As Roman empire collapsed, Christianity served as a cultural foundation

IDENTIFICATION: PEOPLE

What is the contribution of each of the following individuals to world history? (Identification should include answers to the questions *who, what, where, when, how*, and *why is this person important*.)

Zhang Qian

Han Wudi

Gregory the Wonderworker

Mani

Diocletian

Constantine

Attila

Odovacer

St. Augustine

IDENTIFICATION: TERMS/CONCEPTS

State in your own words what each of the following terms means and why it is significant to a study of world history. (Those terms with an asterisk may be defined in the Glossary.)

Silk roads*

Monsoon system

Rhapta

Buddhism*

Hinduism*

Christianity*

Nestorians

Manichaeism*

Epidemic

Yellow Turban

Barracks emperors

Visigoths

Huns

Edict of Milan

Council of Nicaea

STUDY QUESTIONS

1. What developments in the classical era helped reduce the risks inherent in long-distance trade?

2. How did the trade networks of the Hellenistic era help set the stage for the silk roads?

3. In general, what goods from what regions were traded along the silk roads?

4. How did Buddhism become the most popular faith in all of East Asia?

5. How did the silk roads facilitate the spread of Hinduism and Christianity?

6. Why is the rise of Manichaeism such a good example of the relationship between long-distance trade and the spread of religion?

7. What were the long-term effects of the spread of disease along the silk roads?

8. How did China's culture change after the decline of the Han dynasty?

9. What were some of the main causes of the decay and fall of the western Roman empire?

10. How did Europe's culture change during the late Roman empire?

INQUIRY QUESTIONS

1. In what ways did the network of trade routes called the silk roads make life during the classical era a significantly different from life in the preclassical world? Consider all the different effects and the various cultures involved.

2. The textbook states "Christianity was perhaps the most prominent survivor of the western Roman empire." What does this statement mean? How did Christianity manage to survive and thrive after the collapse of the empire?

3. How did the nomadic peoples of Eurasia impede and/or contribute to the development of the silk roads?

STUDENT QUIZ

1. In 139 B.C.E., the Chinese emperor dispatched Zhang Qian to central Asia to
    a. open the silk roads.
    b. seek allies against the Xiongnu.
    c. buy large and strong horses.
    d. spy on his enemies.
    e. none of the above.

2. Which of the following were favorable conditions for developing long-distance trade during the classical era?
    a. Empires ruled vast areas and maintained good social order.
    b. Under imperial rule many roads and bridges were constructed.
    c. Central Asia was pacified by the campaigns of Han Wudi.
    d. The Ptolemies figured out the monsoon system.
    e. all of the above.

3. The monsoon winds in the Indian Ocean
    a. created tremendous difficulty for traders.
    b. blow regularly from the north in the summer.
    c. were actually first discovered by the Romans.
    d. tied southeast Asia, India, Arabia, and east Africa together in a maritime trade route.
    e. all of the above.

4. Which of the following is *not* true with regard to the silk roads?
    a. The silk roads actually had nothing to do with silk.
    b. Because of the silk roads, silk garments became popular among wealthy Romans.
    c. The silk roads linked much of Eurasia and north Africa.
    d. The silk roads also included sea lanes.
    e. The silk roads also carried fine spices.

5. Which of the following would *not* have been on a ship carrying goods in the classical era.
    a. pepper and cotton from India.
    b. silk from Bactria.
    c. olive oil and wine from Rome.
    d. spices from southeast Asia.
    e. slaves from Africa.

6. The principal agents for the spread of Buddhism over the silk roads were
    a. the Buddha himself.
    b. merchants.
    c. Indian monks.
    d. missionaries of the Emperor Ashoka.
    e. mariners.

7. Which of the following is true with regard to the Indian influence in southeast Asia?
    a. Rulers called themselves *rajas* ("kings").
    b. Rulers adopted Indian Sanskrit as their written language.
    c. Rulers appointed Buddhist or Hindu advisors in their governments.
    d. Rulers built temples in the Indian style.
    e. all of the above.

8. By the 3rd century C.E., Christian communities in Mesopotamia and Iran deeply influenced Christian practices in the Roman empire through their
    a. Nestorian beliefs.
    b. Confucian traditions.
    c. ascetic values.
    d. philosophy reflected by St. Augustine.
    e. all of the above.

9. Mani, the founder of Manichaeism, promoted a syncretic blend of
    a. Christianity, Buddhism, and Hinduism.
    b. Zoroastrianism, Christianity, and Buddhism.
    c. Nestorianism, Daoism, and Buddhism.
    d. Hinduism, Daoism, and Confucianism.
    e. Confucianism, Christianity, and Judaism.

10. Manicheism promoted
    a. a highly ascetic lifestyle.
    b. a belief in the struggle between the forces of good and evil.
    c. the possibility of individual salvation.
    d. a strict moral code of behavior.
    e. all of the above.

11. With regard to epidemic diseases on the silk roads, which of the following was *not* true?
    a. The most devastating diseases were smallpox, measles, and bubonic plague.
    b. The diseases seriously weakened the Han and Roman empires.
    c. The diseases caused the greatest population loss in India.
    d. The largest outbreaks occurred in the second and third centuries C.E.
    e. A Roman emperor died during one of the epidemics.

12. Immediately after the dissolution of the Han empire in 220 C.E., China
    a. was taken over by nomadic peoples.
    b. was divided into three large kingdoms.
    c. fell under the domination of the Sui dynasty.
    d. changed its policy on land distribution.
    e. none of the above.

13. Which of the following did *not* contribute to the popularity of Buddhism in post-Han China?
    a. The threats of epidemic diseases turned the Chinese to Buddhism for personal salvation.
    b. After the collapse of the Han dynasty, Confucianism lost its dominant position.
    c. The nomadic peoples who migrated into north China brought their Buddhist faith to the Chinese.
    d. Missionary efforts by Buddhists attracted many native Chinese followers.
    e. Buddhism was familiar because many foreign merchants had practiced it.

14. By dividing the Roman empire into two administrative districts, the emperor Diocletian attempted to
    a. establish more effective control of the empire.
    b. share imperial power with the "barracks emperors."
    c. give up the east half of the empire to Christians.
    d. make up for his lack of skill as an administrator.
    e. none of the above.

15. Which of the following is *not* true with regard to the Visigoths before they invaded the Roman empire?
    a. They adopted Roman law.
    b. They adopted official Roman language and social customs.
    c. They contributed large numbers of soldiers to the Roman armies.
    d. They were driven further west by the Huns.
    e. They converted to Christianity.

16. The invading Huns contributed to the fall of the western Roman empire by
    a. deposing the last emperor of the western Roman empire.
    b. sacking the city of Rome in 410 C.E.
    c. pressing the Germanic peoples into the western Roman empire.
    d. completely disrupting trade along the silk roads.
    e. attacking Constantinople.

17. The emperor who allowed Christians to practice their faith openly for the first time in the Roman empire was
    a. Constantine.
    b. Theodosius.
    c. St. Augustine.
    d. Diocletian.
    e. none of the above.

18. Which of the following was true of the early hierarchy of Christian church?
    a. Bishops presided over the religious affairs of dioceses.
    b. The bishop of Rome became known as the pope.
    c. There were five top religious authorities in the Roman empire.
    d. The church authorities met in councils to resolve theological disputes.
    e. All of the above.

19. St. Cyprian's view of the epidemic of 251 C.E. was that
    a. it would cause the downfall of the Roman empire.
    b. Christians would be protected from the ravages of the disease.
    c. the Jews were responsible for bringing the disease.
    d. it was a welcome event for servants of God.
    e. none of the above.

20. What happened to the silk roads after the decline of the Han and Roman empires?
    a. They no longer carried epidemic diseases.
    b. Activity actually increased along the silk roads.
    c. There was less activity, but trade revived along the routes in the sixth century C.E.
    d. The routes were changed to cross easier terrain.
    e. none of the above.

MATCHING

Match these people and places with their contribution to the trade network.

A. China   E. Parthia
B. Southeast Asia   F. Rhapta
C. India   G. Jews
D. Central Asia   H. Rome

1. ___ Took goods from Palmyra to the Mediterranean basin.

2. ___ Contributed pepper, cotton, and exotic items like pearls.

3. ___ Contributed spices and mariners active in sea trade.

4. ___ Controlled sea trade in the Persian Gulf and overland trade within the empire.

5. ___ Contributed manufactured goods like glass, art, olive oil, and wine and dominated the Mediterranean.

6. ___ Contributed fine silk and spices and was the easternmost extent of the trade route.

7. ___ Contributed horses and jade and dominated overland trade routes.

8. ___ Contributed ivory, tortoise shell, and slaves and dominated East African trade.

SEQUENCING

Place the following clusters of events in chronological order. Consider carefully how one event leads to another, and try to determine the internal logic of each sequence.

A.

____ Han generals divide the empire into three large kingdoms.

____ Han Wudi wages major campaign to subdue nomadic Xiongnu people of central Asia.

____ Buddhism spreads to China.

____ Zhang Qian and his party return to China.

____ Epidemics sweep through Han China.

B.

____ Devastating epidemic breaks out in the Mediterranean basin.

____ The Ptolemies deduce the patterns of the monsoon system in the Indian Ocean.

____ Odovacer deposes the western Roman emperor.

____ Diocletian divides the Roman empire into two administrative units.

____ Constantine converts to Christianity.

____ Christianity spreads throughout the Roman empire and becomes the most popular religion of salvation there.

<u>MAP EXERCISES</u>

1. Add the following information to the map of the silk roads below: the general boundaries of the territories to be traversed (you will need to look at earlier maps in the text for that), the most important trade goods (written in at their places of origin), the people most responsible for carrying the trade goods in each region.

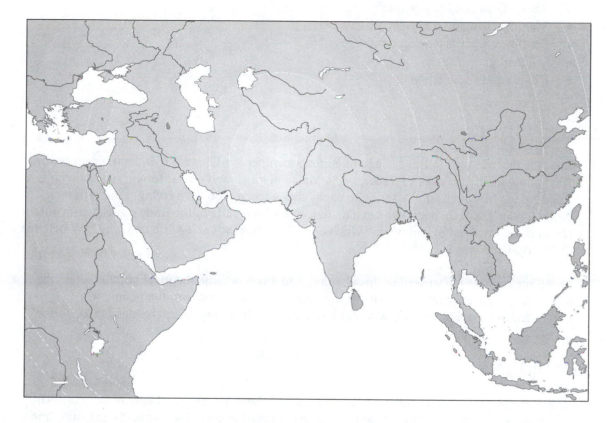

2. Using the map of the Germanic invasions, think about the significance to the Germanic people and the Romans of the invasions of the Huns in the fifth century C.E.

CONNECTIONS

In fifty words or less explain the relationship between each of the following pairs. How does one lead to or foster the other? Be specific in your response. (May be done individually or in small groups.)

- Zhang Qian and the silk roads
- Manichaeism and trade
- Smallpox and the Roman empire
- Silk and glass
- Rhapta and Guangzhou

GROUP ACTIVITIES

1. Imagine that the year is 150 C.E. and one group member is a Chinese merchant, one a central Asian nomad, one a Parthian trader, one a Malay mariner, and one a Roman subject who is a trader in the Middle East. Describe to each other what you do for a living, your religious beliefs, your greatest concerns. On a map, locate which parts of the trade routes you would travel or be involved in and why. Which one of you has the easiest life and why? Which one the hardest and why?

2. Of all the religions discussed in this chapter, Buddhism became the most popular along the silk roads. Discuss why this would be so: address the belief system, the people who converted to it, and the people who did not (Hindus, Christians, Manichaeans).

FEATURE FILMS

The Silk Road (1992). The legendary story of a young scholar's coming of age on the war-torn fringes of a great empire. Dragooned by a Chinese mercenary general, Xingte saves the life of a beautiful princess, and their love and fate is sealed in the woven textures of eleventh-century China. Directed by Junya Sato.

Attila (2000). Very "Hollywood-ized" action movie depiction of the great warrior-king of the Huns and his conflicts with the Roman Empire. Some of the costumes and the sets are worth looking at. With Powers Boothe.

CHAPTER 13
THE COMMONWEALTH OF BYZANTIUM

INTRODUCTION

While the western half of the Roman empire crumbled and fell, the eastern half, which became known as Byzantium, managed to survive and, mostly, to thrive for a millennium. During its long history, the Byzantine empire suffered many serious setbacks because of both internal strife and external pressures. Nevertheless, this culture, which blended Roman and Greek traditions, managed to flourish politically, economically, and socially up until the time it began its centuries-long decline culminating in its conquest by the Islamic Ottoman Turks in 1453. Several unique features of the Byzantine civilization contributed to its prosperity:

- A strategically located capital city called Constantinople that was one of the largest, most influential, and cosmopolitan urban centers in the world.
- A highly centralized and autocratic governmental structure consisting of an exalted emperor with an aura of divinity and a large and intricate bureaucracy.
- A rich Christian tradition elaborated by the emperor and the patriarchs that eventually evolved into an independent and separate faith referred to as Eastern Orthodox.
- An unusual and effective administration system whereby generals governed over free peasants who received small tracts of land to work in exchange for military service.
- The extension of Byzantine cultural traditions to eastern Europe and Russia through political, cultural, and economic relations.

OUTLINE

I.   The early Byzantine empire

  A. The later Roman empire and Byzantium

    1. Fifth century, eastern half of empire remained intact while west crumbled

    2. Challenges: Sasanids and Germans

    3. Highly centralized state

      a. Emperor with aura of divinity—Caesaropapism

      b. Large and complex bureaucracy

  B. Justinian (527–565 C.E.) and his legacy; Theodora (empress)

    1. Rebuilt Constantinople, including Hagia Sophia

    2. Codified Roman law☐ *Corpus iuris civilis* (*The Body of the Civil Law*)

    3. Sent Belisarius to reconquer the western Roman empire (didn't last)

  C. Islamic conquests and Byzantine revival

    1. The emergence of the Islamic state, seventh century

      a. Arab peoples conquered the Sasanid empire and part of Byzantium

      b. Prolonged sieges of Constantinople by Islamic armies

      c.   Byzantium survived partly because of Greek fire

   2. Byzantine society reorganized

      a.   Provinces (*themes*) under generals

      b.   Armies of free peasants helped agricultural economy

  D. Byzantium and western Europe: ecclesiastical and political tensions

II. Byzantine economy and society

  A. Rural economy and society

    1.   Large agricultural base to support cities

    2.   Economy strongest when large class of free peasants (*themes*) existed

    3.   Economy weakened when large landholders consolidated and made peasants dependent

  B. Industry and trade

    1.   Constantinople was major site of crafts and industry

      a.   Glass, linen, textiles, gems, jewelry, gold, and silver

      b.   Silk developed into major industry in sixth century; secrets came from China

    2.   Constantinople was clearinghouse for trade

      a.   Bezant was the standard currency of Mediterranean basin

      b.   Western anchor of trade route revived silk roads

    3.   Banks and partnerships supported commercial economy

  C. Urban life

    1.   Housing in Constantinople varied widely by class

    2.   Attractions of Constantinople: baths, taverns, theaters

      a.   Hippodrome used for mass entertainment

      b.   Chariot races most popular; Greens and Blues rivalry

III. Classical heritage and Orthodox Christianity

  A. The legacy of classical Greece

    1.   Official language went from Latin to Greek

    2.   State-organized school system trained workforce

      a.   Primary education: reading, writing, grammar

      b.   Later education: classical Greek, literature, philosophy, science

      c.   Higher education in Constantinople: law, medicine, philosophy

    3.   Byzantine scholarship emphasized Greek tradition

      a.   Wrote commentaries on Greek literature

      b.   Preserved and transmitted Greek thought to later cultures

B. The Byzantine church

    1. Most distinctive feature was involvement of the emperor

        a. Council of Nicaea (325 C.E.) in which Arianism was declared heresy

        b. Iconoclasm controversy (726–843) was started by Leo III

    2. Greek philosophy applied to Byzantine theology

C. Monasticism and popular piety

    1. Monasticism origins in early Christian ascetics (hermits)

        a. "Pillar saints" like St. Simeon Stylite

        b. St. Basil of Caesarea (329–379 C.E.) organized monastic movement

    2. Mt. Athos, monastery in northern Greece from ninth century to present

    3. Monks/nuns very popular with laity

        a. Provided social services to the community

        b. Opposed iconoclasm

D. Tensions between eastern and western Christianity

    1. Constantinople and Rome: strains mirrored political tensions

    2. Ritual and doctrinal differences, such as iconoclasm

    3. Schism in 1054—Eastern Orthodox versus Roman Catholic

IV. The influence of Byzantium in eastern Europe

A. Domestic problems and foreign pressures

    1. Generals and local aristocrats allied; new elite class challenged imperial power

    2. Western Europe took parts of Byzantium

        a. Normans in southern Italy and Sicily

        b. Crusaders carved out states and sacked Constantinople (1204)

    3. Muslim Saljuq Turks invaded Anatolia, defeated Byzantines at Manzikert, 1071

    4. Ottoman Turks captured Constantinople in 1453, the end of the empire

B. Early relations between Byzantium and Slavic peoples

    1. Byzantines began to influence Bulgarian politics and culture after the eighth century

    2. Missions to the Slavs

        a. Saints Cyril and Methodius, mid-ninth century

        b. Cyrillic writing stimulated conversion to Orthodox Christianity

        c. Education and religion tied together, led to more conversions

C. Byzantium and Russia

    1. Mid-ninth century, Russians started to organize a large state: Kiev

    2. The conversion of Prince Vladimir, 989

      a. Kiev served as a conduit for spread of Byzantine culture and religion

      b. Cyrillic writing and literature and Orthodox missions spread Byzantine culture

      c. Byzantine art and architecture dominated Kiev: icons and onion domes

  3. Princes established caesaropapist control of Russian Orthodox church

  4. Russian culture flourishes from eleventh century

      a. Moscow claimed to be world's "third Rome"

      b. Sent out many missionaries from sixteenth century on

IDENTIFICATION: PEOPLE

What is the contribution of each of the following individuals to world history? (Identification should include answers to the questions *who, what, where, when, how*, and *why is this person important*.)

Procopius

Constantine

Justinian

Theodora

Belisarius

Basil II

Liudprand of Cremona

Arius

Leo III

St. Simeon Stylite

St. Basil of Caesarea

St. Cyril

St. Methodius

Vladimir of Kiev

IDENTIFICATION: TERMS/CONCEPTS

State in your own words what each of the following terms means and why it is significant to a study of world history. (Those terms with an asterisk may be defined in the Glossary.)

Byzantion

Constantinople

Caesaropapism

Hagia Sophia

Corpus iuris civilis

Greek fire

Theme

Bezant

Hippodrome

Greens and Blues

Arianism

Iconoclasm

Pillar saints

Mt. Athos

Eastern Orthodox Church*

Crusades

Battle of Manzikert

Saljuqs

Ottomans

Bulgars

Cyrillic alphabet

Kiev

STUDY QUESTIONS

1. What is the significance of the story of the monks smuggling the silkworm eggs to Byzantium?

2. What elements did Byzantium inherit from the Roman empire that helped it to survive?

3. Describe the Byzantine form of government.

4. What was the significance of Justinian's *Body of Civil Law*?

5. What were the consequences of the rise of the Islamic empire for Byzantium?

6. What was the *theme* system? How did it work? Why was it so successful? What led to its demise?

7. What economic advantages did the Byzantine empire possess?

8. Trace the development of the Byzantine church to the schism. What caused the schism?

9. What kinds of problems eventually led to the constriction and fall of the Byzantine empire?

10. What was the relationship between the Byzantines and the Slavic people, including the Russians?

INQUIRY QUESTIONS

1. Even though the Byzantine empire fell in 1453 and was in decline for centuries before that, it left a strong legacy behind. What was the most important contribution that Byzantium made to world history? Why is that the most important?

2. The book states that Byzantium was the only classical empire to survive. Why did it survive when all the others did not?

3. What role did geographic location play in the history of Byzantium? What were its advantages and disadvantages?

1. According to the Byzantine historian Procopius's account, high-quality silk production was
   a. developed by Byzantine craftsmen by improving the cocoons of wild silkworms.
   b. introduced by two Christian monks to the Byzantine empire.
   c. introduced to the Byzantine empire through several routes.
   d. taught to the Chinese by Byzantine monks.
   e. none of the above.

2. Throughout most of its history the capital of the Byzantine empire was
   a. Byzantion.
   b. Constantinople.
   c. Byzantium.
   d. Istanbul.
   e. none of the above.

3. The term *caesaropapism* refers to the fact that the Byzantine emperors
   a. claimed divine favor and sanction.
   b. claimed divine status.
   c. claimed half human and half divine status.
   d. claimed to be both Roman emperor and pope.
   e. none of the above.

4. Which of the following was *not* true of Theodora?
   a. She was emperor Justinian's wife, advisor, and aid.
   b. She was the daughter of a bear keeper in the circus.
   c. She was the dominant political figure of her age, controlling the empire from behind the scenes.
   d. She was a former stripper.
   e. She advised him to crush a riot in Constantinople.

5. Emperor Justinian is best remembered for his
   a. plan to destroy Constantinople in order to rebuild it.
   b. codification of Roman law, known as *Body of the Civil Law*.
   c. complete reconstitution of the classical Roman empire.
   d. decisive victory over the Muslims.
   e. all of the above.

6. Under the *theme* system,
   a. Byzantine generals used Greek fire to defend their provinces (*themes*).
   b. free peasants received allotments of land in exchange for military service.
   c. generals cooperated with governors in civil administration of provinces (*themes*).
   d. landed aristocrats turned peasants into slaves.
   e. none of the above.

7. The battle of Kleidion in 1014 C.E. was fought between
   a. Byzantium and the Bulgars.
   b. Byzantium and European crusaders.
   c. Byzantium and Muslim Saljuqs.
   d. Byzantium and Islam.
   e. none of the above.

8. Which of the following was *not* an economic policy of the Byzantine government?
   a. preventing land accumulation by wealthy classes in order to protect free peasants.
   b. preventing wealthy and powerful entrepreneurs from monopolizing the silk industry.
   c. issuing the bezant (Byzantine gold coin) as the standard currency.
   d. preventing business partnerships to encourage individual investment.
   e. allowing banks to advance loans for business ventures.

9. Which of the following was *not* a form of entertainment in Constantinople?
   a. perching atop tall pillars.
   b. athletic matches and contests between wild animals.
   c. circuses featuring clowns, jugglers, and dwarfs.
   d. chariot races.
   e. theaters of song and dance.

10. How did the Spanish rabbi Benjamin of Tudela describe Constantinople?
    b. as a corrupt and ungodly place.
    c. as inferior to the city of Baghdad.
    d. as a place where no one is interested in learning.
    d. as the place with the greatest entertainment.
    e. all of the above.

11. After the sixth century, well educated Byzantines
    a. considered themselves the direct heirs of classical Greece.
    b. no longer spoke Latin; they now spoke Greek.
    c. placed more emphasis on the humanities than the sciences.
    d. read commentaries on the Greek classics.
    e. all of the above.

12. Emperor Leo III (reigned 717–741) launched the campaign of iconoclasm because
    a. he wanted to give the ecclesiastical authorities a lesson by destroying paintings and images of Jesus and the saints.
    b. he was convinced that the veneration of religious images was sinful, tantamount to the worship of physical idols.
    c. he suffered from severe mental illness, and the religious images drove him crazy.
    d. he wanted to destroy the influence of the Roman church.
    e. all of the above.

13. Which of the following was *not* true about monasteries of the Byzantine church?
    a. They grew out of the efforts of devout individuals to lead especially holy lives.
    b. They provided social services to their communities.
    c. They were centers of thought and learning.
    d. They opposed the policy of iconoclasm.
    e. Some forbade female humans or animals from entering.

14. In 1054 C.E., the Byzantine patriarch and the pope of Rome mutually excommunicated each other because of their disagreements over matters of
    a. rituals such as whether priests should shave their beards.
    b. the doctrinal dispute about Jesus' relationship to God and the Holy Spirit.
    c. the worship of icons.
    d. who had authority over their jurisdiction.
    e. the appropriateness of the crusades.

15. From the early eleventh century, the most serious domestic problem of Byzantum was
    a. intermarriages between generals' children and local peasants.
    b. the decline of the free peasantry in both number and prosperity.
    c. frequent fights between the Greens and the Blues.
    d. rebellion among the Islamic states.
    e. All were serious problems.

16. Which of the following is true of the crusades launched by the western Europeans during the twelfth and thirteenth centuries?
    a. They were trying to recapture Jerusalem and other holy sites from Muslim control.
    b. They carved out states in parts of the Byzantine empire.
    c. They sacked the city of Constantinople.
    d. They were used to strengthen economic positions in the eastern Mediterranean.
    e. all of the above.

17. The people who finally brought down the Byzantine empire were
    a. crusaders of western Europe.
    b. Muslim Saljuqs.
    c. Ottoman Turks.
    d. Russians and Bulgars.
    e. none of the above.

18. Which of the following was *not* a consequence of the Byzantine missions to the Slavic peoples?
    a. The Cyrillic alphabet became the writing system of the Slavic peoples.
    b. The Byzantine empire and Slavic peoples united to fight against the Islamic armies.
    c. Eastern Orthodox Christianity was adopted by the Slavic peoples.
    d. Schools were organized by the missionaries.
    e. all of the above.

19. How did Alexius I deal with the Bogomil heretics?
    a. He had them all executed by being burned on a cross.
    b. He condemned them to death by crucifixion.
    c. He had them banished from the empire.
    d. He forced them to convert to Manichaeism.
    e. none of the above.

20. The princes of which city established caesaropapist control over the Russian Orthodox Church?
    a. Costantinople
    b. Rome
    c. Moscow
    d. Kiev
    e. St. Petersburg

MATCHING

Match these terms with the statements that follow.

A.	*Theme*	E.	Bezant
B.	Iconoclasm	F.	Caesaropapism
C.	Cyrillic	G.	Hippodrome
D.	Arian	H.	Byzantine

1. ____ Coin that became the standard of currency in the Mediterranean for over five hundred years.

2. ____ Site of mass public entertainments in Constantinople.

3. ____ The alphabet created for the Slavic peoples.

4. ____ A person who believed that Jesus had been a mortal human being.

5. ____ An imperial province under the jurisdiction of a general.

6. ____ A form of government whereby the ruler acts as both a secular and religious authority.

7. ____ The belief that creating and venerating religious images is wrong.

8. ____ A modern term meaning "of unnecessary complexity or intricacy."

SEQUENCING

Place the following clusters of events in chronological order. Consider carefully how one event leads to another and try to determine the internal logic of each sequence.

A.

_____ Emperor Constantine chooses the village of Byzantion as the site of a new capital.

_____ The emperor Diocletian divides the Roman empire into two administrative units.

_____ Justinian orders a systematic codification of Roman law.

_____ Byzantine army is defeated in the Battle of Manzikert.

_____ Constantinople is conquered by the crusaders from western Europe.

_____ Constantinople falls to the Ottoman Turks.

_____ Basil II significantly expands the borders of the empire.

B.

_____ The patriarch and the pope excommunicate each other.

_____ The emperor calls the Council of Niceae.

_____ Iconoclasts abandon their efforts to prohibit the use of images in church.

_____ Monastic reform movement spreads throughout the Byzantine empire.

_____ The western pope calls for a crusade to recapture Jerusalem.

_____ One of the princes of Russia converts to Christianity.

MAP EXERCISES

1. Using the map below, draw in the three boundaries of the Byzantine empire that are illustrated in the two maps in the text. Then explain the shrinking of the Byzantine empire by discussing the roles that the surrounding states played in the process.

2. Study a map of the region and discuss the political, cultural, and economic strategic importance of the location of Constantinople. What other location could Constantine have chosen for his capital that would have been advantageous? Why?

CONNECTIONS

In fifty words or less explain the relationship between each of the following pairs. How does one lead to or foster the other? Be specific in your response. (May be done individually or in small groups.)

- Eastern Orthodoxy and Greek philosophy
- Bezant and silk
- Constantinople and the "third Rome"
- Seljuqs and crusaders
- *Theme* and Islam

GROUP ACTIVITIES

1. Imagine that you are tourists traveling to Constantinople in the ninth century. Plan an itinerary of the sites you want to see and the events you want to participate in during your visit. Visit a website for images of Hagia Sofia.

2. Go to a website that has a translation of the *Body of Civil Law*. As a group see if you can find five laws that you think are still in use in your country today. What does this exercise tell us about the nature of Roman law, the Byzantine culture, and your laws?

CHAPTER 14
THE EXPANSIVE REALM OF ISLAM

INTRODUCTION

The religion of Islam emerged on the Arabian Peninsula in the seventh century C.E. as a result of the vision and the teachings of Muhammad. His message attracted a rapidly expanding circle of devout believers, known as Muslims. After Muhammad's death, Arab conquerors spread the word of Islam throughout a vast territory extending from the Indus River to the Iberian Peninsula within one century. This rapid expansion of Islam contributed to the development of a massive trade and communication network in which goods and ideas spread freely. The realm of Islam became one of the most prosperous and cosmopolitan societies of the postclassical world. This new society was characterized by

- Strong commitment to the monotheistic belief system, resting on the Five Pillars of Islam, first articulated by Muhammad and later elaborated on by scholars and mystics.
- The development of overland and maritime trade and communication routes that facilitated the spread of new crops, trade goods, and ideas, from improved techniques in agriculture to the writings of the classical Greek philosophers.
- Engagement with and sometimes adoption of various cultural traditions encountered by the far-flung realm and its trade contacts. Hence elements of Persian, Indian, Christian, and Greek cultures found their place into Islamic society and thought.

OUTLINE

I. **A prophet and his world**

    A. Muhammad and his message

        1. Arabian peninsula was mostly desert

            a. Nomadic Bedouin people organized in family and clan groups

            b. Important in long-distance trade networks between China/India and Persia/Byzantium

        2. Muhammad's early life

            a. Muhammad ibn Abdullah born to a Mecca merchant family, 570 C.E.

            b. Difficult early life, married a wealthy widow, Khadija, in 595

            c. Became a merchant at age thirty and was exposed to various faiths

        3. Muhammad's spiritual transformation at age forty

            a. There was only one true god, Allah ("the god")

            b. Allah would soon bring judgment on the world

            c. The archangel Gabriel delivered these revelations to Muhammad

        4. The Quran ("recitation")—holy book of Islam

      a. Followers compiled Muhammad's revelations

      b. Work of poetry and definitive authority on Islam

      c. Other works include *hadith* (sayings and deeds of Muhammad)

B. Muhammad's migration to Medina

    1. Conflict at Mecca

      a. His teachings offended other believers, especially the ruling elite of Mecca

      b. Attacks on greed offended wealthy merchants

      c. Attacks on idolatry threatened shrines, especially the black rock at Ka'ba

    2. The *hijra*

      a. Under persecution, Muhammad and followers fled to Medina, 622 C.E.

      b. The move, known as *hijra*, was the starting point of the Islamic calendar

    3. The *umma*: cohesive community of Muslims in Medina

    4. The "seal of the prophets"

      a. Muhammad called himself the "seal of the prophets"—the final prophet of Allah

      b. Held Hebrew scripture and New Testament in high esteem

      d. Determined to spread Allah's wish to all humankind

C. The establishment of Islam in Arabia

    1. Muhammad's return to Mecca

      a. He and his followers conquered Mecca, 630

      b. Imposed a government dedicated to Allah

      c. Destroyed pagan shrines and built mosques

    2. The Ka'ba was not destroyed; it became site of pilgrimage in 632

    3. The Five Pillars of Islam, or obligations taught by Muhammad

    4. Islamic law: the *sharia*, inspired by Quran

      a. Detailed guidance on proper behavior in almost every aspect of life

      b. Through the *sharia*, Islam became more than a religion, it became a way of life

II. **The expansion of Islam**

A. The early caliphs and the Umayyad dynasty

    1. The caliph

      a. Upon Muhammad's death, Abu Bakr served as caliph ("deputy")

      b. Became head of the state, chief judge, religious leader, military commander

    2. Dramatic expansion of Islam

    3. The Shia

      a. The Shia sect originally supported Ali and descendents as caliph

  b. Versus the Sunnis ("traditionalists"), the Shias accepted legitimacy of early caliphs

  c. Different beliefs: holy days for leaders, Ali infallible

  d. Ongoing conflict between the two sects

 4. The Umayyad dynasty (661–750 C.E.)

  a. The dynasty temporarily solved problem of succession

  b. Established capital city at Damascus in Syria

  c. Ruled the *dar al-Islam* for the interests of Arabian military aristocracy

 5. Policy toward conquered peoples

  a. Levied *jizya* (head tax) on those who did not convert to Islam

  b. Even the non-Arab converts were discriminated against

 6. Umayyad decline, due to discontent of conquered and resistance of Shia

B. The Abbasid dynasty

 1. Abu al-Abbas, descendant of Muhammad's uncle

  a. Allied with Shias and non-Arab Muslims

  b. Won battle against Umayyad in 750 after annihilating the clan

 2. The Abbasid dynasty (750–1258 C.E.)

  a. Showed no special favor to Arab military aristocracy

  b. No longer conquering, but the empire still grew

 3. Abbasid administration

  a. Relied heavily on Persian techniques of statecraft

  b. Central authority ruled from the court at Baghdad

  c. Appointed governors to rule provinces

  d. *Ulama* ("people with religious knowledge") and *qadis* (judges) ruled locally

 4. Harun al-Rashid (786–809 C.E.), high point of Abassid dynasty

 5. Abbasid decline

  a. Struggle for succession between Harun's sons led to civil war

  b. Governors built their own power bases

  c. Popular uprisings and peasant rebellions weakened the dynasty

  d. A Persian noble seized control of Baghdad in 945

  e. Later, the Saljuq Turks controlled the imperial family

III. **Economy and society of the early Islamic world**

 A. New crops, agricultural experimentation, and urban growth

  1. Spread of new foods and industrial crops

2. Effects of new crops

    a. Increased varieties and quantities of food

    b. Industrial crops became the basis for a thriving textile industry

3. Agricultural experimentation

4. Urban growth

    a. Increasing agricultural production contributed to the rapid growth of cities

    b. A new industry: paper manufacture

B. The formation of a hemispheric trading zone

1. Overland trade

    a. Trade revived silk roads

    b. Umayyad and Abbasid rulers maintained roads for military and administration

2. Camels and caravans

    a. Overland trade traveled mostly by camel caravan

    b. Caravanserais in Islamic cities

3. Maritime trade

    a. Arab and Persian mariners borrowed the compass from the Chinese

    b. Borrowed the lateen sail from southeast Asian and Indian mariners

    c. Borrowed astrolabe from the Hellenistic mariners

4. Banks

    a. Operated on large scale and provided extensive services

    b. Letters of credit, or *sakk*, functioned as bank checks

5. The organization of trade

    a. Entrepreneurs often pooled their resources in group investments

    b. Traders even went to West Africa, Russia, Scandinavia

6. Al-Andalus with its capital city Cordoba

    a. This area was Islamic Spain, conquered by Muslim Berbers

    b. Claimed independence from the Abbasid dynasty

    c. Products of al-Andalus enjoyed a reputation for excellence

C. The changing status of women

1. The Quran and women

    a. The Quran enhanced security of women

    b. The Quran and *sharia* also reinforced male domination

2. Veiling of women

    a. Adopted veiling of women from Mesopotamia and Persia

b. Women's rights provided by the Quran were reduced through later interpretations

IV. Islamic values and cultural exchanges

A. The formation of an Islamic cultural tradition

1. The Quran and *sharia* were main sources to formulate moral guidelines
2. Promotion of Islamic values

   a. *Ulama, qadis*, and missionaries were main agents

   b. Education also promoted Islamic values

3. *Sufis*, or Islamic mystics

   a. Most effective missionaries

   b. Encouraged devotion to Allah by passionate singing or dancing

   c. Al-Ghazali believed that human reason was too frail and confusing

   d. Sufis led ascetic and holy lives, won respect of the people

   e. Encouraged followers to revere Allah in their own ways

   f. Tolerated those who associated Allah with other beliefs

4. The hajj

   a. The Ka'ba became the symbol of Islamic cultural unity

   b. Pilgrims helped to spread Islamic beliefs and values

B. Islam and the cultural traditions of Persia, India, and Greece

1. Persian influence on Islam

   a. Most notable in literary works

   b. Administrative techniques borrowed from Sasanids

   c. Ideas of kingship: wise, benevolent, absolute

2. Indian influences

   a. Adopted "Hindi numerals," which Europeans later called "Arabic numerals"

   b. Algebra and trigonometry

3. Greek influences

   a. Muslims philosophers especially liked Plato and Aristotle

   b. Ibn Rushd (Averroës) turned to Aristotle in twelfth century

IDENTIFICATION: PEOPLE

What is the contribution of each of the following individuals to world history? (Identification should include answers to the questions *who, what, where, when, how*, and *why is this person important*.)

Muhammad

Abu Bakr

Ali

Abu al-Abbas

Harun al-Rashid

Al-Ghazali

Omar Khayyam

Ibn Rushd

IDENTIFICATION: TERMS/CONCEPTS

State in your own words what each of the following terms means and why it is significant to a study of world history. (Those terms with an asterisk may be defined in the Glossary.)

Islam*

Muslim

Dar al-Islam

Mecca

Quran

Hadith

Medina

Hijra

Umma

Seal of the Prophets

Ka'ba

Five Pillars of Islam

Saria

Caliph

Umayyed

Shia*

Abbasid

Ulama

Qadis

Sultan

Caravanserai

Al-Andalus

Sufis*

Hajj

STUDY QUESTIONS

1. How did Muhammad's background influence his beliefs and the early development of Islam?

2. What were the fundamental tenets of Islam?

3. After Muhammad died, what were the challenges faced by *dar al-Islam* and how were they resolved within the first century?

4. How did the Abbasids come to power, and how did their rule differ from the Umayyads?

5. How did the growth of the realm of Islam contribute to agricultural, industrial, and urban development?

6. What factors contributed to the expansion of Islamic overland and maritime trade?

7. What was the status of women in the early centuries of Islam?

8. What people and institutions helped to promote and spread the values of Islam?

9. What is the significance of the hajj to Islamic religion and culture?

10. How did Persia, India, and Greece influence the realm of Islam?

INQUIRY QUESTIONS

1. Islam spread more rapidly than any other major world religion. Why do you think this was? What aspects of the religion made it appealing? How was the cultural climate conducive to the rapid expansion of Islam?

2. Compare and contrast the beliefs (including the treatment of women) of the major world religions: Judaism, Christianity, Islam, Hinduism, Buddhism.

3. The book states that *dar al-Islam* became "probably the most prosperous and cosmopolitan society of the postclassical world." What does this statement mean? What evidence is there for this statement? Do you agree or disagree?

STUDENT QUIZ

1. The word *Islam* means
   a. submission.
   b. one who has submitted.
   c. the god.
   d. Arabia.
   e. none of the above.

2. The nature of the society into which the prophet Muhammad was born was
   a. an urban-based culture with small manufacturing.
   b. a pastoral society with many camels.
   c. an agricultural society dominated by warriors.
   d. a society made up largely of nomads and merchants.
   e. a society based on maritime trade.

3. Muhammad experienced profound spiritual revelations that led him to believe that
   a. he was chosen by Allah to create a new religion.
   b. he was the last prophet of Allah.
   c. Judaism and Christianity were major offenses to Allah.
   d. Allah was one of many gods.
   e. none of the above.

4. The Quran is to Islam as
   a. Siddhartha is to Buddhism.
   b. the Avesta is to Zoroastrianism
   c. Yahweh is to Judaism.
   d. the New Testament is to Christianity.
   e. none of the above.

5. Under pressure from authorities in Mecca, Muhammad and his followers fled to Medina in 622. Muslims call this move
   a. the *hijra*.
   b. the *umma*.
   c. Yathrib.
   d. the hajj.
   e. none of the above.

6. The Five Pillars are to Muslims as
   a. the *hadith* is to Muslims.
   b. the Noble Eightfold Path is to Buddhists.
   c. the four Vedas are to the Aryans.
   d. the book of Genesis is to Christians.
   e. none of the above.

7. Which of the following is *not* true with regard to the *sharia*?
    a. It offered detailed guidance on proper behavior in almost every aspect of life.
    b. It was created by the prophet Muhammad.
    c. It drew inspiration especially from the Quran.
    d. It drew inspiration from the *hidath*.
    e. It helped to unite the disparate parts of *dar al-Islam*.

8. Which of the following is true of the early caliphs?
    a. The early caliphs quickly rejected many of Muhammad's teachings.
    b. The caliph was strictly a political leader, not a religious one.
    c. The early caliphs were unanimously agreed upon by the *umma*.
    d. The early caliphs concentrated on religious doctrine, not expansion.
    e. None of the above.

9. The Umayyad dynasty was founded by
    a. the Shias.
    b. the Sunnis.
    c. Abu al-Abbas.
    d. Abu Bakr.
    e. none of the above.

10. Which of the following actions was *not* taken by the Umayyad caliphs?
    a. They became more and more lax in their attitudes toward Islamic doctrine.
    b. They levied a special head tax called *jizya* on non-Muslims.
    c. They showed great favor to the Arab military aristocracy.
    d. They temporarily solved the problem of succession to the caliphate.
    e. They maintained their simple lifestyle even in the capital of Damascus.

11. Differing from the Umayyad caliphs, the Abbasid rulers
    a. were from the Shia sect.
    b. did not allow the Arabs to play a large role in government.
    c. paid more attention to administration rather than expansion of the empire.
    d. moved the capital to Mecca.
    e. all of the above.

12. *Ulama* and *qadis* were important in Islamic society because they
    a. developed public policies and heard cases in accordance with the Quran and the *sharia*.
    b. were learned priests in the roles of magistrates and judges.
    c. were effective missionaries encouraging the people's obedience and devotion to Allah.
    d. were part of the military arm of Islam, responsible for its expansion.
    e. all of the above.

13. Which of the following statements is *not* true with regard to the Saljuq Turks?
    a. They invaded the Byzantine empire and seized much of Anatolia.
    b. They converted to Islam in the tenth century.
    c. They usurped the Abbasid caliphate and claimed the title of caliph for themselves.
    d. They were conquered by the Mongols.
    e. They were the true source of power of the Abbasids for about two centuries.

14. During Abbasid times, the Arabs learned from China the technique of making
    a. fine silk.
    b. wood block prints.
    c. gunpowder and cannons.
    d. paper.
    e. all of the above.

15. Islamic Spain, known as al-Andalus, was
    a. controlled by Muslim Berber conquerors.
    b. not part of the Abbasid empire.
    c. the source of a failed invasion of France.
    d. the home of ibn Rashd (Averroes).
    e. all of the above.

16. Which of the following was *not* a right of Islamic women?
    a. They could legally inherit property and divorce husbands.
    b. They could engage in business ventures.
    c. They were equal to men before Allah, not the property of the men.
    d. They could take up to four husbands, just as a man could take up to four wives.
    e. None of the above is true.

17. The veiling of women as a social custom was
    a. not specifically addressed in the Quran.
    b. practiced long before Muhammad was born.
    c. adopted from Byzantine and Sasanid societies by Muslims.
    d. originally practiced by upper-class women.
    e. all of the above.

18. Which of the following was true of Sufis?
    a. They were very effective missionaries.
    b. They sought an emotional and mystical union with Allah.
    c. They used emotional sermons and song and dance to encourage devotion.
    d. They tolerated observances of some non-Islamic customs.
    e. all of the above.

19. The hajj
    a. is one of the Five Pillars of Islam.
    b. helped to unite Muslims from disparate parts of the world.
    c. ends at the Ka'ba in Mecca.
    d. contributed to the spread of Islamic beliefs and values.
    e. all of the above.

20. Which of the following is *not* correct in describing cultural influences on Islam?
    a. Persian literature deeply influenced Islamic literary works.
    b. Indian numerals had a profound influence on the development of mathematical thinking among Muslims.
    c. The caliphs adopted Persian ideas of kingship.
    d. Greek rational reasoning had a long-lasting influence on the theological development of Islam.
    e. None of the above.

MATCHING

Match these Arabic terms with their meaning in Islamic history.

A. *quadis*   G. *hijra*
B. *sharia*   H. *umma*
C. *sakk*   I. *jizya*
D. *hajj*   J. *madrasas*
E. *dar al-Islam*   K. *ulama*
F. *al-Andalus*   L. *sultan*

1. ___ Saljuq Turk ruler who was true source of authority over later Abbasid emperors.

2. ___ Independent Islamic power in Iberian Peninsula.

3. ___ "People with religious authority" who set moral standards in local communities.

4. ___ "House of Islam," referring to the entire Islamic realm.

5. ___ Islamic schools of higher education.

6. ___ One of the Five Pillars of Islam; Muslims must make a pilgrimage to Mecca.

7. ___ The tax that the Umayyad dynasty levied on non-Muslims.

8. ___ A letter of credit that facilitated long-distance trade.

9. ___ "The community of the faithful."

10. ___ Islamic holy law detailing the proper behavior of the faithful.

11. ___ "Migration," Muhammad's move to Medina and the start of the Islamic calendar.

12. ___ Muslim judges who helped resolve disputes in local communities.

SEQUENCING

Place the following clusters of events in chronological order. Consider carefully how one event leads to another, and try to determine the internal logic of each sequence.

A.

_____ Muhammad and his followers attack Mecca.

_____ Muhammad marries a wealthy widow.

_____ Muhammad is pressured to leave Mecca and joins some of his followers in Yathrib.

_____ Muhammad leads first Islamic pilgrimage to the Ka'ba.

_____ Muhammad's revelations are compiled in the Quran.

_____ Muhammad gathers a group of believers around him.

_____ Muhammad has spiritual visions that he interprets as messages from Allah.

B.

_____ Baghdad becomes the artistic and commercial center of Islamic realm.

_____ Saljuq Turks are conquered by the Mongols.

_____ Abu al-Abbas's party seizes control of Persia and Mesopotamia.

_____ Abu Bakr is selected as caliph.

_____ Umayyids bring stability to the Islamic community.

_____ Islamic armies conquer Byzantium and the Sasanid territories.

_____ Caliph Ali is assassinated.

QUOTATIONS

For each of the following quotes, identify the speaker, if known, or the point of view or the subject. What is the significance of each passage?

1. He "is the head of the Muslim religion, and all the kings of Islam obey him; he occupies a similar position to that held by the pope over the Christians."

2. "Lord of all the worlds, Most beneficent, ever merciful, King of the Day of Judgement. You alone we worship, and to You alone turn for help."

3. It "is twenty miles in circumference, situated in a land of palms, gardens, and plantations, the like of which is not to be found in the whole land of Mesopotamia. People come thither with merchandise from all lands."

MAP EXERCISES

1. Using the map of Europe, north Africa, and southwest Asia below, draw the expansion of Islam from 610–632, 632–661, and 661–733. Then draw a boundary around the Umayyad and Abbasid empires.

2. Using the map in conjunction with another that has a scale measurement on it, trace the likely route of a pilgrim going on the hajj from Seville to Mecca and another from Samarkand. Follow the trade routes, which is how most pilgrims traveled. Now calculate the number of miles each pilgrim would have to travel. Make an estimate of how long the trip would be likely to take.

CONNECTIONS

In fifty words or less explain the relationship between each of the following pairs. How does one lead to or foster the other? Be specific in your response. (May be done individually or in small groups.)

- Bedouin and Muslim
- Quran and *Sharia*
- Caravanserai and the Hajj
- Paper and *Umma*
- Sufis and Shia

GROUP ACTIVITIES

1. Go to a website that has a map showing the areas of the world with a majority Islamic population. Speculate about how Islam spread from its realm in the eighth century to those locations.

2. The text lists the new crops that were introduced to the Islamic world by travelers along the trade routes: sugarcane, rice, sorghum and wheat, spinach, artichokes, eggplant, oranges, lemons, limes, bananas, coconuts, watermelons, and mangoes. Now locate some Arabic, Middle Eastern, and North African recipes. What common dishes use those ingredients?

FEATURE FILMS

The Message (Story of Islam) (1976). The story of Muhammad and the early spread of the religion of Islam. With Anthony Quinn and Irene Papas.

CHAPTER 15
THE RESURGENCE OF EMPIRE IN EAST ASIA

INTRODUCTION

After the fall of the Han dynasty, more than 350 years of disruption plagued China. Toward the end of the sixth century, centralized imperial rule returned to China and persisted for almost 700 years under the Sui, Tang, and Song dynasties (589–1279 C.E.). This period witnessed unprecedented economic prosperity for China. In addition, China, as the "Middle Kingdom," made its influence felt throughout the surrounding territories, creating a larger east Asian society centered on China. This period of east Asian history is characterized by

- Rapid economic development because of more advanced agricultural practices, technological and industrial innovations, and participation in sophisticated trade networks throughout east Asia and including the revived silk roads
- The spread of Buddhism beyond its place of origin in India until it became the most popular religious faith in all of east Asia
- The profound influence of Chinese social organization and economic dynamism on the surrounding cultures of Korea, Vietnam, Japan, and central Asia

OUTLINE

I.   **The restoration of centralized imperial rule in China**

A. The Sui dynasty (589–618 C.E.)

1. After the Han dynasty, turmoil lasted for more than 350 years

2. Reunification by Yang Jian in 589

3. The rule of the Sui

a. Construction of palaces and granaries; repairing the Great Wall

b. Military expeditions in central Asia and Korea

c. High taxes and compulsory labor services

4. The Grand Canal integrated economies of north and south

5. The fall of the Sui

a. High taxes and forced labor generated hostility among the people

b. Military reverses in Korea

c. Rebellions broke out in north China beginning in 610

d. Sui Yangdi was assassinated in 618, the end of the dynasty

B. The Tang dynasty (618–907 C.E.)

1. Tang Taizong (627–649)

a. A rebel leader seized Chang'an and proclaimed a new dynasty, the Tang

      b.   Tang Taizong, the second Tang emperor; ruthless but extremely competent

      c.   era of unusual stability and prosperity

  2.   Extensive networks of transportation and communications

  3.   Equal-field system—land allotted according to needs

  4.   Bureaucracy of merit through civil service exams

  5.   Foreign relations

      a.   Political theory: China was the Middle Kingdom, or the center of civilization

      b.   Tributary system became diplomatic policy

  6.   Tang decline

      a.   Casual and careless leadership led to dynastic crisis

      b.   Rebellion of An Lushan in 755 weakened the dynasty

      c.   The Uighurs became de facto rulers

      d.   The equal-field system deteriorated

      e.   A large-scale peasant rebellion led by Huang Chao lasted from 875 to 884

      f.   Regional military commanders gained power and were beyond control of the emperor

      g.   The last Tang emperor abdicated his throne in 907

C. The Song dynasty (960–1279 C.E.)

  1.   Song Taizu (reigned 960–976 C.E.) was the founder

  2.   Song weaknesses

      a.   Financial problems: enormous bureaucracy and high salary devoured surplus

      b.   Military problems: civil bureaucrats in charge of military forces

      c.   External pressures: seminomadic Khitan and nomadic Jurchen

      d.   The Song moved to the south, ruled south China until 1279

II. **The economic development of Tang and Song China**

A. Agricultural development

  1.   Fast-ripening rice increased food supplies

  2.   New agricultural techniques increased production

  3.   Population growth: 45 to 115 million between 600 and 1200 C.E.

  4.   Urbanization

  5.   Commercialized agriculture; some regions depended on other regions for food

  6.   Patriarchal social structure

      a.   Ancestor worship became more elaborate

      b.   Foot binding gained popularity

B. Technological and industrial development

    1. Porcelain (chinaware) diffused rapidly

    2. Metallurgy increased ten times from ninth to twelfth centuries

    3. Gunpowder was used in primitive weapons and diffused through Eurasia

    4. Printing developed from wood block to movable type

    5. Naval technology: "south-pointing needle"—the magnetic compass

C. The emergence of a market economy

    1. Financial instruments: "flying cash" (letters of credit) and paper money

    2. A cosmopolitan society: communities of foreign merchants in large cities

    3. Economic surge in China promoted economic growth in the eastern hemisphere

III. Cultural change in Tang and Song China

A. Establishment of Buddhism

    1. Foreign religions: Nestorians, Manichaeans, Zoroastrians, Muslim communities

    2. Dunhuang, city on silk road, transmits Mahayana Buddhism to China

    3. Buddhism in China

        a. Attraction: moral standards, intellectual sophistication, and salvation

        b. Monasteries became large landowners, helped the poor and needy

        c. Also posed a challenge to Chinese cultural tradition

    4. Buddhism and Daoism

        a. Chinese monks explained Buddhist concepts in Daoist vocabulary

        b. *Dharma* as *dao*, and *nirvana* as *wuwei*

        c. Teaching: one son in monastery would benefit whole family for ten generations

    5. Chan Buddhism

        a. A syncretic faith: Buddhism with Chinese characteristics

        b. Chan (or Zen in Japanese) was a popular Buddhist sect

    6. Hostility to Buddhism from the Daoists and Confucians

    7. Persecution; it survived because of popularity

B. Neo-Confucianism

    1. Buddhist influence on Confucianism

        a. Early Confucianism focused on practical issues of politics and morality

        b. Confucians began to draw inspiration from Buddhism in areas of logic and metaphysics

    2. Zhu Xi (1130–1200 C.E.), the most prominent neo-Confucian scholar

IV. Chines influence in east Asia

A. Korea and Vietnam

1. The Silla dynasty of Korea (669–935 C.E.)

   a. Tang armies conquered much of Korea; the Silla dynasty organized resistance

   b. Korea entered into a tributary relationship with China

2. China's influence in Korea

   a. Tributary embassies included Korean royal officials and scholars

   b. The Silla kings built a new capital at Kumsong modeled on the Tang capital

   c. Korean elite turned to neo-Confucianism; peasants turned to Chan Buddhism

3. Difference between Korea and China: aristocracy and royal houses dominated Korea

4. China and Vietnam

   a. Viet people adopted Chinese agriculture, schools, and thought

   b. Tributary relationship with China

   c. When Tang fell, Vietnam gained independence

5. Difference between Vietnam and China

   a. Many Vietnamese retained their religious traditions

   b. Women played more prominent roles in Vietnam than in China

6. Chinese influence in Vietnam: bureaucracy and Buddhism

B. Early Japan

1. Nara Japan (710–794 C.E.)

   a. The earliest inhabitants of Japan were nomadic peoples from northeast Asia

   b. Ruled by several dozen states by the middle of the first millennium C.E.

   c. Inspired by the Tang example, one clan claimed imperial authority over others

   d. Built a new capital (Nara) in 710 C.E., modeled on Chang'an

   e. Adopted Confucianism and Buddhism, but maintained their Shinto rites

2. Heian Japan (794–1185 C.E.)

   a. Moved to new capital, Heian (modern Kyoto), in 794

   b. Japanese emperors as ceremonial figureheads and symbols of authority

   c. Effective power in the hands of the Fujiwara family

   d. Emperor did not rule, which explains the longevity of the imperial house

   e. Chinese learning dominated Japanese education and political thought

3. *The Tale of Genji* was written by a woman, Murasaki Shikibu

4. Decline of Heian Japan

   a. The equal-field system began to fail

   b. Aristocratic clans accumulated most land

   c. Taira and Minamoto, the two most powerful clans, engaged in wars

   d. Clan leader of Minamoto claimed title *shogun*, military governor; ruled in Kamakura

 C. Medieval Japan was a period of decentralization

  1. Kamakura (1185–1333 C.E.) and Muromachi (1336–1573 C.E.) periods

  2. The samurai

   a. Professional warriors of provincial lords

   b. Valued loyalty, military talent, and discipline

   c. Observed samurai code called *bushido*

   d. To preserve their honor, engaged in ritual suicide called *seppuku*

IDENTIFICATION: PEOPLE

What is the contribution of each of the following individuals to world history? (Identification should include answers to the questions *who, what, where, when, how,* and *why is this person important.*)

Xuanzang

Yang Jian

Sui Yangdi

Tang Taizong

An Lushan

Huang Chao

Du Fu

Song Taizu

Li Bo

Zhu Xi

Murasaki Shikibu

IDENTIFICATION: TERMS/CONCEPTS

State in your own words what each of the following terms means and why it is significant to a study of world history. (Those terms with an asterisk may be defined in the Glossary.)

Sui

Grand Canal

Tang

Chang'an

Equal-field system

Bureaucracy of merit

Middle Kingdom

Uighurs

Song

Khitan

Jurchen

Foot binding

Dunhuang

Chan Buddhism

Neo-Confucianism*

Silla

Vietnam

Nara Japan

Heian period

Tale of Genji

Minamoto

Shogun

Kamakura

Muromachi

Samurai

Bushido

Seppuku

STUDY QUESTIONS

1. What is the significance of the Grand Canal?

2. Compare and contrast the Tang and the Song dynasties.

3. What policies helped to account for the early success of the Tang?

4. Explain how China's view of itself as the Middle Kingdom shaped foreign relations.

5. What factors led to the decline of the Song?

6. What agricultural developments helped to transform the Chinese economy?

7. What important technological, industrial, and commercial innovations occurred during this period?

8. Trace the development of Buddhism in China and how it interacted with Daoism and Confucianism.

9. What was the extent and nature of the influence of China on Korea, Vietnam, and Japan?

10. What is the significance of foot binding?

INQUIRY QUESTIONS

1. The book refers to China and the Byzantine and Abbasid empires as "the political and economic anchor[s] of the postclassical world." What does this phrase mean? What did all three of those powers have in common? How did those factors contribute to their political and economic effectiveness?

2. The Chinese population underwent rapid growth from 600 to 1200. What developments during this period promoted that growth? What were the economic advantages of having such a large population? What are the potential disadvantages?

3. There were many foreign religions in China at this time, but Buddhism is the one that caught on. Why is that? What about Buddhism made it particularly appealing? How did it influence and blend with other belief systems at the time? How did its influence spread from China?

STUDENT QUIZ

1. Xuanzang became a well-known monk of the Tang dynasty because
   a. he was the only Chinese who made the pilgrimage to Mecca.
   b. his travels and study in India helped to popularize Buddhism in China.
   c. he was persecuted by the emperor for his violation of the ban on traveling abroad.
   d. he helped to develop neo-Confucianism.
   e. none of the above.

2. Which of the following does *not* describe the Sui dynasty?
   a. It reunified China and launched military campaigns in central Asia and Korea.
   b. It imposed high taxes and compulsory labor services for construction of the Grand Canal.
   c. It brought about great prosperity in China and long-lived imperial rule.
   d. It only lasted a short period of time.
   e. The last emperor was assassinated, bringing the dynasty to an end.

3. The Tang maintained an efficient communication network, which can be seen by the fact that
   a. the Tang court could communicate with the most distant cities of the empire in about three months.
   b. emperors at Chang'an could have fresh seafood delivered from Ningbo, a city 620 miles away.
   c. the Grand Canal was initiated under Tang rule.
   d. they utilized camels and caravans almost exclusively.
   e. all of the above.

4. Under the equal-field system, the Tang government
   a. allotted land according to the land's fertility and the recipients' needs.
   b. eliminated the possibility of concentrated landholdings among the wealthy.
   c. was able to levy heavy taxes on the recipients.
   d. forbade the Buddhist monasteries from controlling land.
   e. all of the above.

5. The Tang government was run primarily by
   a. hereditary aristocratic families.
   b. royal kinsmen and relatives.
   c. descendents of the Sui.
   d. bureaucrats of intellectual merit.
   e. samurai warriors.

6. "There was always something of a fictional quality to the [tributary] system." By this statement the authors mean that
   a. envoys from subordinate lands were not sincere in performing the ritual kowtow to Chinese emperors.
   b. Chinese authorities had little real influence in the supposedly subordinate lands.
   c. Chinese courts also gave lavish gifts to foreign envoys.
   d. the Chinese did not actually receive any tribute from these lands.
   e. none of the above.

7. One cause for Tang decline during the mid-eighth century was that
    a. the emperors neglected public affairs in favor of music and mistresses.
    b. military campaigns in central Asia, Korea, and Vietnam drained Tang finances.
    c. the central government abolished the equal-field system.
    d. the Mongols continued to invade.
    e. all of the above.

8. Compared with the Tang dynasty, the Song dynasty was
    a. shorter-lived.
    b. less centralized.
    c. equal in size.
    d. less militarized.
    e. all of the above.

9. The Song government moved from north to south in the early twelfth century because of the invasion of
    a. the Khitan.
    b. the Jurchen.
    c. the Uighurs.
    d. the Mongols.
    e. the Muslims.

10. Fast-ripening rice
    a. was introduced to China from Vietnam.
    b. enabled cultivators to harvest two times a year.
    c. increased food supply and supported a large population.
    d. adapted well to southern Chinese soil.
    e. all of the above.

11. The practice of foot binding
    a. was to venerate family ancestors.
    b. discouraged peasant women from working in the fields.
    c. became universal in China by the end of the Song.
    d. placed women of the privileged classes under male supervision.
    e. none of the above.

12. Which of the following was *not* a major technological innovation of Tang and Song China?
    a. Gunpowder.
    b. The magnetic compass.
    c. Movable type printing.
    d. Paper making.
    e. Fine porcelain.

13. The Chinese term *flying cash* meant
    a. paper money printed by the government as a substitute for heavy copper currency.
    b. letters of credit used by merchants.
    c. that money changed hands so quickly it seemed as though it could fly.
    d. runaway inflation.
    e. none of the above.

14. During Tang times, several foreign religions came to China. The foreign faiths that did *not* arrive in China included
    a. Nestorian Christianity and Manichaeanism.
    b. Hinduism and Jainism.
    c. Zoroastrianism and Islam.
    d. Buddhism and Zoroastrianism.
    e. All of the above *did* come to China.

15. In order for Buddhism to be accepted in China, Chinese Buddhists
    a. changed the Buddha and the *boddhisatvas* into Daoist deities.
    b. accommodated Buddhism to Chinese values such as filial piety.
    c. paid high taxes from their monasteries to the Chinese government.
    d. persecuted believers in Daoism and Confucianism.
    e. all of the above.

16. The poet of the Tang who wrote of the social life in cities was
    a. Zhu Xi.
    b. Xuanzang.
    c. Song Taizu.
    d. Li Bo.
    e. Du Fu.

17. Despite cultural borrowing and imitation, Korea was still different from China in that
    a. aristocrats dominated Korean society while bureaucrats dominated Chinese life.
    b. Koreans accepted neo-Confucianism but rejected Buddhism.
    c. the Silla capital at Kumsong did not resemble the Chinese capital at Chang'an.
    d. the Koreans were not nearly as scholarly as the Chinese.
    e. all of the above.

18. Which of the following is true of Vietnam during Tang and Song times?
    a. Many Vietnamese retained their indigenous traditions in preference to Chinese cultural traditions.
    b. Vietnamese authorities established an administrative system and bureaucracy modeled on that of China.
    c. Vietnamese women had more freedoms than their Chinese counterparts did.
    d. The Viets won their independence from China with the fall of the Tang.
    e. all of the above.

19. The earliest phases of Japanese history included
    a. the Kamakura and Muromachi periods.
    b. the Nara and Heian periods.
    c. the Taira and Minamoto periods.
    d. the age of the samurais.
    e. the medieval period.

20. In medieval Japan, professional warriors were called
    a. *samurai.*
    b. *bushido.*
    c. *shogun.*
    d. *seppuku.*
    e. none of the above.

MATCHING

Match these figures with the statements that follow.

A. An Lushan   E. Tang Taizong
B. Xuanzang   F. Zhu Xi
C. Murasaki Shikibu   G. Du Fu
D. Sui Yangdi   H. Song Taizu

1. ____ He began work on the Grand Canal to facilitate trade between the north and the south.

2. ____ Considered one of the greatest poets in Chinese history.

3. ____ Author of the fictitious *Tale of Genji*.

4. ____ Ambitious and ruthless emperor of China in the seventh century.

5. ____ Military leader who led a rebellion that left the Tang in a permanently weakened state.

6. ____ Buddhist monk who was responsible for popularizing his faith in China.

7. ____ Philosopher who blended Confucian values with Buddhist thought.

8. ____ Emperor who consciously weakened the military and built up the bureaucracy.

SEQUENCING

Place the following clusters of events in chronological order. Consider carefully how one event leads to another, and try to determine the internal logic of each sequence.

A.
____ Turkish Uighurs are invited into China to help oust rebels holding the capital.

____ Mongol forces conquer China and incorporate it into their empire.

____ Yang Jian forces abdication of seven-year-old heir and seizes throne for himself.

____ Sui Yangdi assassinated by a disgruntled minister.

____ Capital city of Chang'an is built.

____ Song Taizu convinces generals to retire and live lives of leisure.

B.
____ Samurai loyally serve their overlords and live by the code of *bushido*.

____ One clan seizes power and builds Japanese court modeled after Tang.

____ Clan leader is installed as first *shogun* of Japan.

____ Nomads from northeast Asia migrate to Japan.

____ Chinese literature and writing system are adopted by Japan.

____ Muromachi period lasts for about 240 years.

193

MAP EXERCISES

1. On the map of Asia below, trace the spread of Buddhism from its origins in India to east Asia. Use different colors to illustrate the different periods of its spread.

2. On the map of Asia below, color in the approximate territories of the Tang, the Abbasid, and the Byzantine empires. Why are these three referred to as the "anchors" of the postclassical world? How did the territories they encompassed influence the trade and communications patterns of the postclassical world?

In fifty words or less explain the relationship between each of the following pairs. How does one lead to or foster the other? Be specific in your response. (May be done individually or in small groups.)

- Grand Canal and fast-ripening rice
- Sui and Song dynasties
- Tang and Japan
- Silk roads and Buddhism
- Foot binding and ancestor worship

GROUP ACTIVITIES

6. Go to the Internet and locate a map that shows the distribution of the Buddhist religion in the modern world. Discuss which areas were first exposed to Buddhism through Chinese influence in this period. Speculate about how Buddhism spread to other places after this period. What has become of Buddhism in China?

7. Imagine that one of you is a traditional believer in Confucianism, one is a Daoist, one believes primarily in ancestor worship, and one is a Buddhist (traditional Indian believer). Each of you explain your fundamental beliefs. How could you blend your beliefs in ways that do not seem to compromise your fundamental tenets? How much does your blending reflect what happened in China in this period?

FEATURE FILMS

The Silk Road (1992). The legendary story of a young scholar's coming of age on the war-torn fringes of a great empire. Dragooned by a Chinese mercenary general, Xingte saves the life of a beautiful princess, and their love and fate is sealed in the woven textures of eleventh century China. Directed by Junya Sato.

CHAPTER 16
INDIA AND THE INDIAN OCEAN BASIN

<u>INTRODUCTION</u>

During the postclassical period there emerged in India no long-lasting imperial authority, as there were in China and the Islamic world. Regional kingdoms were the norm. Nevertheless, Indian society exerted a profound influence on the cultures of south and southeast Asia. Through the extensive trade networks of the Indian Ocean basin, Indian forms of political organization, religion, and economic practices spread throughout the region. Several developments in India during this era gradually spread throughout the larger culture zone.

- Dramatic agricultural growth fueled population growth and urbanization. These phenomena, combined with specialized industrial production and trade, resulted in unprecedented economic growth for the region.
- India's central position in the Indian Ocean basin resulted in it becoming a major clearinghouse for products of the voluminous maritime trade network that encompassed east Africa, Arabia, Persia, southeast Asia, and Malaysia as well as the entire Indian subcontinent.
- Islam originally appeared in India through a variety of conduits, and it eventually became the primary religion of one quarter of the population. From India, Islam, along with Hinduism and Buddhism, spread to southeast Asia and the nearby islands.

<u>OUTLINE</u>

I. Islamic and Hindu kingdoms

   A. The quest for centralized imperial rule

      1. North India

         a. Tension among regional kingdoms

         b. Nomadic Turks became absorbed into Indian society

      2. Harsha (reigned 606–648 C.E.) temporarily restored unified rule in north India

   B. Introduction of Islam to northern India

      1. The Sind were conquered by Arab Muslims and passed to Abbasids

      2. Muslim merchants formed small communities in all major cities of coastal India

      3. Turkish migrants and Islam: Turks convert to Islam in tenth century

         a. Some moved to Afghanistan and established an Islamic state

         b. Mahmud of Ghazni, Turk leader in Afghanistan, made expeditions to northern India

      4. The sultanate of Delhi (1206–1526 C.E.)

         a. Mahmud's successors conquered north India, 1206

      b.   Established an Islamic state known as the sultanate of Delhi

      c.   Sultans' authority did not extend far beyond the capital at Delhi

      d.   Islam began to have a place in India

C. The Hindu kingdoms of southern India

    1.   The south: politically divided but relatively peaceful

    2.   The Chola kingdom (850–1267 C.E.) was a larger kingdom; ruled Coromandel coast

      a.   At its high point, conquered Ceylon and parts of southeast Asia

      b.   Navy dominated waters from South China Sea to Arabian Sea

      c.   Not a tightly centralized state; local autonomy was strong

      d.   Began to decline by the twelfth century

D. The kingdom of Vijayanagar (1336–1565 C.E.)

    1.   Established by two Indian brothers

    2.   They renounced Islam in 1336 and returned to their Hindu faith

II. Production and trade in the Indian Ocean basin

A. Agriculture in the monsoon world

    1.   The monsoons (rains in spring and summer)

    2.   Irrigation systems were needed for dry months

      a.   No big river in south India; waterworks included dams, reservoirs, canals, wells

      b.   Stored rainwater in large reservoirs connected to canals

      c.   One reservoir constructed during the eleventh century covered 250 square miles

    3.   Population growth: 53 million in 600 C.E. to 105 million in 1500 C.E.

    4.   Urbanization took place in Delhi and other large port cities

B. Trade and economic development of southern India

    1.   Internal trade

      a.   Self-sufficient in staple food

      b.   Metals, spices, special crops found only in certain regions

      c.   Through trade, south India and Ceylon experienced rapid economic growth

    2.   Temples and society in south India

      a.   Hindu temples served as economic and social centers

      b.   Possessed large tracts of land, hundreds of employees

      c.   Temple administrators were to maintain order, deliver taxes

      d.   Served as banks; engaged in business ventures

C. Cross-cultural trade in Indian Ocean basin

    1.   Dhows and junks—large ships involved in maritime trade in Indian Ocean

2. Emporia, Indian port cities, were clearinghouses of trade and cosmopolitan centers

3. Trade goods

   a. Silk and porcelain from China

   b. Spices from southeast Asia

   c. Pepper, gems, pearls, and cotton from India

   d. Incense and horses from Arabia and southwest Asia

   e. Gold, ivory, and slaves from east Africa

4. Specialized production

   a. Production of high-quality cotton textiles thrived

   b. Other specialized industries: sugar, leather, stone, carpets, iron and steel

5. The kingdom of Axum was a Christian empire centered in Ethiopia

   a. Resisted pressures of Islam; stayed prosperous through trade

   b. Controlled Adulis, most prominent port on Red Sea

D. Caste and society: caste provided guidance in absence of centralized political authority

   1. Caste helped to integrate immigrants (Turks, Muslim merchants) into Indian society

   2. Caste and social change: guilds and subcastes (*jatis*)

   3. Expansion of caste system, especially to southern India

III. **The meeting of Hindu and Islamic traditions**

A. The development of Hinduism

   1. Hinduism predominated in southern India, Islam in the north

   2. Vishnu and Shiva

      a. Decline of Buddhism benefited Hinduism

      b. The growth of Vishnu and Shiva cults (and other gods associated with them)

   3. Devotional cults: to achieve mystic union with gods as a way of salvation

   4. Shankara: philosopher (ninth century) who preferred disciplined logical reasoning

   5. Ramanuja: philosopher (eleventh and twelfth centuries) believed that understanding of ultimate reality was less important than devotion

B. Islam and its appeal

   1. Conversion to Islam occurred in a slow and gradual way

      a. Some converted for improving their lower social statuses

      b. Often an entire caste or subcaste adopted Islam en masse

      c. By 1500, about 25 million Indian Muslims (1/4 of population)

   2. Sufis

      a. The most effective missionaries, they had a devotional approach to Islam

b. Permitted followers to observe old rituals and venerate old spirits

  c. Emphasized piety and devotion

3. The bhakti movement

  a. Sought to erase distinction between Hinduism and Islam

  b. Guru Kabir (1440–1518), important bhakti teacher, taught that Shiva, Vishnu, and Allah were one deity

IV. The influence of Indian society in southeast Asia

A. The states of southeast Asia

  1. Indian influence in southeast Asia

    a. Indian merchants brought their faiths to southeast Asia

    b. Ruling elite of southeast Asia adapted some Indian political traditions

    c. The states sponsored Hinduism and Buddhism

    d. Showed no interest in Indian caste system

  2. Funan (first to sixth century C.E.) in the lower reaches of Mekong River (Cambodia/Vietnam)

    a. Drew enormous wealth by controlling trade

    b. Adopted Sanskrit as official language

    c. Decline of Funan in sixth century

  3. Srivijaya (670–1025 C.E.) was established on Sumatra after the fall of Funan

    a. Maintained sea trade between China and India by navy

    b. Chola kingdom of south India eclipsed Srivijaya in the eleventh century

  4. Angkor (889–1431 C.E.)

    a. Kingdom built by Khmers at Angkor Thom, later Angkor Wat

    b. The city was a microcosmic reflection of Hindu world order

    c. Turned to Buddhism during the twelfth and thirteenth centuries

    d. Thais invaded the capital in 1431, and Khmers abandoned it

  5. Other states: Singosari (1222–1292 C.E.) and Majapahit (1293–1520 C.E.)

B. The arrival of Islam in southeast Asia

  1. Conversion to Islam was slow and quiet

    a. Ruling elite converted in cities while rural residents retained their traditions

    b. Islam was not an exclusive faith in southeast Asia

    c. Sufis appealed to a large public in these countries

  2. Melaka was powerful Islamic state during fifteenth century

IDENTIFICATION: PEOPLE

What is the contribution of each of the following individuals to world history? (Identification should include answers to the questions *who, what, where, when, how,* and *why is this person important.*)

Buzurg ibn Shahriyar

Harsha

Mahmud of Ghazni

Harihara and Bukka

Shankara

Raminuja

Guru Kabir

IDENTIFICATION: TERMS/CONCEPTS

State in your own words what each of the following terms means and why it is significant to a study of world history. (Those terms with an asterisk may be defined in the Glossary.)

Sind

Sultanate of Delhi

Chola kingdom

Vijayanagar

Monsoons

Dhows

Junks

Kingdom of Axum

Caste system*

Vishnu

Shiva

Sufis*

Bhakti

Funan

Srivijaya

Angkor

Melaka

STUDY QUESTIONS

1. What factors led to the collapse of unified, imperial rule in India before and after the reign of Harsha?

2. When and how did Islam enter northern India?

3. How did Indian agriculture improve in the post classical era? What was the impact of these improvements on the population of the subcontinent?

4. What were some of the significant trade goods produced in southern India?

5. What was the function of the Hindu temple within Chola society?

6. How did the seasonal monsoons affect the trade of the Indian Ocean?

7. What were some of the specialized goods and manufactures to emerge from India into the world markets at this time?

8. How is it that Buddhism declined after the Muslim invasions while Hinduism survived?

9. To what extent did Indian culture penetrate southeast Asia before the arrival of Muslim traders in the eighth century?

10. When and how did Islam reach southeast Asia? Where did Islam take root?

INQUIRY QUESTIONS

1. How did India manage to exert such a significant influence on other cultures in the Indian Ocean basin during this era without ever establishing any long-term centralized political institutions?

2. Was the caste system in India during the postclassical era fundamentally a rigid social system or a flexible one? Be able to defend your position.

3. How did Islam become so prevalent and entrenched in Indian society during this period?

STUDENT QUIZ

1. The *Book of the Wonders of India* was
    a. an accurate primary source on Indian history during the tenth century.
    b. a collection of tall tales about foreign lands.
    c. written by an Indian trader.
    d. detailed the overland trade routes to India.
    e. none of the above.

2. Differing from the south, northern India during the postclassical era was
    a. predominantly Buddhist.
    b. one large empire.
    c. wealthy and prosperous.
    d. turbulent and chaotic.
    e. all of the above.

3. Harsha's kingdom
    a. was strongly influenced by Buddhism.
    b. restored unified rule in most of northern India through military force.
    c. supported scholarship through patronage.
    d. collapsed upon Harsha's death.
    e. all of the above.

4. Islam spread in India through
    a. the presence of merchants from the Islamic world.
    b. the Turkish migrations.
    c. Arab expeditions into the Sind.
    d. the influence of the Sultanate of Delhi.
    e. all of the above.

5. The Chola kingdom and the kingdom of Vijayanagar
    a. were states of southeast Asia.
    b. imposed centralized, imperial rules in southern India.
    c. were two of the larger states to form in southern India.
    d. were important Muslim states.
    e. none of the above.

6. Agriculture of the Indian subcontinent relied on
    a. monsoon rains.
    b. irrigation systems.
    c. reservoirs.
    d. dams and canals.
    e. all of the above.

7. According to the account of Cosmas Indicopleustes, southern India and Ceylon during the sixth century were
    a. the world's most urbanized lands.
    b. great markets for imports and exports.
    c. famous for their dhows, junks, and emporia.
    d. places where Christians were persecuted.
    e. all of the above.

8. Besides their religious purpose, Hindu temples also served as
   a. large land owners and banks.
   b. educational institutions.
   c. organizers of irrigation.
   d. economic and social centers.
   e. all of the above.

9. Which of the following was a common trade item seen in India?
   a. cotton from China.
   b. spices from southeast Asia.
   c. slaves from central Asia.
   d. silk from India.
   e. horses from east Africa.

10. The Kingdom of Axum
    a. was one of the most powerful kingdoms in northern India.
    b. was one of the earliest Islamic kingdoms.
    c. prospered from the trade coming through its port city of Adulis.
    d. was unable to resist Arab invasions.
    e. all of the above.

11. Which of the following is true with regard to the development of the caste system during the postclassical era?
    a. It helped to integrate immigrants into Indian society.
    b. Guilds of merchants and manufacturers became powerful castes of India.
    c. It extended to southern India.
    d. It was promoted by powerful temples.
    e. All of the above.

12. Invasions of India by Turkish Muslims hastened the decline of Buddhism because
    a. Buddhists were convinced that Buddha was not helpful for personal salvation.
    b. Muslim rulers banned Buddhism.
    c. the invaders looted and destroyed Buddhist stupas and shrines.
    d. the Hindus persecuted all other religions after the invasions.
    e. none of the above.

13. Shankara and Ramanuja were
    a. two Hindu philosophers with very different ideas about personal salvation.
    b. two brahmin philosophers who promoted the caste system in India.
    c. equally important to the development of devotional cults in popular Hinduism.
    d. philosophers who worshipped Vishnu and Shiva respectively.
    e. all of the above.

14. Islam in India had a strong appeal to members of lower castes because
    a. conversion to Islam made them equal with other caste members.
    b. Islam promised the spiritual equality of all believers.
    c. Allah was more competent than Shiva and Vishnu in terms of salvation.
    d. Islam was less dependent on the written word than other religions were.
    e. all of the above.

15. The bhakti movement was
    a. launched by Guru Kabir in southern India.
    b. a campaign designed to expel Islam from India.
    c. a missionary cult that promoted a personal, emotional approach to Islam.
    d. a religious movement that sought to erase the distinction between Hinduism and Islam.
    e. none of the above.

16. Which of the following was not adopted by ruling elites of southeast Asia?
    a. the Indian caste system.
    b. the model of Indian states.
    c. Hinduism and Buddhism.
    d. Sanskrit.
    e. Islam.

17. Funan was
    a. the first southeast Asian state known to have adopted many Indian practices.
    b. the only Islamic state in southeast Asia.
    c. the only state that did not show Indian influence in southeast Asia.
    d. the only state to control an all-sea trade route between China and India.
    e. the last Hindu state in southeast Asia.

18. The capital of the Angkor state
    a. was a microcosmic reflection of the Hindu world order.
    b. had Buddhist elements added to its architecture.
    c. fell to ruins after the Thais invaded.
    d. was rediscovered in the jungle by Europeans in the mid-ninteenth century.
    e. all of the above.

19. Which of the following is *not* true of Islam in southeast Asia?
    a. It did not arrive there until after the thirteenth century.
    b. It was practiced by foreign merchants in port cities for centuries.
    c. Ruling elites and traders were the first locals to become interested in the faith.
    d. It often blended with other, more traditional religions.
    e. It was promoted by Sufi mystics.

20. Differing from other southeast Asian states, Melaka was predominantly a
    a. Buddhist state.
    b. Confucian state.
    c. Christian state.
    d. Islamic state.
    e. none of the above.

MATCHING

Match these places with the statements that follow.

A. Vijayanagar   E. Axum
B. Melaka   F. Sind
C. Angkor   G. Isthmus of Kra
D. Ceylon   H. Nalanda

1. ___   Portion of the Malay peninsula dominated by wealthy Funan state.

2. ___   Independent Hindu empire of southern India founded in fourteenth century.

3. ___   Christian kingdom in region of Africa now known as Ethiopia that maintained its independence while still being actively involved in Indian Ocean trade.

4. ___   Centrally located island off the southern coast of India and a center of maritime trade.

5. ___   Northwest region of India first invaded by Islamic armies.

6. ___   Buddhist university city destroyed by Muslim invaders.

7. ___   Capital city in southeast Asia built by the kings of the Khmers.

8. ___   Powerful state that sponsored the spread of Islam throughout southeast Asia.

SEQUENCING

Place the following clusters of events in chronological order. Consider carefully how one event leads to another, and try to determine the internal logic of each sequence.

A.

____   Muslim Turks establish Islamic state in Afghanistan.

____   Bhakti movement emerges and attempts to reconcile Hinduism and Islam.

____   Melakan ruling class converts to Islam.

____   Umayyad forces conquer the Sind.

____   Mahmud of Ghazni mounts seventeen raiding expeditions into India.

____   Sultanate of Delhi is established.

MAP EXERCISES

1. On the map of east Asia below, locate the following
   features: Hindu Kush, Kyber Pass, Himalayas, Deccan Plateau, Ceylon, Isthmus of Kra
   bodies of water: Arabian Sea; Bay of Bengal; Indus, Ganges, and Mekong rivers
   cities: Delhi, Cambay, Calicut, Angkor, Melaka, Quilon
   regions: Afghanistan, Punjab, Sind, Bengal, Gujarat

2. On the same map, draw the approximate boundaries and note the dates of the following
   kingdoms:
   Harsha, Chola, Vijayanagar, Sultanate of Delhi, Funan, Srivijaya, Angkor, Melaka

In fifty words or less explain the relationship between each of the following pairs. How does one lead to or foster the other? Be specific in your response. (May be done individually or in small groups.)

- Monsoons and dhows
- Caste and Islam
- Angkor and Buddhism
- Cotton and silk

GROUP ACTIVITIES

1. Imagine that one of you is a traditional believer in Hinduism, one is a Buddhist, one is a traditional believer in Islam, and one is a Sufi. Each of you explain your fundamental beliefs. How could you blend your beliefs in ways that do not seem to compromise your fundamental tenets? How much does your blending reflect what happened in India in this period?

2. Imagine that you are a group of merchants on the island of Ceylon in the twelfth century. Your commercial specialty is warehousing goods imported from different regions and then shipping them out again for export and sale. At various times of the year, what products from what regions would you have in your warehouse? When and where would you ship them out?

CHAPTER 17
THE FOUNDATIONS OF CHRISTIAN SOCIETY IN WESTERN EUROPE

INTRODUCTION

While other parts of the world were experiencing unprecedented prosperity during the postclassical era, Europe's economy underwent a sharp constriction with the fall of the Roman Empire. Long-distance trade did not entirely disappear, significant developments took place in agricultural production, and there were brief periods of government consolidation; nevertheless, early medieval Europe was a world dominated by rural self-sufficiency and political decentralization. In spite of its seeming "backwardness" compared to the other great empires of the postclassical world, Europe was laying the foundation for the development of the powerful society that would emerge during the high middle ages. That foundation rested on

- Hard-won political order, restored out of disruption caused by the fall of the Roman Empire, centuries of destructive invasions, and dramatic depopulation. This order was based on a highly decentralized but flexible system that vested political, military, and judicial authority in local and regional rulers.
- A long, slow process of economic recovery based first on increased agricultural production within the rural manorial system to be followed by gradually increasing trade, industry, and commerce and the eventual reurbanization of Europe.
- The cultural unity provided by the Christian church based in Rome. During this period Roman Christianity provided the impetus for cultural continuity and unity in western Europe. The office of the papacy and the monastic movement were two powerful institutions that helped to preserve Roman traditions and develop and consolidate a uniquely European culture.

OUTLINE

I. **The quest for political order**

   A. Germanic successor states

      1. Germanic kingdoms: Visigoths, Ostrogoths, Lombards, Burgundians, Angles/Saxons

      2. The Franks: center of gravity shifted from Italy to northern lands

   B. The Franks and the temporary revival of empire

      1. Clovis

         a. Led the Franks and wiped out the last vestiges of Roman authority in Gaul

         b. Military campaigns against other Germanic peoples

      2. Clovis's conversion

         a. Many other Germanic peoples converted to Arian Christianity

         b. The Franks converted to Roman Christianity

         c. Alliance with the Roman church greatly strengthened the Franks

3. The Carolingians

    a. Carolingians, an aristocratic clan, asserted authority in the early eighth century

    b. Charles Martel's son claimed the throne for himself, 751

4. Charlemagne (reigned 768–814 C.E.)

    a. Grandson of Charles Martel, founder of Carolingian empire

    b. Control extended to northeast Spain, Bavaria, north Italy

5. Administration

    a. Capital city at Aachen (in modern Germany)

    b. Relied on aristocratic deputies, known as counts

    c. Used *missi dominici* to oversee local authorities

6. Charlemagne as emperor

    a. Pope Leo III proclaimed Charlemagne emperor, 800

    b. The coronation strained relations with Byzantine emperors

C. Decline and dissolution of the Carolingian empire

1. Louis the Pious (reigned 814–840)

    a. Charlemagne's only surviving son; lost control of the counts

    b. His three sons divided the empire into three kingdoms, 843

2. Invasions

    a. Muslims raided south, seized Sicily, parts of northern Italy and southern France

    b. Magyars invaded from the east

    c. Vikings invaded from the north

3. Norse expansion; Scandinavian homelands were Norway, Denmark, and Sweden

    a. Motives: population pressure, resisting Christian missionaries

    b. Most were merchants and migrants

    c. Some mounted raids in many European regions from Russia to Spain

    d. Outstanding seafarers; even established a colony in Canada about 1000

    e. Fleets could go to interior regions via rivers, attacking towns and villages

D. The establishment of regional authorities

1. In England small kingdoms merged into a larger realm against Scandinavian raids

    a. King Alfred (reigned 871–899) expanded to the north

    b. Alfred's successors controlled all England about the mid-tenth century

2. Germany: after Carolingian empire, local lords took matters into their own hands

    a. King Otto I (reigned 936–973) defeated Magyars in 955

    b. Imposed authority in Germany; led armies to support the papacy in Italy

      c.   Otto's coronation by the pope in 962 made him the Holy Roman Emperor

   3. In France counts and other local authorities became local lords

II. Early medieval society

  A. Organizing a decentralized state

     1. After Carolingian empire dissolved, local nobles built decentralized states

     2. Lords and retainers

        a.   Lord provided retainer with a grant known as a benefice (usually land, called fief)

        b.   Enabled retainer to devote time and energy to serve the lord

        c.   Provided resources to maintain horses and military equipment

        d.   Retainers owed lord loyalty, obedience, respect, counsel, and military service

        e.   Lord/retainer relationships become stronger; retainer status became hereditary

     3. Potential for instability

        a.   Multitiered network of lord-retainer relationships

        b.   Sometimes conflicting loyalties led to instability

        c.   But powerful states were built on foundation of lord-retainer relationships

  B. Serfs and manors

    1. Serfs

        a.   Slaves and peasants took agricultural tasks and frequently intermarried

        b.   Free peasants often turned themselves and their lands over to a lord for protection

        c.   Serfs as an intermediate category emerged about the mid-seventh century

    2. Serfs' obligations

        a.   Labor service and rents in kind

        b.   Could not move to other lands without permission

        c.   Once their obligations were fulfilled, serfs had right to work on land and pass it to heirs

     3. Manors were a principal form of agricultural organization

        a.   A manor was a large estate, controlled by the lord and his deputies

        b.   Manors were largely self-sufficient communities

  C. The economy of early medieval Europe

     1. Agriculture production suffered from repeated invasions

     2. Heavy plows

        a.   Heavy plows appeared in the sixth century; could turn heavy northern soils

        b.   Became common from the eighth century; production increased

      c.   Cultivation of new lands; watermills; and rotating crops

   3. Rural society—agricultural surplus not enough to support large cities

   4. Mediterranean trade—Italian and Spanish merchants trade with Muslims

   4. Norse merchant mariners in North and Baltic Seas

      a.   Followed routes of Vikings

      b.   Traded actively with Byzantine and Abbasid empires

      c.   Imported Abbasid silver used in European coinage

   5. Population: 36 million in 200; down to 26 million in 600; back up to 36 million in 1000

III.   The formation of Christian Europe

A. The politics of conversion

   1. The Franks and the Church

      a.   Frankish rulers viewed themselves as protectors of the papacy

      b.   Charlemagne also worked to spread Christianity in northern lands

   2. The spread of Christianity

      a.   Charlemagne's military campaigns forced the Saxons to accept Christianity

      b.   Pagan ways did not disappear immediately

      c.   By 1000 C.E., all western Europe had adopted Roman Christianity

B. The papacy

   1. Pope Gregory I (590–604 C.E.)

      a.   Organized defense of Rome against Lombards' menace

      b.   Reasserted papal primacy over other bishops

      c.   Strongly emphasized the sacrament of penance—confession and atonement

   2. The conversion of England—by 800, England in the Roman church

C. Monasticism

   1. Origin

      a.   Devout Christians practiced asceticism in deserts of Egypt, second and third century

      b.   Monastic lifestyle became popular when Christianity became legal, fourth century

   2. Monastic rules

      a.   St. Benedict (480–547 C.E.) provided a set of regulations

      b.   Virtues of Benedictine monks: poverty, chastity, and obedience

   3. St. Scholastica (482–543 C.E.)

    a.   St. Benedict's sister, a nun

    b.   Adapted the Rule, and provided guidance for religious life of women

4.   The roles of monasteries

    a.   Became dominant feature in social and cultural life of western Europe

    b.   Accumulated large landholdings

    c.   Organized much of the rural labor force for agricultural production

    d.   Provided variety of social services: inns, shelters, orphanages, hospitals, schools

    e.   Libraries and scriptoria became centers of learning

IDENTIFICATION: PEOPLE

What is the contribution of each of the following individuals to world history? (Identification should include answers to the questions *who, what, where, when, how,* and *why is this person important*.)

Clovis

Charles Martel

Charlemagne

Pope Leo III

Gregory of Tours

Louis the Pious

Alfred

Otto I

Pope Gregory I

St. Benedict of Nursia

St. Scholastica

IDENTIFICATION: TERMS/CONCEPTS

State in your own words what each of the following terms means and why it is significant to a study of world history. (Those terms with an asterisk may be defined in the Glossary.)

Franks

Aachen

Missi dominici

Magyars

Vikings

Holy Roman Empire*

Lords

Retainers

Benefice

Manor

Serf

Heavy plow

Papacy

Monasticism

Benedict's Rule

STUDY QUESTIONS

1. What is the significance of Clovis's conversion to Christianity?

2. What were the contributions of Charlemagne's reign, and why did it ultimately fail to last very long?

3. Who were the Vikings? What were the motivations behind their behavior? What were their accomplishments? How did they disrupt European society?

4. What were the obligations of lords toward their retainers and the retainers toward their lords? Why was this arrangement often unstable?

5. What role did the serfs play in early medieval Europe? What was life like on the manor?

6. What was the significance of the invention of the heavy plow for European economy?

7. Although trade constricted in the early middle ages, where and how was it still going on?

8. What was the role of the pope in the early middle ages? How did his role evolve over this period of time?

9. How did monasticism develop in early medieval Europe?

214

10. What was the significance of the monasteries to the European society and economy?

INQUIRY QUESTIONS

1. What were the advantages and disadvantages of the highly decentralized political system that developed in Europe during this period?

2. The economy of Europe underwent sharp constriction after the fall of the Roman empire. What was the nature of that constriction? Where and how was the economy still functioning? What were the impediments to economic development?

3. What was the role of Roman Christianity in early medieval Europe? How did it shape the society? What were its principal channels of influence?

STUDENT QUIZ

1. Abu al-Abbas became well known in the court of Charlemagne as a
    a. distinguished diplomat from the Islamic world.
    b. beloved pet from an Indian king.
    c. gift from the Abbasid court.
    d. Muslim enemy of the king.
    e. none of the above.

2. Historians use the term *middle ages* to refer to
    a. the fact that Europe became mature from 500 to 1500.
    b. the era from about 500 to 1500 C.E., the medieval era of European history.
    c. the crisis of western Europe.
    d. the time between the fall of Rome and the emergence of Christianity.
    e. all of the above.

3. One reason for the Franks' rapid rise in western Europe had to do with Clovis's
    a. conversion to Roman Christianity.
    b. conversion to Arian Christianity.
    c. alliance with the Islamic world.
    d. defeat of the Muslims at the Battle of Tours.
    e. none of the above.

4. Which of the following was one thing done by Charlemagne?
    a. He built an impressive, if relatively short-lived, empire in western Europe.
    b. He rejected coronation by the pope.
    c. He established a large bureaucracy to rule his empire.
    d. He wrote an important book on the art of statecraft.
    e. All of the above.

5. The Carolingian empire dissolved because
    a. Charlemagne's descendants were politically weak and disunited.
    b. Vikings began raiding northern France.
    c. Charlemagne's grandsons divided the empire into three parts.
    d. Magyars raided France from the east.
    e. all of the above.

6. According to Gregory of Tours, which of the following was true of Clovis's conversion?
    a. He was forced to convert by the bishops.
    b. He began to consider conversion when his army was defeated by the Christian Alamanni.
    c. He forced his army to be baptized after he was.
    d. His conversion had much to do with the influence of his wife, the queen Clotilda.
    e. all of the above.

7. In England, ninth-century Scandinavian invasions
    a. promoted various small kingdoms to merge into a larger realm.
    b. led to disintegration of a large realm into smaller kingdoms.
    c. gave way to colonization by the Vikings.
    d. brought down the Anglo-Saxon alliance.
    e. none of the above.

8. The term *feudalism*
    a. means feuds between aristocratic families that had become a social norm.
    b. means a political and social order that was highly centralized.
    c. means the king's power being completely overthrown by the local lords.
    d. is a term that has fallen out of favor among historians.
    e. none of the above.

9. The relationship between lord and retainer was
    a. stable.
    b. exploitative.
    c. reciprocal.
    d. antagonistic.
    e. all of the above.

10. Serfs were
    a. semifree individuals who owed obligations to the lord whose lands they cultivated.
    b. servants of the lord, who provided the lord with domestic and military services.
    c. agricultural slaves who had no rights on the lord's manor.
    d. free peasants who could sell their land and move at will.
    e. none of the above.

11. The rights of serfs included
    a. the right to work on certain land and pass the lands to their heirs.
    b. the right to move from one manor to another.
    c. the right to marry whomever they wanted to marry.
    d. the right to make a profit off of their land.
    e. all of the above.

12. Which of the following does *not* describe a manor?
    a. It was a large plantation operated by free peasants with heavy plows.
    b. It was a large estate supervised by a lord and operated with serf labor.
    c. It was a self-sufficient rural community controlled by the lord and his deputies.
    d. It consisted of fields, meadows, forests, serfs, and their lodgings.
    e. It was the means by which most lords and retainers supported themselves.

13. In the early middle ages, the economic activity of western Europe was
    a. efficient and fast.
    b. predominantly agricultural.
    c. commercial and urban.
    d. based on long-distance trade.
    e. none of the above.

14. The Franks helped to promote Christianity by
    a. destroying the Lombards who threatened Rome.
    b. accepting recognition and backing from the popes.
    c. inviting Christian scholars to the court.
    d. military force.
    e. all of the above.

15. An important pope of the late sixth and early seventh centuries was
    a. Leo III.
    b. Gregory I.
    c. Otto I.
    d. St. Benedict of Nursia.
    e. none of the above.

16. The conversion of England was accomplished through
    a. the military threat of Charlemagne.
    b. marriage of Charlemagne's daughter to the English king.
    c. missionary campaigns of Gregory I.
    d. the encouragement of Clotilda.
    e. all of the above.

17. According to St. Benedict's Rule, monks in monasteries should
    a. live communal, celibate lives.
    b. work hard for personal wealth.
    c. live like hermits, isolated from the outside world.
    d. deprive themselves of all pleasures.
    e. all of the above.

18. St. Scholastica
    a. established a convent and began to accept nuns for the first time in the history of Christianity.
    b. devised an entirely new set of regulations as guidance for the religious life of women in convents.
    c. strongly believed that women should be allowed to become priests and monks.
    d. adapted her brother's Rule as guidance for nuns.
    e. none of the above.

19. Which of the following social services was *not* provided by monasteries?
   a. inns, refuges, orphanages.
   b. banks, shops, factories.
   c. schools.
   d. medical care.
   e. libraries and scriptoria.

20. One of the major differences between India and western Europe during the postclassical era is that
   a. India generated an imperial form of government whereas western Europe did not.
   b. India actively participated in a larger economic and commercial life whereas western Europe was largely a rural and self-sufficient society.
   c. India did not suffer from foreign invasions whereas western Europe had to fight against foreign invaders.
   d. India had a strong religious tradition uniting it and Europe had none.
   e. All of the above are differences.

MATCHING

Match these figures with the statements that follow.

A.	Clovis	E.	Leo III
B.	Benedict	F.	Gregory the Great
C.	Alfred	G.	Otto I
D.	Abu al-Abbas	H.	Charlemagne

1. ___ King who defeated the Magyars, ending their threat to Europe.

2. ___ Led forces to eliminate the vestiges of Roman authority in Gaul.

3. ___ Pope who crowned an emperor on Christmas Day, 800.

4. ___ Albino elephant that was gift from Abbasid emperor.

5. ___ Built a navy and constructed fortresses to protect his people from the Vikings.

6. ___ Wrote a set of guidelines for monastic life.

7. ___ Mobilized local resources and organized defense of Rome against the Lombards.

8. ___ Consolidated the largest empire of early medieval Europe.

SEQUENCING

Place the following clusters of events in chronological order. Consider carefully how one event leads to another and try to determine the internal logic of each sequence.

A.

_____ Charles Martel defeats the Muslims at the Battle of Tours.

_____ Charlemagne is crowned emperor by the pope on Christmas Day.

_____ Carolingian empire is divided into three parts.

_____ Clovis converts to Christianity.

_____ Louis the Pious loses control of the nobility.

_____ Odoacer deposes the last of the western Roman emperors.

B.

_____ Food crops from the Islamic world spread to the Mediterranean through trade.

_____ The heavy plow is invented to better work the heavy soils of northern Europe.

_____ Monasteries take responsibility for clearing large tracts of land for agriculture.

_____ A series of invasions disrupts the economy of Europe, and cities go into decline.

_____ The population of Europe finally surpasses that of the year 200, before the fall of Rome.

QUOTATIONS

For each of the following quotes, identify the speaker, if known, or the point of view. What is the significance of each passage?

1. "And the king was the first to ask to be baptized by the bishop . . . And his army more than 3,000 were baptized."

2. "For our women's work they are to give at the proper time, as has been ordered, the materials, that is the linen, wool, woad, vermillion, madder, wool-combs . . . and the other objects which are necessary."

MAP EXERCISES

1. Draw a graph charting the rise and fall of the European population from the data given to you on page 458. If it continues to grow at about the same rate, what would you expect the population to be in 1200? 1400?

2. On the outline map of Europe below, draw the invasions of the Muslims, the Vikings, and the Magyars in different colored pencils. Where were these groups from? What regions did they invade? What were the effects of these invasions?

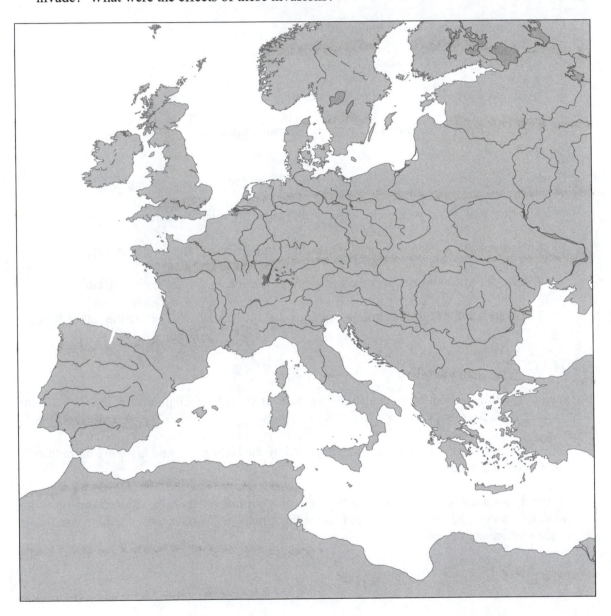

CONNECTIONS

In fifty words or less explain the relationship between each of the following pairs. How does one lead to or foster the other? Be specific in your response. (May be done individually or in small groups.)

- Charlemagne and Otto I
- Gregory I and Benedict of Nursia
- Vikings and Abbasid silver
- Benefices and manors

GROUP ACTIVITIES

1. Now that you have completed the section of the book on postclassical societies, assign each group member a society: Byzantium, Abbasid, Song, Chola Kingdom in India, and France under Charlemagne. Have each person "pitch" a time travel visit back to that society. What would a traveler see? Why would someone want to go there? What are the highlights? After each person does his or her pitch, decide as a group where you would want to go first, second, and so on. Why?

2. As a group, come up with a list of ten explanations for why Europe seems so "backward" in the postclassical era compared to the other regions you have studied. Do not just describe the aspects of the society that seems less developed (for example, long-distance trade) but *explain* the reasons for them.

CHAPTER 18
NOMADIC EMPIRES AND EURASIAN INTEGRATION

<u>INTRODUCTION</u>

Nomadic herders populated the steppes of Asia for centuries during the classical and postclassical eras and periodically came into contact and conflict with the established states and empires of the Eurasian land mass. It was not until the eleventh century, however, that the nomadic peoples like the Turks and Mongols began to raid, conquer, rule, and trade with the urban-based cultures in a systematic and far-reaching manner. While these resourceful and warlike nomads often left a path of destruction in their wake, they also built vast transregional empires that laid the foundations for the increasing communication and exchange that would characterize the period from 1000 to 1500 in the eastern hemisphere. The success of these nomadic empires in this era can be attributed to

- Their unmatched skill on horseback. When organized on a large scale these nomads were practically indomitable in warfare. Outstanding cavalry forces, skilled archers, and well-coordinated military strategy gave these peoples an advantage that was difficult for even the most powerful states to counter.
- Their ability to integrate vast territories through secure trade routes, exceptional courier networks, diplomatic missions, missionary efforts, and resettlement programs.

In spite of these successes and the enormous influence of these nomadic peoples, their leaders were, in general, better at warfare than administration. With the exception of the later Ottoman empire, most of these states were relatively short-lived, brought down by both internal and external pressures.

<u>OUTLINE</u>

I. **Turkish migrations and imperial expansion**

    A. Nomadic economy and society

        1. Turkish peoples were nomadic herders; organized into clans with related languages

        2. Central Asia's steppes: good for grazing, little rain, few rivers

        3. Nomads and their animals; few settlements

            a. Nomads drove their herds in migratory cycles

            b. Lived mostly on animal products

            c. Also produced limited amounts of millet, pottery, leather goods, iron

        4. Nomads and settled peoples sought trade, were prominent on caravan routes

        5. Fluidity of classes in nomadic society

            a. Two social classes: nobles and commoners

            b. Autonomous clans and tribes

        6. Religions: shamans, Buddhism, Nestorian Christianity; by tenth century, Islam

7. Military organization

    a. Khan ("ruler") organized vast confederation of individual tribes for expansion

    b. Outstanding cavalry forces, formidable military power

B. Turkish empires in Persia, Anatolia, and India

  1. Saljuq Turks and the Abbasid empire

    a. Lived on borders of the Abbasid realm, mid-eighth to mid-tenth centuries

    b. Moved further in and served in Abbasid armies thereafter

    c. Overshadowed the Abbasid caliphs by the mid-eleventh century

    d. Extended Turkish rule to Syria, Palestine, and other parts of the realm

  2. Saljuq Turks and the Byzantine empire

    a. Migrated in large numbers to Anatolia, early eleventh century

    b. Defeated Byzantine army at Manzikert in 1071

    c. Transformed Anatolia into an Islamic society

  3. Ghaznavid Turks dominated northern India through sultanate of Delhi

II. The Mongol empires

A. Chinggis Khan and the making of the Mongol empire

  1. Chinggis Khan ("universal ruler") unified Mongol tribes through alliance and conquests

  2. Mongol political organization

    a. Organized new military units and broke up tribal affiliations

    b. Chose high officials based on talent and loyalty

    c. Established capital at Karakorum

  3. Mongol strategy: horsemanship, archers, mobility, psychological warfare

  4. Mongol conquest of northern China

    a. Chinggis Khan, Mongols raided the Jurchen in north China beginning in 1211

    b. Controlled north China by 1220

    c. South China was still ruled by the Song dynasty

  5. Mongol conquest of Persia

    a. Chinggis Khan tried to open trade and diplomatic relations with Saljuq leader Khwarazm shah, the ruler of Persia, 1218

    b. Upon being rejected, Chinggis Khan led force to pursue the Khwarazm

    c. Mongol forces destroyed Persian cities and *qanat*

    d. Chinggis died in 1227, laid foundation for a mighty empire

B. The Mongol empires after Chinggis Khan

1. Division of the Mongol empires: heirs divide into four regional empires
2. Khubilai Khan
   a. Chinggis Khan's grandson, consolidated Mongol rule in China
   b. Promoted Buddhism, supported Daoists, Muslims, and Christians
3. Conquest of southern China
   a. Khubilai extended Mongol rule to all of China
   b. Song capital at Hangzhou fell in 1276, Yuan Dynasty founded in 1279
   c. Unsuccessful conquests of Vietnam, Burma, Java, and Japan
4. The Golden Horde
   a. Group of Mongols overran Russia between 1237 and 1241
   b. Further overran Poland, Hungary, and eastern Germany, 1241–1242
   c. Maintained hegemony in Russia until the mid-fifteenth century
5. The ilkhanate of Persia: Khubilai's brother, Hülegü, captured Baghdad in 1258
6. Mongol rule in Persia
   a. Persians served as ministers, governors, and local officials
   b. Mongols only cared about taxes and order
   c. Ilkhan Ghazan converted to Islam, 1295; massacres of Christians and Jews followed
7. Mongol rule in China
   a. Outlawed intermarriage between Mongols and Chinese
   b. Forbade Chinese from learning the Mongol language
   c. Brought foreign administrators into China and put them in charge
   d. Dismissed Confucian scholars; dismantled civil service examination
   e. Tolerated all cultural and religious traditions in China
8. Mongol ruling elite became enchanted with the Lamaist Buddhism of Tibet

C. The Mongols and Eurasian integration
   1. The Mongols and trade
      a. Mongols worked to secure trade routes and ensure safety of merchants
      b. Elaborate courier network with relay stations
      c. Maintained good order for traveling merchants, ambassadors, and missionaries
   2. Diplomatic missions
      a. The four Mongol empires maintained close diplomatic communications
      b. Established diplomatic relations with Korea, Vietnam, India, Europe
   3. Resettlement

        a. Mongols needed skilled artisans and educated individuals from other places

        b. Often resettled them in different locations to provide services

        c. Uighur Turks served as clerks, secretaries, and administrators

        d. Arab and Persian Muslims also served Mongols far from their homelands

        e. Skilled artisans were often sent to Karakorum; became permanent residents

D. Decline of the Mongols in Persia and China

  1. Collapse of the ilkhanate

        a. In Persia, excessive spending and overexploitation led to reduced revenues

        b. Failure of the ilkhan's paper money

        c. Factional struggle plagued the Mongol leadership

        d. The last ruler died without an heir; the ilkhanate collapsed

  2. Decline of the Yuan dynasty

        a. Paper money issued by the Mongol rulers lost value

        b. Power struggles, assassinations, and civil war weakened Mongols after 1320s

  3. Bubonic plague in southwest China in 1330s, spread through Asia and Europe

        a. Depopulation and labor shortage undermined the Mongol regime

        b. By 1368, the Chinese drove the Mongols back to the steppes

  4. Surviving Mongol khanates

        a. The khanate of Chaghatai continued in central Asia

        b. The Golden Horde survived until the mid-sixteenth century

III. After the Mongols

A. Tamerlane the Whirlwind (1336–1404) built central Asian empire

  1. The lame conqueror, Timur was self-made; rose to power in 1360s; established capital in Samarkand

  2. Tamerlane's conquests

        a. First conquered Persia and Afghanistan

        b. Next attacked the Golden Horde

        c. At the end of the fourteenth century, invaded northern India

        d. Ruled the empire through tribal leaders who relied on existing bureaucrats to collect taxes

  3. Tamerlane's heirs struggled and divided empire into four regions

B. The foundation of the Ottoman empire

  1. Osman

        a. Large numbers of nomadic Turks migrated to Persia and Anatolia

       b.   Osman, a charismatic leader, carved out a small state in northwest Anatolia

       c.   Claimed independence from the Saljuq sultan in 1299

2.   Ottoman conquests in the Balkans in 1350s

       a.   Sultan Mehmed II sacked Constantinople in 1453, renamed it Istanbul

       b.   Absorbed the remainder of the Byzantine empire

       c.   During the sixteenth century, extended to southwest Asia, southeast Europe, and north Africa

IDENTIFICATION: PEOPLE

What is the contribution of each of the following individuals to world history? (Identification should include answers to the questions *who, what, where, when, how*, and *why is this person important*.)

Tughril Beg

Mahmud of Ghazni

Chinggis Khan

Marco Polo

Khubilai Khan

Hülegü

Tamerlane

Osman

Sultan Mehmed II

IDENTIFICATION: TERMS/CONCEPTS

State in your own words what each of the following terms means and why it is significant to a study of world history. (Those terms with an asterisk may be defined in the Glossary.)

Turks

Yurts

Kumiss

Shamans

Khan

Saljuq Turks

Sultan

Manzikert

Karakorum

Khanbaliq

Chaghatai

Golden Horde

Yuan Dynasty

Ilkhanate of Persia

Lamaist Buddhism

Uighur Turks

Bubonic plague*

Ottoman Turks

Istanbul

STUDY QUESTIONS

1. What does the story of Guillaume Boucher represent? How does it fit in with Mongol strategies for Eurasian integration?

2. How did the geography of central Asia affect the development of the nomadic cultures? How did these people adapt to their environment? What advantages did their adaptations give them?

3. Discuss the military organization, techniques, and strategies of these Asian nomads. How did these abilities make their military so formidable?

4. How did the Mongols come to conquer China? What were the key elements in their success?

5. What does the book mean when it states that most of the Mongol leaders were better conquerors than administrators? How was this evident in the various Mongol states? Were there exceptions to that rule?

6. Through what means did the Mongols integrate Eurasian cultures? List and explain at least five ways they did this.

7. Discuss the role of epidemics in the decline of the Mongol empires.

8. Who was Tamerlane, and what was his lasting legacy?

9. How did the Turks come to topple the Byzantine empire?

10. What role did religion(s) play in the nomadic empires? What generalizations can you make? What are the significant differences?

INQUIRY QUESTIONS

1. Why do you think the nomadic peoples of Asia were so successful and influential during this period? What was different from earlier centuries? What were the limits of their success?

2. What do you think were the most significant legacies of this period of nomadic empires? How did these people change history?

3. Marco Polo's account of his travels in the thirteenth century has long been one of the most widely read and beloved sources in history. Why is this? Why is the source so valuable? Why was and is it still so popular?

STUDENT QUIZ

1. By alluding to the story of Guillaume Boucher, the authors of the textbook intend to show that
    a. the goldsmith of Paris was talented in creating a spectacular silver fountain.
    b. the Mongol capital, Karakorum, was magnificent and luxurious.
    c. many roads led to Karakorum during the thirteenth century.
    d. even slaves enjoyed some prestige when they were skilled craftsmen.
    e. all of the above.

2. Which of the following groups were *not* prominent nomadic peoples from the eleventh to the fifteenth centuries?
    a. the Huns.
    b. the Saljuq Turks.
    c. the Mongols.
    d. the Ottomans.
    e. the Golden Horde.

3. Nomadic peoples of central Asia
    a. lived in kumiss and drank yurts.
    b. liked to trade with settled peoples.
    c. did not have any religious beliefs.
    d. had rigid social classes.
    e. none of the above.

4. In nomadic society,
   a. there were only two social classes: nobles and commoners.
   b. clans and tribes were autonomous; they did not obey orders from other clans.
   c. the statuses of nobles and commoners were hereditary and unchanging.
   d. nobles tended to govern with iron fists.
   e. none of the above.

5. Nomadic peoples of Asia could wield massive military power because of their
   a. outstanding horsemanship.
   b. accuracy with bows and arrows.
   c. maneuverability as cavalry units.
   d. ability to retreat quickly.
   e. all of the above.

6. Saljuq Turks who lived in Abbasid Persia and took over Byzantine Anatolia during the early eleventh century were
   a. equal corulers with the Abbasid caliphs.
   b. led by sultans who were responsible for most of the governance.
   c. resented by the peasants of Anatolia.
   d. responsible for defeating the Abbasid army at Manzikert.
   e. all of the above.

7. During the eleventh and twelfth centuries, Ghaznavid Turks
   a. invaded Afghanistan.
   b. converted to Buddhism and Hinduism.
   c. invaded northern India.
   d. were constantly expanding their territory.
   e. all of the above.

8. The man who united all the Mongol tribes into a single confederation in 1206 was
   a. Khubilai Khan.
   b. Hülegü.
   c. Teghril Beg.
   d. Chinggis Khan.
   e. Mahmud of Ghazni.

9. With regard to Mongols' military strategies, they
   a. would travel more than 100 kilometers (62 miles) per day to surprise an enemy.
   b. could shoot arrows behind them while riding at a gallop.
   c. could shoot arrows and fell enemies within 200 meters (656 feet).
   d. would spare their enemies if they surrendered without resistance.
   e. all of the above.

10. According to the eyewitness account of Marco Polo, the Mongols' military tactics included
    a. gathering up forces and meeting the enemy face-on.
    b. refusing to ever retreat.
    c. making even the lowest soldier report to the one high officer in charge of the battle.
    d. carrying little by way of food supplies; they would rely on their horses' blood if needed.
    e. all of the above.

11. Chinggis Khan led his army to Persia and wreaked massive destruction on the conquered land. The immediate reason for this havoc was
    a. to eliminate Islam.
    b. to seek revenge against the shah and eliminate the possibility of his survival.
    c. to make Persian lands into Mongol pastureland.
    d. to learn how to use the *qanat* irrigation system.
    e. none of the above.

12. After Chinggis Khan's death, the Mongol empire was divided into four regional empires. China, as one of the regional empires, was ruled by
    a. the great khans.
    b. the khans of the Golden Horde.
    c. the ilkhans.
    d. the khans of Chaghatai.
    e. none of the above.

13. Which of the following did *not* contribute to the failure of Khubilai's ventures in Japan and southeast Asia?
    a. The Mongol forces did not adapt well to the environment of southeast Asia.
    b. Bubonic plague erupted and took great tolls among the conquered populations.
    c. The Mongol navies were destroyed by Japanese kamikaze.
    d. The Mongols were unable to combat the guerilla tactics of the defenders.
    e. all of the above.

14. Observing Mongol rule in Persia and China, one can say that the Mongols were
    a. good administrators.
    b. ferocious plunderers.
    c. intolerant of religious diversity.
    d. isolationist.
    e. none of the above.

15. As for their rule in China, the Mongols
    a. resisted assimilation to Chinese cultural traditions.
    b. executed Confucian scholars and promoted Buddhism.
    c. encouraged intermarriage between Mongols and Chinese.
    d. used local Chinese people as administrators.
    e. all of the above.

16. During the thirteenth century, long-distance trade in Eurasia increased primarily because
    a. the Mongols worked to secure trade routes and ensure the safety of merchants passing through their vast territories.
    b. Mongol rulers adopted the same paper currency that could be used within all the four regional empires.
    c. Mongol policies encouraged economic growth and specialization of production in various regions.
    d. Mongol people settled down and began creating agricultural surpluses.
    e. all of the above.

17. All of the following caused the decline of Mongol rule in China *except*
    a. peasant rebellions.
    b. bubonic plague.
    c. the mandate of Heaven.
    d. sharply rising inflation.
    e. weak administration.

18. The real name of the most famous Turkish leader, known as the lame conqueror, was
    a. Tamerlane.
    b. Timur.
    c. Tamerlane the Whirlwind.
    d. Temujin.
    e. Osman.

19. Ottomans were
    a. descendants of the Mongols.
    b. Turkish people.
    c. Persians.
    d. Indo-Europeans.
    e. none of the above.

20. The man who led the Turkish army and captured Constantinople in 1453 was
    a. Osman.
    b. Tamerlane.
    c. Mehmed II.
    d. Istanbul.
    e. none of the above.

MATCHING

Match these figures with the statements that follow.

A. Chabi	E. Chinggis Khan
B. Mahmud of Ghazni	F. Teghril Beg
C. Tamerlane	G. Osman
D. Marco Polo	H. Khubilai Khan

1. ___ Saljuq leader recognized by caliph of Abbasid empire as sultan.

2. ___ Venetian merchant who served in administrative position during Yuan dynasty.

3. ___ Reorganized army and began conquest of China and Persia.

4. ___ Favorite wife of Mongol emperor; she was a Nestorian Christian.

5. ___ Spent most of his adult life in conquest; sacked the city of Delhi.

6. ___ Charismatic leader who carved out a state in Anatolia and founded Ottoman empire.

7. ___ Founder of Yuan dynasty and ruler of China.

8. ___ He led the Turks of Afghanistan on raids of northern India.

SEQUENCING

Place the following clusters of events in chronological order. Consider carefully how one event leads to another, and try to determine the internal logic of each sequence.

A.

_____ Song capital in southern China falls to the Mongol conquerors.

_____ Mongol emperor defeats the shah of Persia and destroys the conquered land.

_____ Temujin is born into a noble family on the steppes.

_____ Khubilai Khan dies.

_____ Mongol ruler begins conquest of China by invading the Jurchen realm.

_____ Grandson of Chinggis is named great khan of China.

MAP EXERCISES

Study Map 18.1, Map 18.2, and Map 18.3 (pages 476, 481, and 488 in your textbook) and complete the following exercise, matching the nomadic groups on the left with the *correct* description on the right:

Nomads	Description
Suljuq Turks led by Tughril Beg	Replaced Chaghatai khanate in 1370; built a magnificent capital in Samarkand.
Turks who migrated to Anatolia	Established Yuan dynasty in China, but campaigns of conquering southeast Asia and Japan failed.
Ghaznavid Turks	Overran Russia; mounted expeditions into Poland, Hungary, and eastern Germany.
Mongols of the great khans	Controlled Abbasid caliphs; extended Turkish rule to Syria, Palestine, and other parts of Abbasid realm.
Mongols of Chaghatai khanate	Toppled Abbasid empire; sacked Baghdad; executed caliph; massacred 200,000 residents
Mongols of the ilkhanate	Established a foothold in Balkan peninsula during 1350s; captured Constantinople in 1453
The Golden Horde	Established khanate in central Asia that was replaced by Tamerlane's empire.
Turks led by Tamerlane	Established Turkish sultanate in Delhi; claimed authority over all of northern India.
Ottomans	Defeated Byzantine army at Manzikert in eastern Anatolia and took Byzantine emperor captive.

CONNECTIONS

In fifty words or less explain the relationship between each of the following pairs. How does one lead to or foster the other? Be specific in your response. (May be done individually or in small groups.)

- Horses and yurts
- Golden Horde and Khubilai Khan
- Bubonic plague and Yuan dynasty
- Uighur Turks and Guillaume Boucher
- Tamerlane and Ottomans

GROUP ACTIVITIES

1. Assign each group member to represent each of the societies discussed in Part III of the textbook, "*The Postclassical Era, 500–1000 C.E.*" Those societies are Byzantium, Islam, China, India, and western Europe. Each one of you should present an overview of how the central Asian nomads had an impact on your culture after 1000. When you are finished, discuss and try to form consensus on which culture was most severely affected by nomadic incursions and why.

2. To better understand the lifestyle of the nomads of the steppes, go to a website on the Mongols to see images of how they probably lived. What would families carry with them? How long would they stay in one place? What did they eat? What did they do with their leisure time? What was the significance of the horse to their culture?

FEATURE FILMS

The Conqueror (1956). The story of Chinggis Khan, a little-known John Wayne adventure movie.

The Mongols (1960). Son of Chinggis Khan slashes and burns his way across Europe. With Jack Palance.

Marco Polo (1961). Italian explorer rescues khan's daughter, meets hermit who has invented gunpowder, and builds cannon. With Rory Calhoun.

Marco the Magnificent (1965). Story of Polo's travels to China. With Orson Welles as a Venetian servant.

CHAPTER 19
STATES AND SOCIETIES OF SUB-SAHARAN AFRICA

INTRODUCTION

Agriculture and herding spread gradually throughout sub-Saharan Africa from about 2000 B.C.E. until the end of the first millennium C.E. through a process known as the Bantu migrations. After about 500 B.C.E. the knowledge of iron metallurgy was also disseminating throughout Africa. As a result of these movements, of the introduction of new nutritious foods such as bananas, and of long-distance trade, the population of Africa grew dramatically, and increasingly complex forms of government began to emerge. Most sub-Saharan African cultures were kin-based and organized into relatively small villages that were loosely allied into districts governed by a chief. Occasionally larger and more structured kingdoms and empires appeared. These larger states generally consolidated their position through controlling long-distance trade in their regions. In general, the history of sub-Saharan Africa from 1000 to 1500 C.E. is noted for

- The introduction and widespread dissemination of the Islamic religion. In many cases the belief in Islam supplemented rather than supplanted traditional religious practices. Some sub-Saharan societies became important centers of worship and learning in the Islamic world.
- A regular and reliable flow of trade goods: gold, ivory, and slaves being the most important exports. These trade networks were both overland—particularly notable was the trans-Saharan camel caravan routes—and maritime, where east African city-states became important stops on the Indian Ocean seaways.
- The emergence and growth of states that became highly influential in the cross-cultural interactions of this period. The states of Kongo, Zimbabwe, Ghana, Mali, and the Swahili city-states became trade and religious centers whose fortunes were clearly tied into those of Eurasia.

OUTLINE

I. **Effects of early African migrations**

A. Agriculture and population growth

1. Bantu and other migrations from 2000 B.C.E.–1000 C.E.

a. Spread agriculture and herding throughout Africa

b. Displaced and/or absorbed hunting/gathering/fishing people

c. Iron metallurgy after 500 B.C.E. facilitated clearing more land

d. Yams, sorghum, and millet cultivated

e. Introduction of bananas after 500 C.E. caused migration and population surge

2. Population growth: from 3.5 million in 400 B.C.E. to 22 million by 1000 C.E.

B. African political organization

1. Kin-based society the norm (sometimes called "stateless society")

      a.   Early societies did not depend on elaborate bureaucracy

      b.   Societies governed through family and kinship groups

      c.   Village council consisted of male family heads

      d.   Chief of a village was from the most prominent family head

      e.   A group of villages constituted a district

      f.   Villages chiefs negotiated intervillage affairs

  2. Chiefdoms

      a.   Population growth strained resources and increased conflict

      b.   Some African communities began to organize military forces, 1000 C.E.

      c.   Powerful chiefs overrode kinship networks and imposed authority and conquered

      d.   Examples: Ife and Benin

  3. Kingdom of Kongo

      a.   Villages formed small states along the Congo River, 1000 C.E.

      b.   Small states formed several larger principalities, 1200 C.E.

      c.   One of the principalities overcame its neighbors and built kingdom of Kongo

      d.   Maintained a centralized government with a royal currency system

      e.   Provided effective organization until the mid-seventeenth century

II. Islamic kingdoms and empires

  A. Trans-Saharan trade and Islamic states in west Africa

    1. After 300 C.E. camels replaced horses and donkeys as transport animals

      a.   Camels' arrival quickened pace of communication across the Sahara

      b.   Islamic merchants crossed desert and established relations

    2. The kingdom of Ghana became the most important commercial site in west Africa

      a.   Provided gold (most important), ivory, and slaves for traders from north Africa

      b.   Exchanged for horses, cloth, manufactured goods, and salt

      c.   Koumbi-Saleh, capital city of Ghana, a thriving commercial center

      d.   Ghana kings converted to Islam by the tenth century, didn't force on others

      e.   Nomadic raids from the Sahara weakened the kingdom in the early thirteenth century

    3. Sundiata, or lion prince, built Mali empire (reigned 1230–1255 C.E.)

    4. Mali empire and trade

      a.   Controlled and taxed almost all trade passing through west Africa

      b.   Enormous caravans linked Mali to north Africa

      c.   Besides the capital Niani, many other prosperous cities on caravan routes

5. Mansa Musa, Sundiata's grandnephew (reigned 1312–1337 C.E.)

    a. Made his pilgrimage to Mecca in 1324–1325 with huge caravan

    b. Upon return to Mali, built mosques

    c. Sent students to study with distinguished Islamic scholars in northern Africa

    d. Established Islamic schools in Mali

6. Decline of Mali due to factions and military pressure from neighbors and nomads

7. The Songhay empire replaced Mali by the late fifteenth century

B. The Indian Ocean trade and Islamic states in east Africa

  1. *Swahili* is an Arabic term meaning "coasters"

    a. Dominated east African coast from Mogadishu to Sofala

    b. Spoke Swahili, a Bantu language, supplemented with some Arabic words

    c. Trade with Muslim merchants became important by the tenth century

  2. The Swahili city-states

    a. Chiefs gained power through taxing trade on ports

    b. Ports developed into city-states governed by kings, eleventh and twelfth centuries

  3. Kilwa: good example of busy city-state on east coast; exported gold

  4. Zimbabwe was powerful kingdom of east Africa

    a. By the ninth century, chiefs began to build stone residences (*Zimbabwe*)

    b. Magnificent stone complex known as Great Zimbabwe in the twelfth century

    c. Eighteen thousand people lived in Great Zimbabwe in the late fifteenth century

    d. Kings organized flow of gold, ivory, and slaves

  5. Islam in east Africa

    a. Ruling elite and wealthy merchants converted to Islamic faith

    b. Conversion promoted close cooperation with Muslim merchants

    c. Conversion also opened door to political alliances with Muslim rulers

III. African society and cultural development

A. Social classes

  1. Diversity of African societies: villages, kingdoms, empires, city-states

  2. Kinship groups: extended families and clans as social and economic organizations

    a. Communities claimed rights to land; no private property

    b. Village council allocated land to clan members

  3. Sex and gender relations

    a. Men undertook heavy labor

    b. Women were responsible for child rearing, domestic chores

    c.   Men monopolized public authority, but women enjoyed high honor as the source of life

    d.   Aristocratic women could influence public affairs

    e.   Women merchants commonly traded at markets

    f.   Sometimes women organized all-female military units

    g.   Islam did little to curtail women's opportunities in sub-Saharan Africa

4. Age grades

    a.   Assumed responsibilities and tasks appropriate to their age grades

    b.   Age group formed tight circle of friends, later allies

5. Slavery

    a.   Most slaves were captives of war, debtors, criminals

    b.   Worked as agricultural labor or sold in slave markets

    c.   Slave trade increased after the eleventh century

    d.   Demand for slaves outstripped supply from eastern Europe

    e.   Slave raids of large states against small states or villages

    f.   Zanj slave revolt in Mesopotamia in tenth century

B. African religion

1. Creator god as source of world order

2. Lesser gods and spirits

    a.   Often associated with natural features

    b.   Intervened in the workings of the world

    c.   Believed in ancestors' souls; had many rituals

3. Diviners mediated between humanity and supernatural beings

    a.   Interpreted the cause of the people's misfortune

    b.   Used medicine or rituals to eliminate problems

    c.   African religion was not theological but practical

C. The arrival of Christianity and Islam

1. Early Christianity in north Africa

    a.   Christianity reached north Africa during the first century C.E.

    b.   Christian kingdom of Axum in Ethiopia (fourth century C.E.)

2. Ethiopian Christianity

    a.   Missionaries translated Bible and popularized Christianity there

    b.   Carved churches out of solid rock

    c.   Solomonic dynasty claimed descent from Israelite kings (thirteenth century)

d. *Kebra Negast* fictionalized account of lineage; was popular with Rastafarians

3. African Islam

    a. Appealed strongly to ruling elite and merchants of sub-Saharan Africa

    b. Converts took their religion seriously; they built mosques and schools, invited experts

    c. Accommodated African gender relations; women retained more freedoms

    d. Supplemented rather than replaced traditional religions

IDENTIFICATION: PEOPLE

What is the contribution of each of the following individuals to world history? (Identification should include answers to the questions *who, what, where, when, how*, and *why is this person important*.)

Sundiata

Mansa Musa

Ibn Battuta

Ali ibn Muhammad

IDENTIFICATION: TERMS/CONCEPTS

State in your own words what each of the following terms means and why it is significant to a study of world history. (Those terms with an asterisk may be defined in the Glossary.)

Griots

Bananas

Kin-based society*

Chiefdom

Kingdom of Kongo

Camels

Gao

Kingdom of Ghana

Koumbi-Saleh

Mali empire

Swahili

Kilwa

Zimbabwe

Age grades

Zanj revolt

Diviners

Axum

Solomonic dynasty

Kebra Negast

STUDY QUESTIONS

1. What was the function of the *griot* in sub-Saharan African culture?

2. Why were bananas and camels so significant in early African history? What do they represent? How did they change the way people lived?

3. How are kin-based societies structured? How are they organized politically?

4. Compare and contrast the Kingdom of Kongo with the Kingdom of Ghana.

5. Where and how did Islam spread to sub-Saharan Africa? How was it different from north African and southwest Asian Islam? Why?

6. What was the role of the Mali empire in the Eurasian trade network?   How did Mansa Musa influence its development?

7. In what ways was Kilwa a good example of a Swahili city-state?

8. What was the important of gender and age grades in sub-Saharan African societies?

9. Discuss the history of slavery in Africa. How did the developments in the slave trade from 1000 to 1500 set the stage for the Atlantic slave trade to come?

10. How did Christianity and Islam supplement native African religions in this period?

INQUIRY QUESTIONS

1. Why do you think we have so few names to associate with sub-Saharan African history in this period? How did the nature of the societies contribute to this phenomenon? How did their cultural traditions contribute?

2. List and explain at least five reasons why Islam became such a prevalent religion in sub-Saharan Africa in this period. Use examples to justify each point.

3. Compare and contrast the development of the Swahili city-states with the west African empires in the years from the eleventh to the fifteenth centuries.

STUDENT QUIZ

1. The remarkable oral tradition of sub-Saharan Africa was preserved primarily by
    a. Muslim African scholars.
    b. professional singers and griots.
    c. village chiefs and diviners.
    d. women.
    e. none of the above.

2. The story of Sundiata was about
    a. the heroic deeds of the lion prince in establishing the Mali empire.
    b. the misery of slaves captured and traded in the Mediterranean basin network.
    c. the coming of Islam as a dominant faith in sub-Saharan societies.
    d. the rise of the Swahili city-states.
    e. none of the above.

3. Trade and communications networks were slower to penetrate sub-Saharan Africa compared to other regions because
    a. Africans had little contact with each other.
    b. Africans did not have any goods that others wanted to trade for.
    c. there was a language barrier.
    d. there were formidable geographic barriers to overcome.
    e. all of the above.

3. The earliest Bantu migrants were
    a. aggressive warriors.
    b. hunting and gathering peoples.
    c. fishing peoples.
    d. agriculturalists.
    e. horsemen.

4. All of the following stimulated African migrations *except*
    a. iron metallurgy.
    b. bubonic plague.
    c. bananas.
    d. population pressure.
    e. agriculture.

6. Before the tenth century, the dominant form of social organization in sub-Saharan Africa was the
    a. city-state.
    b. empire.
    c. kin-based system.
    d. kingdom.
    e. theocracy.

7. Which of the following statements typically describes a kin-based society?
    a. Male heads of families presided over village affairs.
    b. The most prominent of the family heads acted as chief.
    c. A group of villages constituted a district.
    d. Ethnic loyalties were focused at the district level.
    e. All of the above.

8. The kingdom of Kongo
    a. emerged as a powerful state through trading with Muslim merchants of north Africa.
    b. maintained a royal currency system based on cowries from the Indian Ocean.
    c. was a loosely organized government with little authority over officials.
    d. was destroyed by the expansion of the Swahili.
    e. none of the above.

9. The arrival of camels in Africa
    a. made communication across the Sahara possible.
    b. quickened the pace of communication across the Sahara.
    c. replaced elephants as the preferred transport animals throughout the Sahara.
    d. still made travel across the Saharan impossible.
    e. is unknown because they have always been there.

10. Koumbi-Saleh was to the kingdom of Ghana as
    a. Mansa Musa was to the Mali empire.
    b. Niani was to the Mali empire.
    c. Sundiata was to the Mali empire.
    d. Zaire was to the Kongo.
    e. Axum was to the Christians.

11. The conversion to Islam of rulers of the kingdom of Ghana and the Mali empire
    a. stimulated commercial relations with Muslim merchants.
    b. meant that Islamic faith was imposed forcibly on their entire societies.
    c. facilitated the export of Muslim African slaves by these two states to other Islamic countries.
    d. transformed the role of women in those cultures.
    e. all of the above.

12. Swahili
    a. was an Arabic language.
    b. refers to the peoples of the east African coast.
    c. refers to the slave traders of Africa.
    d. is a dead language.
    e. was the language of the Mali empire.

13. All of the following were Swahili city-states except
    a. Sofala, Mogadishu.
    b. Zimbabwe, Ife.
    c. Malindi, Kilwa.
    d. Zanzibar, Mozambique.
    e. All of the above *are* Swahili city-states.

14. Great Zimbabwe was
    a. a powerful guild of gold merchants.
    b. the king of an empire.
    c. an anti-Islamic organization of Zimbabwe.
    d. a capital city built of stone.
    e. none of the above.

15. According to Ibn Battuta, Mogadishu
    a. had only hunters, gatherers, and fishers.
    b. was a large, inland, overland trade city.
    c. had not yet converted to Islam.
    d. was hostile to strangers.
    e. none of the above.

16. In societies of the sub-Sahara,
    a. slaves did not exist.
    b. private ownership of land did not exist.
    c. gender differentiation did not exist.
    d. war did not exist.
    e. currency did not exist.

17. After the eleventh century, the slave trade became increasingly important in Africa because
    a. demand for slaves in foreign markets outstripped the supply.
    b. a population explosion created a ready surplus.
    c. slaves were needed on the other side of the Atlantic.
    d. Africans readily sold their children into slavery.
    e. all of the above.

18. Unlike many other religions, African religion
    a. did not concern itself with morality and proper behavior.
    b. did not concern itself with matters of theology.
    c. did not concern itself with world order.
    d. did not worship a creator god.
    e. did not include religious specialists in society.

19. Compared with Islam, Christianity in sub-Saharan Africa was
    a. located in a much smaller region.
    b. equally important.
    c. more true to original Christian theology than African Islam was to original Islamic theology.
    d. had little to do with merchants or missionaries.
    e. none of the above.

20. Upon adopting Islamic faith, African women
   a. were increasingly confined in their social and economic activities.
   b. did not experience much change in their social status.
   c. enjoyed higher honor than before.
   d. took the veil.
   e. no longer could talk to men in public.

MATCHING

Match these terms with the statements that follow.

A. Zanj   E. Gao
B. *zimbabwe*   F. *Kebra Negast*
C. griot   G. swahili
D. Benin   H. Kilwa

1. ___ Early kingdom in western Nigeria.

2. ___ Fictional work tracing lineage of Ethiopian kings to King David.

3. ___ Sub-Saharan African slaves who staged revolt against slaveholders in Mesopotamia.

4. ___ One of the busiest and most prosperous city-states on east African coast.

5. ___ Originally referred to wooden residences of chiefs in central Africa.

6. ___ "Coasters," or those who engaged in sea trade along the east African coast.

7. ___ Professional singer or storyteller who orally transmitted sub-Saharan African history.

8. ___ Ancient established trade center that served as terminus for caravan routes.

SEQUENCING

Place the following clusters of events in chronological order. Consider carefully how one event leads to another, and try to determine the internal logic of each sequence.

A.
_____ Sundiata returns from exile.

_____ Bananas are introduced to Africa.

_____ Sub-Saharan Africans independently develop iron metallurgy.

_____ Special saddle for camels is invented.

_____ Bantu people begin their migrations from their homelands.

_____ Islam arrives in west Africa.

_____ Mansa Musa goes to Mecca.

MAP EXERCISES

1. On the outline map of Africa below, write in the following locations: Sahara Desert, Nile River, Lake Chad, Lake Victoria, Congo River, Zambezi River, Niger River, Madagascar, Red Sea, Cairo, Mogadishu, Niani, Koumbi-saleh, Sofala, Mombasa, Timbuktu, Kilwa, Gao, Axum, Great Zimbabwe, Ife, Jenne, Malindi.

    On the same map, draw in different colors the following: Ghana empire, Swahili city-states, Zimbabwe, Kingdom of Kongo, Egypt, Mali empire, Ethiopia.

    Now draw the trans-Saharan and maritime trade routes. Which cultures got wealthy from the trans-Saharan trade? Which ones from maritime trade? Speculate about what factors might be most likely to cause the downfall of these societies based on their geographic locations.

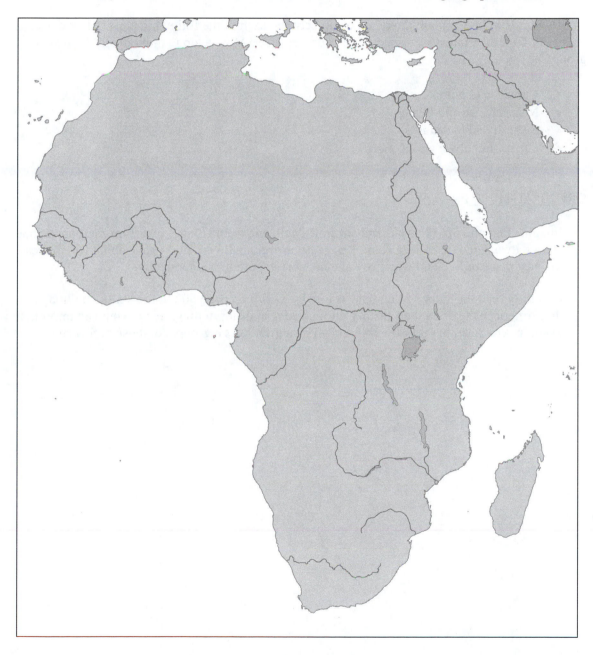

2. Based on the population data given on page 495 in the textbook, draw a graph of sub-Saharan population growth from 400 B.C.E. to 2200 C.E. Put the years in 200-year increments on the X axis and the population in millions on the Y axis. Continue the graph with projected population growth to 1500, factoring in a 10-million-person decrease for the slave trade between 1000 and 1500. Go onto the Internet or consult a reference book for the population of sub-Saharan Africa around 2000 and plot that on the graph. That number too should reflect at least a 10-million-person decrease for the Atlantic slave trade from about 1700 to 1800. Next, consult a source on the potential population drop over the next 200 years because of diseases such as AIDS. Factor that in to a projection to 2200. What conclusion can you draw from this exercise about Africa and population patterns?

CONNECTIONS

In fifty words or less explain the relationship between each of the following pairs. How does one lead to or foster the other? Be specific in your response. (May be done individually or in small groups.)

- Camels and gold
- Mansa Musa and Islam
- Swahili and bananas
- Great Zimbabwe and Kongo

GROUP ACTIVITIES

1. Imagine that one of you is a merchant from Mali, one from Kongo, one from Zimbabwe, one from Kilwa, and one from Axum. Re-create an argument you might have about which area is the best place to live and which area is the most important economically.

2. Carefully read the story of Sundiata as told by a griot on page 502 in the textbook. Imagine that Americans learned their history through song and storytelling. How would an important event in American history sound if recited by a griot? As a group, compose such a story.

CHAPTER 20
WESTERN EUROPE DURING THE HIGH MIDDLE AGES

INTRODUCTION

Europeans, during the high middle ages, built a vibrant and prosperous society. Rising from the foundations laid during the early middle ages—lord-retainer relationships, agricultural innovation, and the Roman Catholic Church—Europe emerged from its long period of relative political instability and economic and intellectual stagnation. The hallmarks of high medieval European culture included

- The consolidation and expansion of regional states. These powerful states sometimes were organized by local rulers and based on lord-retainer relationships, as in France. Other times they were direct conquests, as with the Norman invasion of England. At other times, they were supported or encouraged by the Roman church, like the Holy Roman Empire.
- Economic revitalization. With renewed agricultural surplus, the population expanded and Europe began to reurbanize. Cities grew, and with them grew business, industry, trade, and educational institutions. Long-distance trade networks reappeared, especially in the Mediterranean and Baltic and North Sea regions.
- Continued presence of the Roman Catholic Christianity in virtually all aspects of high medieval life. Through both traditional church institutions and the mass appeal of popular religious practices, the church prospered during this period. The Roman church's influence was felt in education, philosophy, literature, conquest, and travel.

In the high middle ages Europe began to interact with increasing regularity with the other regions of the eastern hemisphere. Its days of relative isolation were over.

OUTLINE

I. The establishment of regional states

   A. The Holy Roman Empire

   1. Otto I

      a. Otto of Saxony rose in northern Germany by the mid-tenth century

      b. Pope John XII proclaimed him emperor in 962: birth of Holy Roman Empire

   2. Investiture contest

      a. Formerly, important church officials were appointed by imperial authorities

      b. Pope Gregory VII ordered an end to the practice

      c. Emperor Henry IV was excommunicated because of his disobedience

   3. Frederick Barbarossa

      a. Sought to absorb Lombardy in north Italy

      b. Papal coalition forced Barbarossa to relinquish his rights in Lombardy

B. Regional monarchies in France and England

    1. Capetian France: Hugh Capet founded dynasty from 987, lasted three centuries

    2. The Normans were descendents of Vikings in Normandy, France

        a. Duke William of Normandy invaded England in 1066

        b. Introduced Norman style of political administration to England

C. Regional states in Italy and Iberia

    1. Popes ruled a good-sized territory in central Italy

    2. Prosperous northern Italian city-states: Florence, Bologna, Genoa, Milan, Venice

    3. Normans conquered southern Italy, brought Roman Catholic Christianity

    4. Christian and Muslim states in Iberia

        a. Muslim conquerors ruled most of the peninsula, eighth to the eleventh centuries

        b. Christian kingdoms took the peninsula (except Granada) by late thirteenth century

II. Economic growth and social development

A. Growth of the agricultural economy

    1. Expansion of arable land

        a. Population pressure by the late tenth century

        b. Serfs and monks began to clear forests and swamps

        c. Lords encouraged such efforts for high taxes

    2. Improved agricultural techniques

        a. Crop rotation methods

        b. Cultivation of beans increased and enriched the land

        c. More domestic animals also enriched the land

        d. Books and treatises on household economy and agricultural methods

    3. New tools and technology

        a. Extensive use of watermills and heavy plows

        b. Use of horseshoe and horse collar increased land under cultivation

    4. New food supplies

        a. Before 1000, European diet was mostly grains

        b. After 1000, more meat, dairy products, fish, vegetables, legumes

        c. Spain, Italy, Mediterranean got new foods through Islamic world

    5. Population growth: from 29 million to 79 million between 800 C.E. and 1300 C.E.

B. The revival of towns and trade

    1. Urbanization: peasants and serfs flocked to cities and towns

2. Textile production, especially in north Italy and Flanders

3. Mediterranean trade: Italian merchants dominated and established colonies

4. The Hanseatic League—an association of trading cities

   a. Hansa dominated trade of northern Europe

   b. Major European rivers linked Hansa to the Mediterranean

5. Improved business techniques

   a. Bankers issued letters of credit to merchants

   b. Commercial partnerships for limiting risks of commercial investment

C. Social changes

1. The three estates

   a. "Those who pray"—clergy of Roman Catholic church, the spiritual estate

   b. "Those who fight"—feudal nobles, the military estate

   c. "Those who work"—mostly peasants and serfs

2. Chivalry

   a. Widely recognized code of ethics and behavior for feudal nobles

   b. Church officials directed chivalry toward Christian faith and piety

3. Troubadours

   a. Aristocratic women promoted chivalric values by patronizing troubadours

   b. Troubadours drew inspiration from the love poetry of Muslim Spain

4. Eleanor of Aquitaine was most celebrated woman of her day

   a. Supported troubadours, promoted good manners, refinement, and romantic love

   b. Code of chivalry and romantic poetry softened manners of rough warriors

5. Independent cities: urban populations increasingly resisted demands of feudal nobles

6. Guilds

   a. Regulated production and sale of goods

   b. Established standards of quality for manufactured goods

   c. Determined prices and regulated entry of new workers

   d. Social significance: friendship, mutual support, built halls

7. Urban women: most guilds admitted women, and women also had own guilds

III. European Christianity during the high middle ages

A. Schools, universities, and scholastic theology

1. Cathedral schools

   a. Bishops and archbishops in France and northern Italy organized schools

   b. Cathedral schools had formal curricula, concentrated on liberal arts

      c. Some offered advance instruction in law, medicine, and theology

  2. Universities

      a. Student guilds and faculty guilds

      b. Large cathedral schools developed into universities

  3. The influence of Aristotle

      a. Obtained Aristotle's works from Byzantine and Muslim philosophers

      b. Scholasticism: St. Thomas Aquinas harmonized reason with Christianity

B. Popular religion

  1. Sacraments; the most popular was the Eucharist

  2. Devotion to saints for help; Virgin Mary most popular (cathedrals)

  3. Saints' relics were esteemed; pilgrimages (Rome, Compostela, Jerusalem)

C. Reform movements and popular heresies

  1. Dominicans and Franciscans were urban-based mendicant orders

      a. Organized movements to champion spiritual over materialistic values

      b. Zealously combated heterodox movements

  2. Popular heresy: the movements of Waldensians and Cathars (Albigensians)

IV. The Medieval Expansion of Europe

A. Atlantic and Baltic Colonization

  1. Vinland

      a. Scandinavian seafarers turned to North Atlantic Ocean, ninth and tenth centuries

      b. Colonized Iceland and Greenland

      c. Leif Ericsson traveled to modern Newfoundland, called Vinland

  2. Christianity in Scandinavia: Denmark and Norway (tenth century), then spread

  3. Crusading orders and Baltic expansion

      a. Teutonic Knights most active in the Baltic region

      b. Baltic region was absorbed into Christian Europe from the late thirteenth century

B. The reconquest (for Christianity) of Sicily and Spain

  1. Reconquest of south Italy by Norman Roger Guiscard, 1090

  2. Roger (also Norman) conquers Sicily

  3. The *reconquista* of Spain began in 1060s

      a. By 1150, took over half the peninsula

      b. By the thirteenth century, took almost all the peninsula except Granada

C. The crusades

  1. Pope Urban II called Christian knights to take up arms and seize the holy land, 1095

     a. Peter the Hermit traveled in Europe and organized a ragtag army

     b. Campaign was a disaster for the crusaders

2. The first crusade

     a. French and Norman nobles organized military expedition, 1096

     b. Jerusalem fell to the crusaders, 1099; Muslims recaptured, 1187

3. Later crusades

     a. By the mid-thirteenth century, five major crusades had been launched

     b. The fourth crusade (1202–1204) conquered Constantinople

     c. The crusades failed to take over Palestine from the Muslims

4. Consequences of the crusades

     a. Crusaders established some states in Palestine and Syria

     b. Encouraged trade with Muslims; demands for luxury goods increased

     c. Muslim ideas filter to Europe: Aristotle, science, astronomy, numerals, paper

IDENTIFICATION: PEOPLE

What is the contribution of each of the following individuals to world history? (Identification should include answers to the questions *who, what, where, when, how,* and *why is this person important.*)

Marco Polo

Otto I

Pope John XII

Pope Gregory VII

Henry IV

Frederick Barbarossa

Hugh Capet

Duke William of Normandy

King Louis IX

Eleanor of Aquitaine

St. Thomas Aquinas

St. Dominic

St. Francis

Pope Innocent III

Eric the Red

Leif Ericsson

Robert Guiscard

Roger Guiscard

Pope Urban II

Peter the Hermit

Saladin

IDENTIFICATION: TERMS/CONCEPTS

State in your own words what each of the following terms means and why it is significant to a study of world history. (Those terms with an asterisk may be defined in the Glossary.)

Holy Roman Empire*

Investiture contest

Capetian dynasty

Normans

Champagne fairs

Hanseatic League

Three estates

Chivalry

Troubadours

Guilds*

Cathedral schools

Universities

Scholasticism

Sacraments

Saints

Relics

Pilgrimages

Waldensians

Cathars (Albigensians)

Vinland

Teutonic Knights

Reconquista

Crusades

STUDY QUESTIONS

1. What do the journeys of the Polos represent about European society during the high middle ages?

2. What was the Holy Roman Empire? What did each one of those words (*holy, Roman,* and *empire*) mean to Europeans in this period? How was the Holy Roman Empire none of those?

3. What did the monarchies that emerged in France and England have in common? How were they different?

4. What were the significant innovations in agriculture in Europe during this period? How did each one lead to increased yield?

5. What was the role of the textile industry in the European economy during this period?

6. Where were the centers of the trade networks for Europe? Why there?

7. How did the development of chivalry affect the noble classes?

8. During this period Europe saw the emergence of a new social class in the cities. Who were they? What roles did they play? How did they make a place for themselves in the medieval social order?

9. What is scholasticism and what broader intellectual movements did it reflect? How did it contrast with popular religion?

10. Where and how did Europe expand during the high middle ages?

1. Consider the northern Italian city-states that emerged during this period. How did they become so successful and prosperous? What roles did they play in the economy, politics, and religion of Europe?

2. The Roman Catholic Church encountered many challenges during this period. What were they? How did the Church manage to meet each challenge and still thrive? What do you predict will happen to the church after this period?

3. Some historians believe that the institutional foundations of *modern* Europe (and by extension North America) first appeared during this period. What political, economic, and social institutions can you see emerging of during this period? Explain their beginnings.

STUDENT QUIZ

1. In the investiture contest, the winner was
   a. Otto I.
   b. Henry IV.
   c. Gregory VII.
   d. Frederick Barbarossa.
   e. Hugh Capet

2. The Holy Roman Empire was "neither holy, nor Roman, nor an empire" because
   a. the emperors were not crowned by the popes.
   b. the Byzantine emperors did not acknowledge the Holy Roman Empire.
   c. the people who lived there did not practice Christianity.
   d. it did not restore imperial unity to western Europe.
   e. all of the above.

3. During the high middle ages, the Normans
   a. conquered England in 1066.
   b. built a tightly centralized state.
   c. commissioned a tapestry.
   d. took southern Italy and Sicily back from the Muslims.
   e. all of the above.

4. Which of the following did *not* contribute to the expansion of arable land in Europe during the high middle ages?
   a. population pressure.
   b. use of the horseshoe and horse collar.
   c. increased cultivation of beans.
   d. the shift from horses to oxen.
   e. clearing of forests and draining of swamps.

5. According to Pegolotti,
   a. European long-distance trade with China was perfectly safe.
   b. local lords always robbed traveling merchants.
   c. by using paper money in China, Europeans paid higher prices for their goods.
   d. traders should try to bargain for the cheapest guide.
   e. none of the above.

6. The Hanseatic League was
   a. known for its determination to reconquer Spain and wrest it from Muslim control.
   b. responsible for curbing the expansion of the Holy Roman Empire.
   c. an association of trading cities of northern Europe.
   d. a military religious order.
   e. none of the above.

7. In medieval Europe, the three estates meant
   a. England, Scotland, and Ireland.
   b. the three royal estates of the Capetian kings.
   c. the three social classes.
   d. the big three city-states in north Italy.
   e. none of the above.

8. During the high middle ages the European nobility
   a. had their manners softened.
   b. practiced the code of chivalry.
   c. drew their literary inspiration from Muslim Spain.
   d. was one of the three estates.
   e. all of the above.

9. During the high middle ages, the development of towns and cities "fit awkwardly in the framework of a medieval political order" because
   a. their citizens demanded autonomy from local lords.
   b. unlike feudal manors, cities were egalitarian societies.
   c. unlike the organization of the workforce on feudal manors, women became part of the working class in cities.
   d. townspeople included all three estates.
   e. none of the above.

10. Guilds of European cities and towns could do all of the following *except*
    a. set standards of quality for manufactured goods.
    b. administer justice on behalf of the city government.
    c. determine the prices at which members had to sell their products.
    d. build large halls in the cities.
    e. regulate the entry of new workers into their groups.

11. Curricula of cathedral schools concentrated on
    a. liberal arts.
    b. theology.
    c. law and medicine.
    d. the writings of Aquinas.
    e. none of the above.

12. During the high middle ages, European scholars' rediscovery of Aristotle's work led to
    a. the growing dynamism of popular heresies.
    b. the development of scholasticism.
    c. the rise of the Dominicans and Franciscans.
    d. a rejection of the Latin classics.
    e. a decline in Christian belief.

13. The most famous scholastic theologian was
    a. Eucharist.
    b. St. Francis.
    c. St. Thomas Aquinas.
    d. Saladin.
    e. St. Dominic.

14. Christians' devotion to saints was very much like
    a. the Bantu people's devotion to the creator god.
    b. Buddhists' devotion to Bodhisattvas.
    c. Muslims' devotion to Mecca.
    d. the Jews' devotion to the Torah.
    e. all of the above.

15. Which of the following did *not* belong to the popular heresies of medieval Europe?
    a. Waldensians.
    b. Cathars.
    c. Albigensians.
    d. mendicants.
    e. All of the above were heresies.

16. The Albigensian crusade was
    a. a military campaign against the Muslims.
    b. a military expedition against the Cathars.
    c. a military venture against the pagan Slavic peoples in the Baltic region.
    d. a military coup in Sicily.
    e. none of the above.

17. Vinland was
    a. conquered by the Teutonic Knights.
    b. reconquered by European crusaders.
    c. colonized by Scandinavian seafarers.
    d. continuously occupied until the present day.
    e. none of the above.

18. The reconquest of Sicily from the Muslims was accomplished by
    a. Eric the Red.
    b. Roger Guiscard.
    c. Robert Guiscard.
    d. William the Conqueror.
    e. none of the above.

19. The term *reconquista* specifically referred to
    a. the reconquest of Spain.
    b. the reconquest of Sicily.
    c. the recapture of Palestine.
    d. the colonies in Greenland.
    e. the Albigensian crusade.

20. Which one of the following statements does *not* describe the crusades?
    a. The campaigns showed European military superiority to Muslim armies.
    b. One of the crusades conquered Constantinople instead of recapturing Palestine.
    c. The crusaders traded eagerly with Muslim merchants in the eastern Mediterranean.
    d. The crusaders brought many Muslim ideas back to Europe with them.
    e. The crusaders introduced to Europe new agricultural products they learned about from the Muslims.

MATCHING

Match these figures with the statements that follow.

A. Thomas Aquinas   E. Peter the Hermit
B. Eleanor of Aquitaine   F. Saladin
C. Gregory VII   G. William of Normandy
D. Hugh Capet   H. Francis of Assisi

1. ___ Led disastrous first campaign to reclaim the holy land from the Muslims.

2. ___ King and founder of dynasty in France that gradually expanded its political influence.

3. ___ Led successful invasion of England and established new dynasty there.

4. ___ Founder of highly successful mendicant religious order.

5. ___ Muslim leader who defeated crusaders and recaptured Jerusalem.

6. ___ Pope who excommunicated Henry IV during the investiture conflict.

7. ___ Teacher at the university of Paris who attempted to reconcile reason and faith.

8. ___ Powerful patron of the arts, especially the troubadours.

SEQUENCING

Place the following clusters of events in chronological order. Consider carefully how one event leads to another, and try to determine the internal logic of each sequence.

A.

____ The Holy Roman emperor begs the pope for mercy while standing barefoot in the snow.

____ The pope proclaims Otto of Saxony emperor.

____ The popes encourage Dominican friars to assist in *reconquista* of Spain.

____ The pope calls for the first crusade.

____ A papal coalition forces the emperor to relinquish rights to Lombardy.

B.

____ The textile industry booms in Flanders and cities of Italy.

____ The volume of trade encourages development of banking, credit, and partnerships.

____ Genoa gets wealthy from its Mediterranean sea trade.

____ The growth of cities brings about increasing specialization of labor.

____ Agricultural expansion creates population growth.

QUOTATIONS

For each of the following quotes, identify the speaker, if known, or the point of view. What is the significance of each passage?

1. "The road you travel from Tana to Cathay [China] is perfectly safe, whether by day or by night, according to what the merchants say who have used it."

2. "Who curses a poor man does an injury to Christ, whose noble image he wears, the image of him who made himself poor for us in this world."

3. "He alone may depose bishops and reinstate. [He] is the only person whose feet are kissed by all princes. His title is unique in the world. He may depose emperors."

4. "This royal city, however, situated at the center of the earth, is now held captive by the enemies of Christ and is subjected, by those who do not know God, to the worship of the heathen . . . God has conferred upon you above all other nations great glory in arms. Accordingly, undertake this journey eagerly for the remission of your sins."

5. "Almost up to the twenty-fifth year of his age, he squandered and wasted his time miserably…[After his conversion] his greatest concern was to be free from everything of this world, lest the serenity of his mind be disturbed even for an hour by the taint of anything that was mere dust."

6. "The existence of God can be proved in five ways. The first and more manifest way is the argument from motion."

MAP EXERCISES

1. Use the maps in this chapter supplemented by maps on the Internet to locate the following places on the outline map of Europe below: Normandy; Aquitaine; Holy Roman Empire; northern Italian cities: Venice, Genoa, Florence, Milan, Bologna; Papal states; Naples; Sicily; the region of the Hanseatic League; Granada; Portugal; Castile; Aragon; Champagne; Constantinople.

Study the map and determine why the Italian city-states and the Hanseatic League were the centers of trade networks. Why were the Champagne fairs so successful? How did the Normans launch so many successful conquests?

2. Based on the population data given on page 525 in the textbook and on the additional fact that in 1400 the population of Europe stood at 60 million (see chapter 22), draw a graph of European population growth from 800 to 1400. Put the years in 100-year increments along the X axis and the population in millions on the Y axis.

CONNECTIONS

In fifty words or less explain the relationship between each of the following pairs. How does one lead to or foster the other? Be specific in your response. (May be done individually or in small groups.)

- Investiture conflict and Cathars
- Guilds and universities
- Scholasticism and crusades
- Vinland and Sicily
- Troubadours and cathedrals

GROUP ACTIVITIES

1. Assign each group member to represent one of the three estates and one more member to represent a merchant guild member. Discuss how you each make your living, what your realistic aspirations would be, what life was like for women in your order, and which group wields the most power.

2. Imagine you could go back in time and plan a sixth crusade to the holy land. Paying attention to the successes and failures of the previous ones, how would you plan this one? Consider who would go, how they would travel, what the goals would be, when would be the best time, and a good military strategy.

FEATURE FILMS

Becket (1964). Henry II of England promotes best friend Thomas Becket to archbishop and a power struggle ensues. With Peter O'Toole and Richard Burton.

The Lion in Winter (1968). Intrigue and squabbling between King Henry II of England and his wife, Eleanor of Aquitaine, over who will be Henry's heir. With Katharine Hepburn and Peter O'Toole.

Monty Python and the Holy Grail (1975). Hilarious British film that pokes fun at all things medieval (and many modern).

Name of the Rose (1986). A murder mystery set in a medieval monastery. From the best-seller by Umberto Eco. With Sean Connery.

The Sorceress (1988). Set in a rural French village. A Dominican friar comes to the area to root out heresy. Excellent depiction of peasant life.

CHAPTER 21
WORLDS APART: THE AMERICAS AND OCEANIA

<u>INTRODUCTION</u>

This chapter presents the evolution of complex societies in the Americas and the Pacific Islands up through the sixteenth century. Isolation and varied resources led to a wide range of social structures from simple hunting and gathering to settled agricultural villages to the highly complex urban societies like those of the Aztecs and the Incas. Common aspects of these societies include:

- Isolation from one another and from the cultures of the Eastern Hemisphere.
- Absence of metallurgy, although the peoples of Mesoamerica and South America mined gold and silver.
- Few domesticated animals—the llama and alpaca of the Andes Mountains being the notable exceptions—and, as a result, no wheeled transport.
- Lack of a written language. The Aztec had mathematics, precise calendars, and a symbolic system of record keeping, but no formal written literature. The Inca kept accounts with *quipu*, a system of knotted cord.

Study of these societies is limited by the lack of written sources. The earliest accounts of the Aztec and Inca come from the Spanish conquerors and missionaries and are distorted by their prejudices. Nevertheless, those accounts plus oral traditions and archaeological evidence make it possible to describe those societies in some detail.

<u>OUTLINE</u>

I. **States and empires in Mesoamerica and North America**

    A. The Toltec and the Mexica

        1. Toltecs emerge in the ninth and tenth centuries after the collapse of Teotihuacan

            a. Established large state, powerful army mid-tenth to the mid-twelfth century

            b. Tula was the Toltec capital city and center of trade

            c. Maintained close relations with societies of the Gulf coast and the Maya

        2. Toltec decline after twelfth century

            a. Civil strife at Tula, beginning in 1125

            b. Nomadic invaders after 1175

        3. Arrival of the Mexica (or Aztecs) in central Mexico mid-thirteenth century

            a. Warriors and raiders

            b. Built capital city, Tenochtitlan (modern Mexico City), about 1345

            c. Developed productive *chinampas* style of agriculture

        4. Fifteenth century, Aztecs launched military campaigns against neighboring societies

            a. Conquered and colonized Oaxaco in southwestern Mexico

  b. Made alliance with Texcoco and Tlacopan

  c. Built an empire of twelve million people, most of Mesoamerica

 5. Controlled subject peoples with oppressive tribute obligations

  a. Empire had no bureaucracy or administration; local administrators enforced tributes

  b. Allies did not have standing army

  c. Tribute of 489 subject territories flowed into Tenochtitlan

B. Mexica society

 1. Most information comes from Spanish sources, recorded after the conquest

 2. Mexica warriors were the elite at the top of a rigid social hierarchy

  a. Mostly from the Mexica aristocracy

  b. Enjoyed great wealth, honor, and privileges

 3. Mexica women had no public role, but were honored as mothers of warriors

  a. Mexica women active in commerce and crafts

  b. Primary purpose to bear children: women who died in childbirth celebrated

 4. Priests also among the Mexica elite

  a. Read omens, presided over rituals, monitored ritual calendar

  b. Advisers to Mexica rulers, occasionally became supreme rulers

 5. Most of the Mexica were either cultivators or slaves

  a. Cultivators worked on *chinampas* (small plots of reclaimed land) or on aristocrats' land

  b. Paid tribute and provided labor service for public works

  c. Large number of slaves who worked as domestic servants

 6. Artisans and merchants enjoyed prestige

  a. Artisans valued for skill work, especially luxury items

  b. Trade could be profitable, but also risky

C. Mexica religion

 1. Mexica deities adopted from prior Mesoamerican cultures

  a. Tezcatlipoca

  b. Quetzalcóatl

 2. Ritual bloodletting common to all Mesoamericans

  a. Human sacrifice to Huitzilopochtli

  b. Large temple at the center of Tenochtitlan, thousands of skulls

D. Peoples and societies of the north

1. Pueblo and Navajo: large settled societies in American southwest
   a. Agriculture and irrigation
   b. By about 700 C.E., began to build stone and adobe buildings
2. Iroquois peoples: an agricultural society in the eastern woodlands
   a. Five Iroquois nations emerged from Owasco society, 1400 C.E.
   b. Male/female roles
3. Mound-building peoples in eastern North America
   a. Built enormous earthen mounds for ceremonies and burials
   b. Largest mound at Cahokia, Illinois
   c. Fifteen thousand to thirty-eight thousand people lived in Cahokia society during the twelfth century
   d. No written records: burial sites reveal existence of social classes and trade

II. States and empires in Andean South America

A. The coming of the Incas
   1. Kingdom of Chucuito dominated Andean South America after the twelfth century
      a. Cultivation of potatoes; herding of llamas and alpacas
      b. Traded with lower valleys; chewed coca leaves
   2. Chimu, powerful kingdom in the lowlands of Peru before the mid-fifteenth century
      a. Irrigation networks; cultivation of maize and sweet potatoes
      b. Capital city at Chanchan had massive brick buildings
   3. The Inca settled first around Lake Titicaca in the Andean highlands
      a. Ruler Pachacuti launched campaigns against neighbors, 1438
      b. Built a huge empire stretching four thousand kilometers from north to south
   4. Inca ruled as a military and administrative elite
      a. Use of *quipu* for record keeping
      b. Capital at Cuzco, which had as many as three hundred thousand people in the late fifteenth century
      c. Extensive road system linked north and south
      d. Official runners carried messages; spread of Quecha language

B. Inca society and religion
   1. Trade limited
      a. Local barter in agricultural goods
      b. Fewer specialized crafts
   2. Inca society was also a hereditary aristocracy

a. Chief ruler viewed as descended from the sun, owned everything on earth

b. After death, mummified rulers became intermediaries with gods

c. Aristocrats enjoyed fine food, embroidered clothes, and wore ear spools

d. Priests led celibate and ascetic lives, very influential figures

3. Peasants worked the land and gave over a portion of their produce to the state

   a) Besides supporting ruling classes, revenue also used for famine relief

   b) Peasants also provided heavy labor for public works

4. Inca priests served the gods

   a) Venerated sun god called Inti

   b) Creator god, Viracocha

   c) Ritual sacrifices practiced, but not of humans

   d) Inca religion had a strong moral dimension: rewards and punishments

III. The societies of Oceania

A. The nomadic foragers of Australia

1. Nomadic, foraging societies; did not take up agriculture

   a. Exchanged surplus food and small items during their seasonal migrations

   b. Peoples on north coast had limited trade with mariners of New Guinea

2. Aboriginal culture and religious traditions

   a. Intense concern with immediate environments

   b. Stories and myths related to geographical features

B. The development of Pacific Island society

1. Trade between island groups such as Tonga, Samoa, and Fiji

2. Distant islands more isolated, especially eastern Pacific

3. Polynesian mariners took long voyages

   a. Settled Easter Island about 300 C.E.

   b. Reached west coast of South America

   c. Brought back sweet potato, new staple crop in Polynesia

   d. Settled Hawaiian Islands early centuries C.E.; also twelfth- and thirteenth-century voyages

4. Population growth on all larger Pacific islands

   a. Result of diversified farming and fishing

   b. Hawai`i may have had five hundred thousand people in the late eighteenth century

   c. On Easter Island, conflict and environmental degradation from overpopulation

5. More complex social and political structures

    a. Sandeluer dynasty at Pohnpei in Carolina Islands, 1200–1600

    b. Workers became more specialized; distinct classes emerged

    c. Social classes: high chiefs, lesser chiefs, priests, commoners

6. Powerful chiefs created centralized states in Tonga and Hawai`i

    a. *Ali'i nui:* high chiefs of Hawai`i

    b. Chiefs allocated lands, organized men into military forces

7. In Polynesian religion, priests were intermediaries between gods and humans

    a. Gods of war and agriculture were common

    b. The *marae* Mahaiatea on Tahiti was a huge step pyramid for religious rituals

IDENTIFICATION: PEOPLE

What is the contribution of each of the following individuals or groups to world history? (Identification should include answers to the questions *who, what, where, when, how,* and *why is this person or group important.*)

Toltec

Mexica

Huitzilopochtli

Quetzalcóatl

Pueblo

Iroquois

Inca

IDENTIFICATION: TERMS/CONCEPTS

State in your own words what each of the following terms means and why it is significant to a study of world history. (Those terms with an asterisk are defined in the glossary.)

Tenochtitlan

Chinampas

Quipu

Cahokia Mound

Marae

Nan Madol

Ali'i nui

STUDY QUESTIONS

1. How did the Mexica people establish their authority over the peoples of central Mexico? How did the Mexica treat conquered peoples?

2. What are some of the distinctive features of Mexica agriculture? Why was it so productive?

3. What are some of the typical trade goods within the Aztec empire? Which items particularly impressed the Spanish?

4. What are the distinctive features of the Mexica social structure?

5. What are the expectations for men and women in Mexica society? What does the midwife's speech on page 553 indicate about gender roles?

6. What are the distinctive aspects of Mexica religion? What is the purpose of human sacrifice?

7. Which of the societies of North America had developed settled agriculture by the fifteenth century? What kind of agriculture was typical?

8. What are some of the distinctive features of the agriculture and animal husbandry to emerge in the Andes Mountains?

9. What are some of the distinctive features of Inca society and religion?

10. What are some of the notable achievements of Inca society?

11. What are the distinctive features of the agricultural societies to emerge in the Pacific Islands before western contact?

INQUIRY QUESTIONS

1. Why did the peoples of North America not achieve the population density of the societies of Mesoamerica?

2. What aspects of Mexico society made them vulnerable to attack with the arrival of the Spanish in the sixteenth century?

3. Compare the Aztec and Inca societies with those of the Pacific Islands. What were the similarities? What were the significant differences?

1. What is the correct chronological order?
    a. Toltecs, Teotihuacan, Mexica, Spanish.
    b. Toltecs, Teotihuacan, Spanish, Mexica.
    c. Teotihuacan, Mexica, Toltecs, Spanish.
    d. Teotihuacan, Toltecs, Mexica, Spanish.
    e. Teotihuacan, Toltecs, Spanish, Mexica.

2. Which of the following was probably *not* a factor in the collapse of the Toltec civilization?
    a. conflict between the various ethnic groups living at Tula.
    b. immigration of various nomadic peoples to central Mexico.
    c. a large fire that destroyed much of Tula.
    d. defeat by the Mexica in the thirteenth century.
    e. All of the above contributed to the Toltec collapse.

3. The *chinampa* system of agriculture
    a. introduced new Mexica crops into the central valley.
    b. required the Mexica to move on to new lands after the soil had been exhausted.
    c. was based on the rotation of crops to replenish the soil.
    d. was similar to the slash-and-burn agriculture practiced by the Maya.
    e. created fertile plots of land from the mud dredged off the bottom of Lake Texcoco.

4. Which of the following was *not* a typical trade item found in the Mexica markets?
    a. iron and brass implements.
    b. gold and silver jewelry.
    c. vanilla beans and cacao.
    d. jaguar skins and parrot feathers.
    e. cotton cloth.

5. In order to maintain control over conquered peoples, the Mexica
    a. maintained a large standing army.
    b. appointed Mexica governors in each province of their empire.
    c. threatened subject peoples with brutal reprisals.
    d. appointed an elaborate bureaucracy to collect tributes.
    e. all of the above.

6. The most honored class in Mexica society were
    a. the priests.
    b. the warriors.
    c. the merchants.
    d. the large landowners.
    e. the royal family.

7. In order to maintain clear class distinctions, Mexica sumptuary laws held that persons of different social classes should have no interaction.
    a. persons of different social classes could not intermarry.
    b. commoners should wear rough cloth, while aristocrats could wear cotton.
    c. conquered people could not speak the Mexica language.
    d. all of the above.

8. The Aztecs offered human sacrifices in order to
    a. honor the gods and forestall the destruction of the world.
    b. terrorize conquered people into submission .
    c. provide nourishment to the moon and the stars.
    d. mark off the days of their ritual calendar.
    e. all of the above.

9. Most of those sacrificed were
    a. criminals.
    b. war captives.
    c. tribute from conquered people.
    d. all of the above.
    e. none of the above.

10. Which of the following statements does *not* describe the Iroquois peoples?
    a. They lived in the woodlands east of the Mississippi River.
    b. They cultivated maize and beans.
    c. They lived in settled communities with defensive walls.
    d. Women were in charge of villages and longhouses.
    e. Their system of pictographic writing has not yet been deciphered.

11. The great earthen mounds like Cahokia were probably used for
    a. marketplaces.
    b. urban complexes.
    c. defense.
    d. rituals and burials.
    e. all of the above.

12. Between the thirteenth and the fifteenth centuries, the Andean kingdom of Chucuito governed an agricultural society based on
    a. maize farming.
    b. potato farming.
    c. cotton manufacture.
    d. coca farming.
    e. all of the above.

13. Which of the following was *not* a method by which the Inca were able to effectively administer their empire?
    a. a complex system of record keeping with knotted cord.
    b. taking hostages from the ruling families of conquered peoples.
    c. a vast network of paved roads to unite their empire.
    d. relocating loyal colonists in troublesome territories.
    e. granting autonomy to local chieftains.

14. Which city and state are incorrectly paired?
    a. Iroquois and Cahokia.
    b. Toltec and Tula.
    c. Chucuito and Teotihuacan.
    d. Inca and Cuzco.
    e. Mexica and Tenochtitlan.

15. The Inca government maintained storehouses of agricultural surplus for
    a. the private reserve of the royal family.
    b. payment to the military.
    c. public relief and social welfare.
    d. payments to governmental officials.
    e. all of the above.

16. Commoners in the Inca kingdom were required to
    a. work assigned lands on behalf of the state.
    b. pay a portion of their earnings to the state.
    c. work on the public roads and irrigation systems.
    d. deliver pottery, textiles, and other handmade goods.
    e. all of the above.

17. Unlike the Aztec religion, Inca religion
    a. was monotheistic.
    b. had a moral dimension.
    c. revered a sun god.
    d. had no priest class.
    e. had no sacrificial rituals.

18. The aboriginal people of Australia subsisted by
    a. cultivating root crops.
    b. herding swine and poultry.
    c. cultivating taro and sweet potato.
    d. building fish traps.
    e. none of the above.

19. Which island population was most isolated from the rest of Polynesia?
    a. Easter Island.
    b. Fiji.
    c. Hawai`i.
    d. Tahiti.
    e. Tonga.

20. The peoples of the Pacific islands did *not*
    a. develop metallurgy.
    b. develop agriculture.
    c. build complex societies.
    d. interact with one another.
    e. develop any transportation technologies.

MATCHING

Match these figures with the statements that follow.

A.	Toltec	F.	Polynesians
B.	Maya	G.	Huitzilopochtli
C.	Mexica	H.	Quetzalcóatl
D.	Inca	I.	Ali'i nui
E.	Iroquois	J.	Pueblo

1. ___ They dominated the central valley of Mexico between the tenth and the twelfth centuries.

2. ___ They built large earthen mounds for ceremonies and burials.

3. ___ These settled cultivators lived in stone and adobe villages in the southwest of North America.

4. ___ These were the traditional chieftains of Hawai`i.

5. ___ This Mexica god of war required the sacrifice of human blood.

6. ___ By the fifteenth century, their Yucatan empire had faded into obscurity.

7. ___ The "Feathered Serpent" was a Mexica deity who protected arts, crafts, and farming.

8. ___ Navigating only by wind and stars, these maritime people successfully negotiated thousands of miles of open water.

9. ___ This warrior society established control over a vast Andes Mountains empire.

10. ___ These invaders from the north seized control of central Mexico in the fourteenth century and built there a wealthy and powerful empire.

SEQUENCING

Place the following clusters of events in chronological order. Consider carefully how one event leads to another, and try to determine the internal logic of each sequence.

A.

_____ From their capital city of Tula, Toltec armies dominate central Mexico.

_____ Tribute, taxes, and hostages pour into Tenochtitlan from conquered provinces.

_____ Newcomers, Mexica invaders, settle on Lake Texcoco and build their capital city, Tenochtitlan, there.

_____ Spanish conquistadors marvel at the wealth of the Mexica marketplace.

_____ Tula erupts in civil war, and the empire is invaded by nomadic tribes.

B.

_____ Complex political and social structures emerge, including specialized trades and ruling elites.

_____ Traveling in open boats using celestial navigation, Polynesian mariners reach most of the island groups of the Pacific Ocean.

_____ High chiefs lead raids on neighboring islands to create larger states.

_____ Diversified agriculture and easy fishing prompt rapid population growth.

1. On the map of the central valley of Mexico below, indicate the domain and the capital city of each of these empires: Teotihuacan, the Tolmec, and the Aztec (see Map 21.1, page 551). Indicate also the significant topographic features: the Sierra Madre Mountains, Lake Texcoco, and the River Tula. What geographic features supported the emergence of three separate empires in this region?

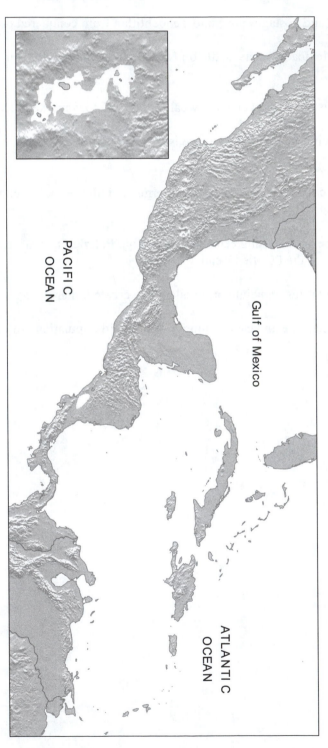

2. On the map of the Pacific Ocean below, identify the following: Easter Island, Fiji, Galapagos, Hawai'i, Samoa, Tahiti, Tonga, Marquesas Islands, Mariana Islands (see Map 21.3, page 564). Include a mileage key so that you can estimate the distances between the Pacific Islands. Now, consider the following questions:

    •   Which islands are the closest to one another? What are the approximately distances?
    •   Which islands are furthest apart? What are the approximate distances?
    •   Note the pattern of the Pacific trade winds (found in Volume II on page 612). How might these patterns facilitate long-distance travel?
    •   Based on this information, which islands do you think would have the closest ties to one another?
    •   Which islands would be most culturally isolated? Explain your answers.

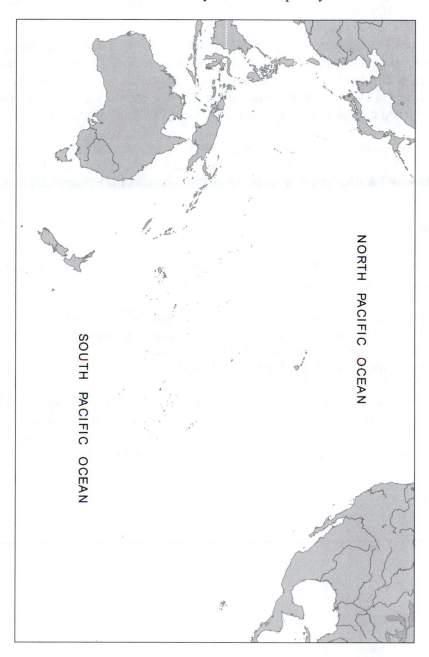

CONNECTIONS

In fifty words or less explain the relationship between each of the following pairs. How does one lead to or foster the other? Be specific in your response. (May be done individually or in small groups.)

- Human sacrifice and the marketplace at Tenochtitlan
- *Chinampas* and Mexica warriors
- Inca roads and royal mummies
- Ali'i nui and long-distance travel

GROUP ACTIVITIES

1. Each group will represent a cross-section of Aztec society. Decide among yourselves who will be: a priest to Huitzilopochtli, an Aztec warrior, a *chinampa* farmer, a warrior's mother, a goldsmith, a merchant/trader, and a slave assigned to public works. Determine what each one contributes to the prosperity and preservation of the empire. Come to class prepared to convince the rest of your group that you are the most valuable member of Mexica society.

2. Oral traditions in Hawai`i speak of intermittent travel between Tahiti and Hawai`i. Consider the legend of Mo'ikeha's voyage on page 568. What aspects of Hawaiian life are explained by this story? What does this story reveal about the quality of Hawaiian life?

FEATURE FILMS

Song of Hiawatha (1997). Film portrays the life of the legendary Iroquois culture-hero from a Native American perspective.

Rapa Nui (1994). Rapa Nui is the traditional name for Easter Island. This film attempts to explain some of the mysteries surrounding Easter Island: the huge stone images, the rapid population decline. Shot on location, the film is cited for gorgeous scenery, if a somewhat improbable plot. With Jason Scott Lee; in English.

Windwalker (1980). In the late eighteenth century, an aging Cheyenne warrior, Windwalker (played by Trevor Howard, the only non-Indian in the cast), reflects back on his life. A powerful, beautifully rendered tale of family, duty, and honor in traditional Native American culture. Entirely in Cheyenne and Crow with English subtitles.

CHAPTER 22
REACHING OUT: CROSS-CULTURAL INTERACTIONS

INTRODUCTION

This chapter explores the cross-cultural networks that linked Europe and Asia between 1000 and 1500. The Mongol conquests of the thirteenth century disrupted commerce along the ancient silk route through central Asia, but eventually trade and travel were restored and even strengthened. Although travel was slow and costly, international trade grew significantly with the exchange of crops, technologies, and ideas. Ironically, that same traffic helped spread the bubonic plague, the Black Death, which ravaged much of Eurasia in the mid-fourteenth century. Common elements of these cross-cultural networks include:

- Diplomacy. Different states used trade routes to send envoys abroad seeking either to form alliances or to impress potential rivals.
- Religion. Islamic law and culture were common to societies from north and west Africa to southeast Asia and the Philippines. Travel for Muslim pilgrims and scholars was common under Mongol rule. Christian missionaries also traveled to East Asia, but less frequently.
- Cultural diffusion. These routes became an important source of new ideas and information throughout Eurasia. New crops, such as sugarcane, and new technologies, such as gunpowder, the magnetic compass, and the printing press, transformed western societies.
- European exploration. Portugal sought to bypass Muslim-controlled trade routes by mounting expeditions to India around the Cape of Good Hope. In 1492, the Spanish attempted to beat the Portuguese at this game by sending Columbus west across the Atlantic.

OUTLINE

I. Long-distance trade and travel

    A. Patterns of long-distance trade

        1. Trading patterns between 1000 and 1500 in Eurasia

            a. Luxury goods of high value traveled overland on the silk roads

            b. Bulkier commodities traveled the sea lanes of the Indian Ocean

        2. Trading cities and ports grew rapidly

            a. Large trading cities had communities of foreign merchants

            b. Cities like Melaka: orderly, strategically located, with reasonable custom fees

            c. Mongol conquests in thirteenth century disrupted trade, but they later restored order

        3. Marco Polo (1253–1324), Venetian traveler to Asia

            a. Traveled to Mongol court of Khubilai Khan in China

       b. Back to Venice in 1295 after seventeen years in China

       c. Narrative of his travels a best-seller, inspiring many European merchants

B. Political and diplomatic travel

   1. Mongol-Christian diplomacy across Eurasia in thirteenth century

       a. Mongols and western Europeans, potential allies against Muslims

       b. Pope Innocent IV's invitation to the Mongols to become Christians rejected

   2. Rabban Sauma's mission to Europe, 1287

       a. Sent by ilkan of Persia to win allies against Muslims

       b. Met kings of France and England and the pope, but the mission failed

       c. Ilkan Ghazan's conversion to Islam in 1295 ended possibility of alliance

   3. Ibn Battuta (1304–1369)

       a. A Moroccan Islamic scholar who served as *qadi* to the sultan of Delhi

       b. Later served on Maldive Islands and traveled to east and west Africa

       c. Consulted with Muslim rulers and offered advice on Islamic values

C. Missionary campaigns

   1. Sufi missionaries (Muslim) visited recently conquered or converted lands

   2. Christian missionaries in eastern Europe after 1000

   3. John of Montecorvino: mission to convert the Mongols and Chinese, 1291–1328

       a. The first archbishop of Khanbaliq (Beijing) in 1307

       b. Translated the New Treatment; built several churches in China

       c. Baptized some Mongol and Chinese boys, but won few converts

D. Long-distance travel and cross-cultural exchanges

   1. Cultural exchanges included science, ideas, art, and music

   2. New technology spread by travelers and facilitated their travel—for example, magnetic compass

   3. New crops introduced to sub-Saharan Africa by Muslims: citrus fruits, rice, cotton

   4. Sugarcane originated in southwest Asia and north Africa

       a. Introduced to Europeans during the crusades

       b. Sugarcane plantations spread all over the Mediterranean basin

       c. Plantations operated through slave labor, Muslim captives, and Africans

   5. Gunpowder technologies spread west from China by Mongol armies in thirteenth century

       a. Used for catapults, primitive cannons

       b. Changed warfare dramatically

II. Crisis and recovery

A. Bubonic plague

   1. Plague in China

      a. Crises of the fourteenth century: global climate cooled, declining productivity, famine

      b. Bubonic plague began in southwest China, spread rapidly through interior

      c. In 1331, 90 percent of population in Hebei province killed

      d. Continued through 1350s, two-thirds of population killed in other provinces

   2. Spread of plague west along trade routes

      a. Reached Black Sea in 1346, Italy in 1347, and western Europe in 1348

      b. Terrifying symptoms of the Black Death

      c. Mortality: often 60 percent to 70 percent of population, sometimes whole villages

      d. Scandinavia and India less effected; bypassed sub-Saharan Africa

   3. Population decline

      a. Chinese population dropped by 10 million from 1300 to 1400

      b. European population dropped by about 25 percent

      c. Islamic societies also devastated, slower to recover

   4. Social and economic effects

      a. Massive labor shortages led to social unrest

      b. In western Europe, workers demanded higher wages

      c. Authorities resisted change; peasant rebellions

B. Recovery in China: the Ming dynasty

   1. Hongwu overthrew Mongol rule and established the Ming dynasty in 1368

   2. Ming centralization of government and reviving of Chinese traditions

      a. Reestablished Confucian educational and civil service systems

      b. Emperor ruled China directly, without the aid of chief ministers

   3. Mandarins and eunuchs maintained absolute authority of emperors

      a. Mandarins represented central government to local authorities

      b. Eunuchs in government could not build family fortunes

   4. Ming dynasty promoted economic recovery

      a. Repaired irrigation systems, agricultural productivity surged

      b. Promoted manufacture of porcelain, silk, and cotton textiles

      c. Trade within Asia flourished with increased production

   5. Cultural revival

a. Actively promoted neo-Confucianism

b. *Yongle Encyclopedia*, massive anthology of Chinese cultural traditions

C. Recovery in western Europe: state building

1. Taxes and armies as instruments of national monarchies by late fifteenth century

2. Italian city-states flourished with industries and trade

   a. Each with independent administration and army

   b. Levied direct taxes on citizens

3. France and England

   a. Fought Hundred Years' War (1337–1453) over control of French lands

   b. Imposed direct taxes to pay the costs of war

   c. Asserted authority of central government over feudal nobility

   d. Unlike France, England did not maintain a standing army

4. Spain united by the marriage of Fernando of Aragon and Isabel of Castile

   a. Sales tax supported a powerful standing army

   b. Completed the *reconquista* by conquering Granada from Muslims

   c. Seized southern Italy in 1494

   d. Sponsored Columbus's quest for a western route to China

5. Competition among European states

   a. Frequent small-scale wars

   b. Encouraged new military and naval technology

   c. Technological innovations vastly strengthened European armies

D. Recovery in western Europe: the Renaissance

1. Italian renaissance art

   a. Renaissance, or rebirth of art and learning, 1400–1600

   b. City-states sponsored innovations in art and architecture

   c. Painters (Macaccio and Leonardo) used linear perspective to show depth

   d. Sculptors (Donatello and Michelangelo) created natural poses

2. Renaissance architecture

   a. Simple and elegant style, inherited from classical Greek and Roman

   b. Magnificent domed cathedrals such as Brunelleschi's cathedral of Florence

3. Humanists drew inspiration from classical models

   a. Scholars interested in literature, history, and moral philosophy

   b. Recovered and translated many classical works

III. Exploration and colonization

A. The Chinese reconnaissance of the Indian Ocean basin

   1. Zheng He's expeditions

      a. Ming emperor permitted foreigners to trade at Quanzhou and Guangzhou

      b. Refurbished the navy and sent seven large expeditions to the Indian Ocean basin

      c. Purposes: to control foreign trade and impress foreign peoples

      d. Admiral Zheng He's ships were the largest marine crafts in the world

      e. Visited southeast Asia, India, Ceylon, Arabia, and east Africa

   2. Chinese naval power

      a. Zheng He's voyages diplomatic: exchanged gifts, envoys

      b. Also military: used force to impress foreign powers, for example, against coastal pirates

      c. Expeditions enhanced Chinese reputation in the Indian Ocean basin

   3. End of the voyages, 1433

      a. Confucian ministers mistrusted foreign alliances

      b. Resources redirected to agriculture and defense of northern borders

      c. Technology of building large ships was forgotten, nautical charts destroyed

B. European exploration in the Atlantic and Indian Oceans

   1. Portuguese exploration

      a. European goals: to expand Christianity and commercial opportunities

      b. Portuguese mariners emerged as the early leaders

      c. Prince Henry of Portugal determined to increase Portuguese influence

      d. Seized Moroccan city of Ceuta in 1415

   2. Colonization of the Atlantic Islands

      a. Portuguese ventured into the Atlantic, colonized Madeiras, Azores, other islands

      b. Italian investors, Portuguese landowners cultivated sugarcane on the islands

   3. Slave trade expanded fifteenth century

      a. Portuguese traders ventured down west coast of Africa

      b. Traded guns, textiles for gold and slaves

      c. Thousands of slaves delivered to Atlantic island plantations

   4. Indian Ocean trade

      a. Portuguese searched for sea route to Asian markets without Muslim intermediaries

      b. Bartolomeu Dias reached Cape of Good Hope, entered the Indian Ocean, 1488

      c. Vasco da Gama arrived at Calicut in 1498, returned to Lisbon with huge profit

      d.   Portuguese mariners dominated trade between Europe and Asia, sixteenth century

      e.   Portuguese ships with cannons launched European imperialism in Asia

5. Cristoforo Colombo (Christopher Columbus) hoped to reach Asia by sailing west

      a.   Plan rejected by Portuguese king but sponsored by king and queen of Spain

      b.   1492, led three ships to the Caribbean Sea, believed he was near Japan

      c.   Other mariners soon followed Columbus and explored American continents

IDENTIFICATION: PEOPLE

What is the contribution of each of the following individuals to world history? (Identification should include answers to the questions *who, what, where, when, how,* and *why is this person important?*)

Ibn Battuta

Marco Polo

Rabban Sauma

John of Montecorvino

Hongwu

Zheng He

Prince Henry

Bartolomeu Dias

Vasco da Gama

Fernando and Isabel

Christopher Columbus

IDENTIFICATION: TERMS/CONCEPTS

State in your own words what each of the following terms means and why it is significant to a study of world history. (Those terms with an asterisk may be defined in the glossary.)

Qadi

Sufi

Melaka

Little Ice Age

Black Death

Ming dynasty

Reconquista*

Renaissance

Humanism*

STUDY QUESTIONS

1. Identify the most significant land and sea routes in the fourteenth century. What societies tended to control and profit from these routes?

2. What was the role of religion in the cultural interactions of this era? Which religion had the greater international impact, Christianity or Islam? Explain.

3. Give some specific examples of agricultural and technological diffusion along the trade routes.

4. Summarize the origins and the progress of the bubonic plague of the fourteenth century. Which regions were hit the hardest? Which regions were largely spared?

5. What were the social and economic outcomes of the plague?

6. How did the Ming dynasty rebuild the economy of China?

7. Note the kind of state to emerge in the fifteenth century in northern Italy, France, England, and Spain. Which was the most powerful state at this time?

8. What were some of the distinctive elements of the artistic Renaissance of western Europe in the fifteenth century?

9. How were the Ming Chinese able to establish a forceful presence in the Indian Ocean in the fifteenth century? When and why did this presence cease?

10. What were the Portuguese objectives in the exploration of the coast of west Africa? What did they accomplish?

11. What did Columbus hope to accomplish when he set forth across the Atlantic in 1492? What did he achieve?

1. Try to imagine the impact of a catastrophe such as the bubonic plague on European society. How did people behave? What was the impact on social relations? (Consider this: how would *you* behave in such a crisis? Would you live your life any differently?)

2. What are some of the common elements in the process of European state building? What specific measures did the national monarchies take in order to establish and maintain their authority? Who did they need to control?

3. What were some of the common concerns of the Renaissance humanists? How would these goals be expressed today? Does the word *humanism* mean the same thing today as it did then?

STUDENT QUIZ

1. Ibn Battuta was able to travel extensively across Asia and Africa in the early fourteenth century because
   a. he was welcomed as an Islamic judge in many Muslim kingdoms.
   b. new maritime technology made long-distance travel more common.
   c. he was able to take advantage of existing trade routes.
   d. the Mongol kingdoms provided safe passage for merchants and travelers.
   e. all of the above.

2. Which of the following was *not* a well-traveled trade route in the thirteenth and fourteenth centuries?
   a. from Morocco across the Sahara Desert to Mali.
   b. from Arabia down the east coast of Africa.
   c. from Portugal down the west coast of Africa.
   d. from India across the Indian Ocean to southeast Asia.
   e. from China overland to Constantinople.

3. The primary significance of Marco Polo's travels is the fact that
   a. he was the first European to live and work in China.
   b. he opened European markets to Chinese merchants.
   c. he introduced Chinese technologies to Europe.
   d. his adventures inspired European readers to seek profit and adventure abroad.
   e. all of the above.

4. Which of the following was *not* a serious diplomatic mission of the thirteenth century?
   a. The Persian khan proposed an alliance with European powers against Muslims in Jerusalem.
   b. The pope invited the Mongol khans to convert to Christianity.
   c. The sultan of India proposed an alliance with the Byzantine empire against the Mongols.
   d. An envoy of the khans declared that European Christians should submit to Mongol rule or face destruction.
   e. All of the above were diplomatic ventures of the thirteenth century.

5. Efforts to forge an alliance between the Mongols and the powers of Europe ended when
    a. the Mongols converted to Islam.
    b. Rabban Sauma was denied access to the pope.
    c. Christian crusaders attacked Muslims at Jerusalem.
    d. the Mongols invaded Russia.
    e. Marco Polo's memoirs revealed a Mongol plan to invade Europe.

6. On his visit to Mali, Ibn Battuta expressed disapproval at
    a. the tolerance of paganism by the emperor of Mali.
    b. the immodesty of African Muslim women.
    c. the corruption of the local courts.
    d. the failure to observe Muslim rituals, such as prayer and fasting.
    e. all of the above.

7. One of the most significant impacts of sugarcane production on global economies was
    a. widespread deterioration in diet and nutrition.
    b. the increased demand for slave labor.
    c. increased demand for tea and coffee.
    d. increased demand for other luxury goods, such as porcelain.
    e. all of the above.

8. The first military use of gunpowder was mainly for
    a. psychological terror: making unexpected loud noises .
    b. fireworks display to celebrate a victory.
    c. unmanned torpedoes against enemy vessels.
    d. bombs lobbed by catapults into cities under siege.
    e. large mounted cannons on merchant ships.

9. The bubonic plague started in
    a. western Europe.
    b. southwest China.
    c. Mediterranean seaports.
    d. central Asia.
    e. southwest Asia.

10. One region relatively unaffected by the plague was
    a. western Europe.
    b. north Africa.
    c. China.
    d. India.
    e. the Byzantine empire.

11. Mongol rule in China was ended in a rebellion led by
    a. a destitute orphan.
    b. a Confucian scholar.
    c. a Buddhist monk.
    d. a eunuch in service to the Yuan dynasty.
    e. a brilliant naval commander.

12. Under Hongwu, the Ming dynasty was established as
    a. a feudal state dominated by local warlords.
    b. a military state with a puppet emperor.
    c. a constitutional monarchy.
    d. a decentralized empire with considerable autonomy for local authorities.
    e. a highly centralized, autocratic state.

13. Chinese economic recovery was aided by all of the following steps *except*
    a. increased agricultural productivity.
    b. increased production of porcelain, silk, and other luxury goods.
    c. active state support of foreign trade.
    d. the involvement of Chinese merchants in foreign trade.
    e. restoration of irrigation systems.

14. In the fifteenth century, the nation-states of western Europe were strengthened by
    a. a long period of peace among the nations of Europe.
    b. direct taxes and standing armies.
    c. increasing reliance on knights as a military force.
    d. the ideals of Renaissance humanism.
    e. all of the above.

15. In Spain, the process of state building was accelerated by
    a. Columbus's quest for a western route to China.
    b. the reconquest of Granada from the French.
    c. an alliance with the Islamic states of northern Africa.
    d. the marriage of Fernando of Aragon and Isabel of Castile.
    e. all of the above.

16. The European Renaissance is characterized by all of the following *except*
    a. a revival of classical learning.
    b. domed cathedrals.
    c. naturalistic painting and sculpture.
    d. repudiation of Christian values.
    e. translations of the New Testament.

17. A Renaissance humanist is one who
    a. seeks to reconcile Christian values with a public life.
    b. considers Christianity to be an outmoded superstition.
    c. holds that personal glory is the only true value.
    d. withdraws from the world to study ancient texts.
    e. rejects the past and embraces all that is new.

18. Which of the following was the *primary* goal of Zheng He's expeditions?
    a. to eliminate foreign trade with China.
    b. to establish Chinese trading cities on the Indian Ocean.
    c. to impress foreign people with the power and might of the Ming dynasty.
    d. to establish diplomatic relations with the Muslim states trading on the Indian Ocean.
    e. to offer military protection and support to Chinese merchants in the Indian Ocean.

19. Chinese naval expeditions were abruptly ended in 1433 because
    a. Zheng He was suspected of building his personal power.
    b. maintaining the fleet was considered a needless waste of national resources.
    c. the voyages had led to several humiliating defeats.
    d. the large Chinese vessels proved to be unseaworthy.
    e. all of the above.

20. Portugal led Europe in maritime exploration for all the following reasons *except*
    a. they had long years of experience fishing in the Atlantic.
    b. they took an early lead in the African slave trade.
    c. Prince Henry hoped to convert the peoples of Africa to Christianity.
    d. they discovered and colonized a number of Atlantic islands early in the fourteenth century.
    e. they had more people and a more advanced economy than the other states of Europe.

MATCHING

Match these figures with the statements that follow.

A. Ibn Battuta	F. Rabban Sauma
B. Hongwu	G. Erasmus
C. Zheng He	H. Marco Polo
D. Prince Henry	I. Christopher Columbus
E. Vasco da Gama	J. Bartolomeu Dias

1. ____ Dutch humanist, one of the greatest Christian philosophers of the Renaissance

2. ____ Venetian merchant and traveler who lived at the court of the khans in China and later described his travels to a western audience

3. ____ Moroccan diplomat and scholar who traveled throughout Asia and Africa and recorded his travels

4. ____ Commoner who overthrew the Mongols and founded the Ming dynasty

5. ____ Encouraged Portuguese mariners and missionaries to take the lead in overseas exploration and expansion

6. ____ Portuguese mariner who sailed down the west coast of Africa and around the Cape of Good Hope into the Indian Ocean

7. ____ Portuguese mariner who first reached India by sailing around the tip of Africa

8. ____ Genoese mariner who crossed the Atlantic Ocean and reached the Caribbean in 1492

9. ____ Chinese mariner who led a number of expeditions into the Indian Ocean

10. ____ Nestorian Christian priest sent by the ikhan of Persia as an envoy to the pope and European political leaders

SEQUENCING

Place the following clusters of events in chronological order. Consider carefully how one event leads to another, and try to determine the internal logic of each sequence.

A.

_____ Prince Henry's promotion of overseas exploration

_____ Vasco da Gama's voyages

_____ Bartolomeu Dias's voyages

_____ Portuguese conquest of Ceuta

B.

_____ Ibn Battuta travels to India, to the Maldives, and to Africa as a visiting *qadi*.

_____ Mongol states in southwest Asia convert to Islam.

_____ Islamic law and practice provide an important common culture across Eurasia and into Africa.

_____ New Islamic states seek judges and Islamic scholars to help administer *sharia*.

C.

_____ Italian entrepreneurs establish sugarcane plantations on the islands in the Mediterranean.

_____ European crusaders develop a taste for refined sugar.

_____ Sugar production fuels a greater demand for slave labor, either Muslim war captives or African slaves.

_____ Sugar production originates in southwest Asia and spreads to north Africa.

MAP EXERCISES

1. Study the travels by Marco Polo in the thirteenth century and Ibn Battuta in the fourteenth century (see Map 22.1, pages 576–577). Based on this evidence, what appear to be some of the more frequently visited places by the end of the fourteenth century? What regions seem to be relatively unexplored?

2. Compare the routes traveled by Zheng He (Map 22.2, pages 596–597) in the fifteenth century with the travels of Marco Polo and Ibn Battuta. Has Zheng He expanded travel in the Indian Ocean? Based on this evidence, what can you conclude about the purpose of the Chinese expeditions?

3. Trace the course of the Black Death as it moved from China across Asia to western Europe. A little research will reveal specific dates of outbreak. Based on this evidence (and foreknowledge, of course), what could a European trading city have done to protect itself against the plague?

CONNECTIONS

In fifty words or less explain the relationship between each of the following pairs. How does one lead to or foster the other? Be specific in your response. (May be done individually or in small groups.)

Black Death and humanism
- Islamic *sharia* and Marco Polo
- *Reconquista* and Columbus
- Marco Polo and Vasco da Gama

GROUP ACTIVITIES

1. Read the letter from John of Montecorvino on page 583. Imagine that the Franciscans have responded by sending a young missionary to replace him (which, sadly, they did not do). What advice would John give to his replacement? What difficulties confront a Christian missionary in China? Develop a set of instructions on how best to proceed in this work.

2. Consider the impact of gunpowder on world history. Review the technology and tactics of warfare at the time of the crusades (see chapter 20). How will warfare change after the fifteenth century with the introduction of gunpowder arms? Who will be advantaged by this change? Who will be disadvantaged? Develop a list of pros and cons that addresses these questions.

FEATURE FILMS

Artemisia (1998). True story of talented Renaissance painter Artemisia Gentileschi, whose career and independence were restricted because she was a woman. In Italian with English subtitles.

1492: Conquest of Paradise (1992). Generally considered the best of the Columbus bio-pics. Directed by Ridley Scott and starring Gerard Depardieu as Columbus and Sigourney Weaver as Queen Isabella. Visually stunning, historically reasonably accurate.

The Agony and the Ecstasy (1965). Rex Harrison as Pope Julius II and Charlton Heston as Michelangelo. The clash of two powerful wills at the height of the Renaissance.

The Seventh Seal (1956). A masterpiece by Swedish filmmaker Ingmar Bergman. Max von Sydow plays a fourteenth-century knight who returns to Sweden after the crusades to find his homeland ravaged by a plague. In a classical allegorical sequence, the knight plays chess with the Devil in order to prolong his life. In stark black-and-white with English subtitles.

GLOSSARY

Agricultural Transition: The gradual transition from a dependence on hunting and gathering for subsistence to a dependence on cultivation and animal husbandry. First evidence of transition is from around 12,000 B.C.E.

Ancestor Worship: Belief that dead ancestors can influence one's fortunes in this life. People who practice ancestor worship characteristically practice rituals and ceremonies to the memory or remains of their ancestors.

Austronesians: Peoples from Asia who speak related languages. Austronesians were seafaring people who migrated from southeast Asia and settled many of the Pacific islands and as far west as Madagascar.

Bubonic Plague: Epidemic that swept Eurasia, causing devastating population loss and economic disruption. It was known as the Black Death in Europe after around 1350 C.E.

Buddhism: A religious doctrine that first emerged in India in the sixth century B.C.E. From there it spread widely to China, Japan, and southeast Asia. It taught that life is suffering but that extinction of desire can culminate in a state of illumination.

Caste: A social class system with distinctions that are transferred through generations or through occupation. Restrictions are placed on marriage, occupation, handling of food, and other matters, according to caste. Caste usually refers to the social system of India.

Christianity: Religious doctrine that emerged in southeast Asia in the first century C.E. and then spread through Europe, north Africa, parts of Asia, and eventually to the Americas. Central to the religion is the belief that Jesus was the son of God and sacrificed himself on behalf of humankind.

Confucianism: Chinese philosophy based on the teachings of Confucius (551–479 B.C.E.). It emphasizes personal virtue, devotion to family, justice, duty, and tradition. China's civil service examinations were based on Confucianist principles.

Daoism: *Dao* means "the way" and refers to the Chinese philosophical school that stressed disengagement from the affairs of the world in order to live simply and seek harmony with the natural order.

Eastern Orthodox Christianity: An eastern branch of Christianity that evolved after the division of the Roman Empire and the subsequent development of the Byzantine Empire in the east and the medieval European society in the west. The Eastern Orthodox Church acknowledged what became known as the Byzantine rite and recognized the primacy of the patriarch of Constantinople.

Guild: Organizations whose membership is based on occupation. They often regulate the production and sale of goods and serve as mutual aid societies for their members. They were particularly powerful in medieval European cities.

Hellenistic Age: The age of Alexander of Macedon and his successors (from around the fourth century B.C.E. until the first century B.C.E. The Hellenistic Age was an era when Greek cultural traditions expanded their influence beyond Greece itself, particularly eastward into southeast Asia and along the eastern Mediterranean and Egypt.

Hinduism: A diverse body of religious practices native to India, characterized by beliefs in successive reincarnations and supreme beings of many forms and natures.

Holy Roman Empire: A confederation of states mostly in central and western Europe. It began in 962 C.E. with the crowning of Otto I by the pope.

Humanism: Cultural movement during the Renaissance that drew inspiration from the humanities, that is, literature, history, philosophy, and the arts. In contrast to medieval theologians, humanists argued that one could live a moral life and still be actively engaged in the affairs of the world.

Hunting/Gathering Culture: Any culture whose primary means of subsistence is through hunting and gathering from the environment. Humans survived this way for millions of years before the agricultural transition, and some hunting/gathering cultures persisted into the twenty-first century C.E.

Islam: Religion based on the teachings of Muhammad (570–632 C.E.). It consists of the belief in only one god, Allah, and the need for all believers to fully submit to his will. Islam began on the Arabian peninsula but spread throughout Africa, much of Asia, and parts of Europe.

Judaism: The monotheistic religion of the Jewish people that traces its origins to Abraham (ca. 2000 B.C.E.). It emerged in the Middle East, and constitute a majority, believers were widespread in Europe, north Africa, and southeast Asia.

Kin-Based Society: A society that governs itself primarily through family and clan relationships; many existed in sub-Saharan Africa throughout history.

Legalism: Chinese political philosophy that promoted a practical and ruthlessly efficient approach to statecraft. It emerged in the late fourth century B.C.E. and was embraced by various emperors and ministers thereafter.

Manichaeism: Dualistic religion that blended elements of Zoroastrianism, Christianity, and Buddhism. It spread throughout Persia during the third century C.E.

Mesopotamia: Geographic region located in modern-day Iraq, which includes the river valleys of the Tigris and Euphrates rivers. Literally translates as "between the rivers."

Metallurgy: The process of extracting metal from ores, or purifying metals, and of creating objects from metals.

Mithraism: Dualistic religion of salvation that originated in Persia and spread to much of the Roman Empire. It was especially popular with Roman soldiers.

Neo-Confucianism: A Chinese philosophy that emerged in the twelfth century C.E. that adapted Buddhist themes and reasoning to Confucian interests and values. Neo-Confucianism enjoyed the status of an officially recognized creed until the early twentieth century.

Patriarchy: A system of social organization in which males dominate the family and in which the public institutions and descent and succession are traced through the male line.

Renaissance: The cultural flowering of western Europe in the fourteenth and fifteenth centuries. Arts and literature of this period reflected greater individualism and secularism than in the medieval period and often drew inspiration from classical models.

Shia: A sect of Islam that supported the descendents of the line of Ali to the caliphate. They developed rituals and doctrines that distinguished themselves as distinct from the Sunnis ("traditionalists").

Silk Roads: A network of sea and land trade routes that linked east Asia to the Mediterranean.

Stoicism: A Hellenistic philosophy that emphasized strict adherence to duty and personal self-discipline. It became very popular among the Roman upper classes.

Sufis: A sect of Islam that sought emotional and mystical union with Allah rather than an intellectual understanding. Sufis were important missionaries of Islam throughout Asia.

Zoroastrianism: A dualistic Persian religion of salvation that emerged in the sixth century B.C.E. It was popular in Persia and spread to the Mediterranean basin and parts of Asia.

ANSWER KEY

CHAPTER 1: ANSWERS

STUDENT QUIZ

1. C	6. C	11. C	16. D
2. C	7. B	12. D	17. C
3. B	8. E	13. E	18. A
4. A	9. A	14. B	19. B
5. C	10. D	15. C	20. A

MATCHING

1. G	5. H
2. D	6. A
3. C	7. F
4. E	8. B

SEQUENCING

A. 1, 6, 4, 2, 5, 3
B. 1, 3, 2, 4, 5

CHAPTER 2: ANSWERS

STUDENT QUIZ

1. E	6. C	11. E	16. C
2. B	7. D	12. E	17. A
3. E	8. C	13. B	18. A
4. D	9. D	14. E	19. D
5. C	10. B	15. A	20. A

MATCHING

1. A	5. D	9. I
2. G	6. B	
3. H	7. F	
4. E	8. J	

SEQUENCING

A. 3, 2, 5, 1, 4
B. 1, 5, 3, 2, 4, 7, 6

QUOTATIONS

1. Kings 5, Old Testament: Solomon, king of the Israelites, sends message to Hiram, Phoenician king of Tyre
2. The Sumerian flood story found in the *Epic of Gilgamesh*
3. From Hammurabi's code of laws
4. From the Ten Commandments, conveyed to the Israelites by Moses

CHAPTER 3: ANSWERS

STUDENT QUIZ

1. C	6. E	11. A	16. C
2. D	7. B	12. D	17. E
3. C	8. A	13. E	18. B
4. B	9. D	14. D	19. D
5. A	10. E	15. D	20. E

MATCHING

1. E	5. F
2. D	6. B
3. G	7. H
4. C	8. A

SEQUENCING

A. 2, 3, 4, 6, 1, 5
B. 1, 6, 5, 3, 2, 4

QUOTATIONS

1. From *The Great Hymn to Aten* during period when Akhenaten was trying to impose monotheism in Egypt
2. A hymn to the pharaoh; this one dates from nineteenth century B.C.E.
3. A hymn to the Nile ("Hapy"), from an early period in Egyptian history
4. Harkhuf's description of his expedition to Nubia

CHAPTER 4: ANSWERS

STUDENT QUIZ

1. C	6. B	11. A	16. B
2. A	7. E	12. D	17. E
3. B	8. E	13. E	18. C
4. D	9. B	14. A	19. C
5. C	10. C	15. D	20. E

MATCHING

1. D	7. C
2. J	8. G
3. A	9. E
4. F	10. F
5. I	11. B
6. K	12. H

SEQUENCING

A. 2, 3, 6, 5, 4, 1

QUOTATIONS

1. Passage from the *Rig Veda* on the creation of the first four castes
2. From the *Lawbook of Manu*
3. *Brhadaranyaka Upanishad* on the explanation of karma
4. *Chandogya Upanishad* on the nature of reality, or Brahman

CHAPTER 5: ANSWERS

STUDENT QUIZ

1. C	6. D	11. E	16. A
2. B	7. A	12. B	17. D
3. A	8. B	13. C	18. B
4. D	9. B	14. B	19. B
5. A	10. A	15. D	20. A

MATCHING

1. A	5. F
2. H	6. E
3. G	7. B
4. C	8. D

SEQUENCING

A. 2, 3, 1, 5, 4

QUOTATIONS

1. *Book of Songs* on family
2. Another name for the Yellow River
3. Question for the oracle bones
4. *Book of Songs* on a bride

CHAPTER 6: ANSWERS

STUDENT QUIZ

1. C	6. C	11. D	16. A
2. B	7. A	12. D	17. D
3. D	8. A	13. A	18. E
4. C	9. E	14. A	19. B
5. E	10. D	15. E	20. C

MATCHING

1. B	5. G
2. E	6. D
3. H	7. F
4. A	8. C

SEQUENCING

A. 3, 2, 4, 1
B. 1, 3, 2, 4

CHAPTER 7: ANSWERS

STUDENT QUIZ

1. D	6. B	11. D	16. E
2. E	7. B	12. E	17. B
3. E	8. C	13. C	18. C
4. B	9. B	14. E	19. A
5. A	10. A	15. E	20. D

MATCHING

1. H	5. A
2. E	6. D
3. C	7. G
4. F	8. B

SEQUENCING

A. 5, 2, 3, 1, 4
B. 1, 5, 4, 2, 3

QUOTATIONS

1. A quote from Zarathustra
2. A quote about an Achaemenid ruler
3. A belief of Zoroastrianism
4. From the oracle at Delphi to Croesus, king of the Lydians

CHAPTER 8: ANSWERS

STUDENT QUIZ

1. C	6. B	11. E	16. B
2. A	7. D	12. B	17. A
3. D	8. B	13. E	18. C
4. A	9. D	14. B	19. C
5. B	10. E	15. D	20. A

MATCHING

1. C	5. G
2. D	6. A
3. H	7. B
4. F	8. E

SEQUENCING

A. 2, 5, 3, 1, 4
B. 4, 1, 3, 2

QUOTATIONS

1. Confucius
2. Mencius
3. Han Feizi
4. Laozi
5. On the subordination of women

CHAPTER 9: ANSWERS

STUDENT QUIZ

1. C	6. A	11. B	16. B
2. C	7. E	12. D	17. E
3. D	8. E	13. A	18. A
4. A	9. C	14. A	19. D
5. C	10. E	15. D	20. A

MATCHING

1. G	6. C
2. F	7. A
3. I	8. E
4. J	9. H
5. D	10. B

SEQUENCING

A. 4, 2, 3, 6, 5, 1
B. 3, 2, 4, 5, 1

QUOTATIONS

1. *Mahabharata* on the role of the warrior/aristocratic caste
2. *Ashokavadana*, Ashoka on Buddhist philosophy
3. *Kamasutra* on *kama* (physical/sexual pleasure)
4. Jainism
5. On a *boddhisatva*
6. *Bhagavad Gita* on reincarnation

CHAPTER 10: ANSWERS

STUDENT QUIZ

1. A	6. C	11. C	16. A
2. B	7. A	12. E	17. D
3. B	8. D	13. D	18. C
4. E	9. B	14. C	19. B
5. C	10. A	15. E	20. E

MATCHING

1. C	6. H
2. G	7. A
3. F	8. D
4. J	9. E
5. I	10. B

SEQUENCING

A. 5, 1, 3, 6, 2, 4

QUOTATIONS

1. Arrian on Alexander of Macedon
2. Socrates from Plato's *Apology*
3. Pericles from Thucydides' account of his Funeral Oration
4. The words of an Athenian wife from Xenophon
5. Epicurean philosophy by Epicurus
6. On Alexander of Macedon, written by Richard Stoneman

CHAPTER 11: ANSWERS

STUDENT QUIZ

1. B	6. B	11. E	16. A
2. D	7. B	12. D	17. C
3. C	8. E	13. E	18. E
4. A	9. B	14. C	19. A
5. D	10. D	15. B	20. D

MATCHING

1. F	5. C
2. H	6. G
3. A	7. B
4. E	8. D

SEQUENCING

A. 5, 2, 1, 4, 3
B. 1, 3, 4, 2

QUOTATIONS

1. Jesus in his Sermon on the Mount
2. Cicero on his education
3. Plautus from the point of view of a slave
4. Tacitus on corruption in the early Roman empire
5. Paul of Tarsus
6. Polybius on the consuls of Rome

CHAPTER 12: ANSWERS

STUDENT QUIZ

1. B	6. B	11. C	16. C
2. E	7. E	12. B	17. A
3. D	8. C	13. A	18. E
4. A	9. B	14. A	19. D
5. B	10. E	15. B	20. C

MATCHING

1. G	5. H
2. C	6. A
3. B	7. D
4. E	8. F

SEQUENCING

A. 5, 2, 3, 1, 4
B. 3, 1, 6, 4, 5, 2

CHAPTER 13: ANSWERS

STUDENT QUIZ

1. B	6. B	11. E	16. E
2. B	7. A	12. B	17. C
3. A	8. D	13. C	18. B
4. C	9. A	14. D	19. B
5. B	10. D	15. B	20. D

MATCHING

1. E	5. A
2. G	6. F
3. C	7. B
4. D	8. H

SEQUENCING

A. 2, 1, 3, 5, 6, 7, 4
B. 6, 1, 3, 2, 5, 4

CHAPTER 14: ANSWERS

STUDENT QUIZ

1. A	6. B	11. C	16. D
2. D	7. B	12. A	17. E
3. B	8. E	13. C	18. E
4. B	9. B	14. D	19. E
5. A	10. E	15. E	20. D

MATCHING

1. L	7. I
2. F	8. C
3. K	9. H
4. E	10. B
5. J	11. G
6. D	12. A

SEQUENCING

A. 5, 1, 4, 6, 7, 3, 2
B. 6, 7, 5, 1, 4, 2, 3

QUOTATIONS

1. Benjamin of Tudela on the caliph
2. The Quran on Allah
3. Benjamin of Tudela on Baghdad

CHAPTER 15: ANSWERS

STUDENT QUIZ

1. B	6. B	11. D	16. D
2. C	7. A	12. D	17. A
3. B	8. D	13. B	18. E
4. A	9. B	14. B	19. B
5. D	10. E	15. B	20. A

MATCHING

1. D	5. A
2. G	6. B
3. C	7. F
4. E	8. H

SEQUENCING

A. 4, 6, 1, 2, 3, 5
B. 5, 2, 4, 1, 3, 6

CHAPTER 16: ANSWERS

STUDENT QUIZ

1. B	6. E	11. E	16. A
2. D	7. B	12. C	17. A
3. E	8. E	13. A	18. E
4. E	9. B	14. B	19. A
5. C	10. C	15. D	20. D

MATCHING

1. G	5. F
2. A	6. H
3. E	7. C
4. D	8. B

A. 2, 5, 6, 1, 3, 4

CHAPTER 17: ANSWERS

STUDENT QUIZ

1. C	6. D	11. A	16. C
2. B	7. A	12. A	17. A
3. A	8. D	13. B	18. D
4. A	9. C	14. E	19. B
5. E	10. A	15. B	20. B

MATCHING

1. G	5. C
2. A	6. B
3. E	7. F
4. D	8. H

SEQUENCING

A. 3, 4, 6, 2, 5, 1
B. 4, 2, 3, 1, 5

QUOTATIONS

1. Gregory of Tours's *The History of the Franks* on Clovis's conversion
2. From the "Capitulary de Villis," a guide for stewards on Carolingian estates

CHAPTER 18: ANSWERS

STUDENT QUIZ

1. E	6. B	11. B	16. A
2. A	7. C	12. A	17. C
3. B	8. D	13. B	18. B
4. A	9. E	14. E	19. B
5. E	10. D	15. A	20. C

MATCHING

1. F	5. C
2. D	6. G
3. E	7. H
4. A	8. B

SEQUENCING

A. 5, 3, 1, 6, 2, 4

CHAPTER 19: ANSWERS

STUDENT QUIZ

1. B	6. C	11. A	16. B
2. A	7. E	12. B	17. A
3. D	8. B	13. B	18. B
4. D	9. B	14. D	19. A
5. B	10. B	15. E	20. B

MATCHING

1. D	5. B
2. F	6. G
3. A	7. C
4. H	8. E

SEQUENCING

A. 6, 4, 2, 3, 1, 5, 7

CHAPTER 20: ANSWERS

STUDENT QUIZ

1. C	6. C	11. A	16. B
2. D	7. C	12. B	17. C
3. E	8. E	13. C	18. B
4. D	9. A	14. B	19. A
5. A	10. B	15. D	20. A

MATCHING

1. E	5. F
2. D	6. C
3. G	7. A
4. H	8. B

SEQUENCING

A. 2, 1, 5, 4, 3
B. 3, 5, 4, 2, 1

<u>QUOTATIONS</u>

1. Francesco Balducci Pegolotti on trade between Europe and China
2. Words spoken by St. Francis of Assisi as quoted in Thomas of Celano's biography of him
3. Pope Gregory VII from his letters on the power of the papacy
4. Pope Urban II's plea for a crusade at the Council of Clermont
5. About St. Francis of Assisi, from Thomas of Celano's biography
6. St. Thomas Aquinas from the *Summa Theologica*, using reason to prove the existence of God